O'CONNOR, Richard.   The First Hurrah; a Biography of Alfred E. Smith.   Putnam, 1970.   318p il bibl 70-97091.   6.95
A colorfully written job by a former newspaperman geared primarily to the general reader.   But it is based largely upon previously published materials and provides little or no new information or insights. College libraries would be better advised to get *Al Smith: Hero of the Cities* (see above).

CHOICE   *APR. '70*

History, Geography &

Travel

  North America

ALFRED E. SMITH
1873–1944

The Author

RICHARD O'CONNOR was a newspaper reporter for twenty-five years before devoting full time to writing. He is the author of many books, including *Pacific Destiny, The German-Americans, Ambrose Bierce, Bret Harte,* and *Jack London,* and his articles have appeared in such publications as *Life, American Heritage,* and *McCall's.* Mr. O'Connor now makes his home in Ellsworth, Maine.

THE FIRST HURRAH

HURRAH

A Biography
of Alfred E. Smith

by RICHARD O'CONNOR

G. P. Putnam's Sons, New York

Contents

Illustrations appear after page 160.

PART I

Happy Warrior

This is the Happy Warrior; this is he
Whom every Man in arms should wish to be.
—WILLIAM WORDSWORTH

1

Under the Brooklyn Bridge

NO one could tell Alfred Emanuel Smith that his country would deny the Presidency to a man simply because he was an Irish Catholic. He could not be convinced that a man who climbed the slippery slope of ward politics under the sponsorship of Tammany Hall would be regarded with suspicion in the Bible Belt. Nor could his advisers urge on him the necessity of not pronouncing radio as "raddio," hospital as "horspital," first as "foist," because they fell so unkindly on the Middle Western ear. No one could tell him that the brown derby and the old hurdy-gurdy tune "The Sidewalks of New York" may have been respectable enough in his youth but were now regarded as vulgar reminders of his Lower East Side background. Nor could he believe that a red-faced, banana-nosed, cigar-chomping fellow with New York politician written all over him would not fit in with the American people's conception of a proper President; nor that he and his Bronx-born wife would remind all too many people of the popular comic strip "Maggie and Jiggs."

Al Smith also refused to believe that his beloved country would deny its highest office to a man simply because he had only an eighth-grade education or that it was so intolerant— this in the decade of the Ku Klux Klan resurgence, of the Scopes "monkey trial" in Tennessee, of the Chautauqua tents and the

Main Street psychology and the "booboisie" outlook so thoroughly reported in the "Americana" column of Mencken's *American Mercury*—it would scorn him because, if he were elected, the Vatican might be moved stone by stone to Pennsylvania Avenue, Washington, D.C.

Smith was not a bookish man, or he might have learned a great deal about his countrymen from the works of Sinclair Lewis and H. L. Mencken. He had denounced as an impudent lie the report that he had never read a book from cover to cover, replying, as much in truth as in jest, that "I've read *The Life and Battles of John L. Sullivan* from cover to cover." He had his share of the politician's cynicism and often expressed it pungently, but he refused to believe that it was impossible for a Catholic, a Jew, or anyone but a certified white, preferably Anglo-Saxon Protestant to be elected to the White House.

One night more than forty years ago he learned, as the crushing news poured in from the polls, that he was wrong about his fellow Americans. It was—then—impossible for a Catholic to reach the White House. When another Catholic did become President thirty-two years later, it was at least partly because John F. Kennedy had acquired an Anglo-Saxon overlay of social and intellectual distinction. Yet without Smith's groundbreaking attempt to attain the Presidency—without, perhaps, the guilt many Americans must have felt over the denial of that office to Alfred E. Smith—a Kennedy might not have reached the White House in 1960 and two of the leading candidates for the Democratic nomination in 1968 might not have been Senators Robert F. Kennedy and Eugene McCarthy.

Everything about Al Smith might be forgotten except for that largely symbolic brown derby and his sobriquet of the Happy Warrior, but what should remain indelible in the American memory is his touching, ill-rewarded faith in the tolerance of the American people. His eloquent faith in Americanism, as Oscar Handlin has written, was "more than a matter of fife-and-drum patriotism; it was also a way of life that encouraged the diversity he had known from the time he was a boy on the East Side and that evaluated a man for what he was—otherwise, he would himself never have climbed out of the day laborer's category."

Until that election night in 1928 when his faith in the democratic process—which from his viewpoint was at issue, not the prosperity attributed to two Republican administrations, as political historians would have it—he had evidence that it was possible, in his pragmatic and often boisterous way, to be a man for all seasons and for all men. He had discovered the ecumenical spirit before its time had come—another element of his personal tragedy. As a legislator and governor, he had worked closely and associated intimately with people not of his faith. A Jewish woman was one of his closest advisers and undoubtedly his most fervent political supporter. A German Lutheran was his best friend, tutor, and roommate during his early years in Albany. A Miss Frances Perkins and a Mr. Robert Moses were most prominent, along with Mrs. Belle Moskowitz, in his administrations as governor.

As a boy raised on the Lower East Side, he had experienced at firsthand how people of diverse religious and national origins could live and work together amicably. If there was one thing he believed in, it was the homogeneity of Americanism, which was the basis and essence of his political credo. Without the American capability for amalgamation, everything that his patchwork party, his melting-pot world of the sidewalks of New York, and his country stood for was meaningless.

His faith in the wide compass of American acceptance of differing peoples was severely damaged that election night in 1928. If the country could show so little tolerance in a moment of high prosperity, how could it survive under greater social and economic pressures? The question went unanswered and would present itself with even greater urgency forty years later.

More was lost that night than a national election or one man's shot at the Presidency. That it has since been recouped

mitigates the sense of loss. But for that tragic moment, because it was more than a personal tragedy, Smith deserves to
be remembered and the paramount lesson of his life studied.

In one decade, between 1873 and 1882, three male infants
were born in New York State who grew up to be the most elec-
trifying, appealing, and controversial figures in modern
American political history. Each was born on a different social
and economic level that only pointed up the convergence, then
the conflict of their political ambitions. The firstborn, in 1873,
was Alfred E. Smith. Next (1881) came James J. Walker, the
son of a Greenwich Village alderman. The third, Franklin D.
Roosevelt, was born a year later in Hyde Park among the
Hudson River aristocracy.

Few men could have had less in common than the three men
who received their higher political education almost simultaneously in the statehouse at Albany. Jimmy Walker was a
dapper, witty little sybarite with a gift for amusing and diverting the populace of the largest city in the world. He and Smith
were both Irish, but the resemblance ended there; Walker
hung around stage doors and became known as the night
mayor of New York, while Smith was a serious-minded family
man and churchgoer. Roosevelt was a member of the quality
who traced his ancestry to the patroons and merchant-venturers
of Old New York. Smith came out of the Fulton Fish Market,
Walker out of Tin Pan Alley, and Roosevelt out of Harvard. In
the long run, Harvard proved to be the best of the three finishing schools.

On the last day of 1873, the New York newspapers found
space for stories about charges that Civil War veterans were
being employed as servants in the White House and that General Ulysses S. Grant, now President, was taking steps to end
such degradation of men who had fought to preserve the
Union. The New York *Herald* devoted several columns on its
front page to a dispatch from its Havana correspondent de-

scribing underground efforts to win Cuban independence, the Spanish being the current oppressors of the island's people. Memorial services were to be held in Gloucester for the 174 fishermen who lost their lives off the Grand Banks that year. Augustin Daly was starring in *The Parricide* at his Fifth Avenue Theater, the famous Gus Williams was appearing at Tony Pastor's on the Bowery, *The Merchant of Venice* was being produced at Wood's Museum with "a galaxy of stars," and at Niblo's Garden on Houston Street "A Grand Fairy Spectacle" was being offered for children's holiday parties.

Nowhere in all those dozen daily newspapers, which in coming years would devote thousands of columns to his activities, was there any mention of the birth of one Alfred Emanuel Smith the day before.

That event, with the assistance of the neighborhood midwife, took place at 174 South Street, on the third floor of a tenement above a German grocery store. The boy was the first-born of Alfred Emanuel Smith, Sr., a boss truckman, and his wife, the former Catherine Mulvehill, both native New Yorkers. Their only other child would be a daughter, born exactly two years later.

New York then was the world capital—the Mecca—of the immigrant, but the infant Al Smith boasted both a father and mother born in this country, which in 1873 made them practically old settlers. On the mother's side of the house, his lineage could be traced clearly enough back to Westmeath, Ireland, from which his grandparents, Thomas and Maria Mulvehill, migrated in 1841 aboard a clipper ship of the Black Ball Line. The Mulvehills disembarked at the foot of Beekman Street, and found a home on the second floor of a tenement on the corner of Dover and Water streets several blocks away. The first floor was occupied by a German grocer named Dammerman and his family. (The site is now a vacant lot bounded by the Mongolia Importing Company.) In that second-floor tenement the Mulvehills settled down to make the best of their humble lot in the new world. "My mother was born in that house," her son later wrote, "and so was the daughter of the Dammerman family. The girls were about the same age and their friendship lasted through the years."

His mother, Catherine Mulvehill, was born in 1850 and brought up, strictly enough, in a world bounded by home, church, and school. At the age of twenty-two, she married Alfred Emanuel Smith, a truckman (that is, the driver of a wagon drawn by horses) and a widower fifteen years older than she. Smith lived on Oliver Street but kept his horses in a stable next door to the Dammerman grocery.

Less—nothing, in fact—is known about Alfred E. Smith, Sr.'s ancestry. He was born on Oliver Street between Water and South streets but, according to his son, never mentioned "where his parents came from." This was odd, because if there is one thing an Irishman knows, and is often eloquent on the subject of, it is the county in Ireland, if not the village itself, where his people came from. Later, to his son's ribald amusement, political enemies circulated the rumor that Alfred E. Smith, Sr., actually had changed his name from Schmidt. The rumor was published in the *Gaelic-American,* with so much harumphing and ahaing that its readers, in 1926, were given to understand that a Smith suspected of being a Schmidt couldn't possibly aspire to higher office. By way of replying to the canard, a newspaper reporter friendly to Smith burrowed into old records and came up with the evidence that Smith, Sr., in 1857, had joined a volunteer fire company as Smith, not Schmidt, and the same name had graced the muster roll of that colorful Civil War regiment the Bowery Boys.

Smith, Sr., as his son recalled him was a tall, heavyset man, slightly more than six feet tall and weighing more than 225 pounds, "well known and very well liked in the old neighborhood." An old photograph of him standing on a South Street dock with a friend shows a brawny man with a long face and a drooping mustache. He was a skillful boatman and an excellent swimmer and spent as much time as possible on the water.

Every Sunday in the summer he took his wife, son, and daughter, Mary (born December 30, 1875), to Staten Island or Coney Island. Most of his son's memories of the father, who died when Al was twelve, were concerned with the water, with his father's prowess as an oarsman and swimmer. "I remember my mother telling of an incident that happened in the summer of 1871 while they were keeping company. He found fault with her because she was not ready on time to catch a given boat on schedule for Staten Island. That boat was the *Westfield,* the boilers of which blew up that day while she was in her slip before starting to Staten Island."

The boy saw little of his father because "his day's work was done when he delivered all the freight for that day, and not before, no matter what the hour. Trucking was then a very hard job. A man engaged in that line of business had little chance to be with his family except on Sunday, and even on that day my father went to the stable in the morning to see that the men taking care of the horses were on the job."

He would also recall trips to a German beer garden with his father. The Atlantic Garden was largely patronized by the German families then living on Chrystie, Forsyth, Eldridge, Broome, Delancey, Rivington, and Houston streets. The entertainment was provided by Professor Esher and his band of lady musicians. "My sister and I were given chocolate to drink, and huge slices of cake, while the elders drank their beer, gossiped and listened to the entertainment."

He would also remember his father's talent as a storyteller, which was displayed in Morganweck's barbershop on the second floor of the tenement in which they lived, where the Sandy Hook pilots came to be shaved and listen to the elder Smith's anecdotes.

It was undoubtedly a fascinating neighborhood for a growing boy. Just across cobbled South Street the sailing ships tied up at their East River dock after voyages to Asian, South American, and European ports. He could almost lean out the parlor window and touch the bowsprits of the ships at their open docks.* South Street was lined with pier sheds, warehouses, sailors' dives and lodging houses, saloons, sailmaker's lofts, ship chandlers, nautical instrument companies, and from morning to night wagons and drays clattered over its cobbles with boxes and bales from distant ports. The waterfront was Al's play-pen, but a watchful mother saw to it that he did not become one of the young wharf rats who ran wild along South Street.

Long after his political career ended, he recalled for a Boy Scout meeting that "the great playground, the great organiza-tion center in my boyhood was along the waterfront. . . . the rigging of the sailing vessels afforded a very good gym-nasium—just as good as they have today. The ship would be at the dock about two months. It would take a month to unload it. Everything was taken out with a block and fall, and the tow-horse pulled it up the dock; and as the ship load was lighten-ing the ship raised and it was out of reach, but that adjusted itself because at the next dock another one came in loaded down; so we just shifted from one gymnasium to the other, and in that way we were well satisfied!"

Al learned to swim when his father, using the instructional method then in standard usage, tied a rope around his middle and simply heaved the boy into the East River. He also learned to play baseball, stickball, and handball in the open lots around the warehouses on South Street.

The great spectacle, the overriding interest of his boyhood, however, was the construction of the Brooklyn Bridge. The lower Manhattan approaches to the bridge were being built as he grew up, almost under the front windows of the Smith flat.

"The bridge and I," he would recall, "grew up together. I spent a lot of time superintending the job. I have never lost the memory of the admiration and envy I felt for the men

---

* 174 South Street has long since vanished, and Al Smith's birthplace is now part of the low-cost housing project which bears his name. A small park in the center of the project stands like an oasis, with tree-shaded benches, among the towering apartment buildings. It contains a statue of Smith.

swarming up, stringing the cables, putting in the roadways as the bridge took shape."

The bridge was formally opened on May 24, 1883, with a parade across the span during the day and fireworks exploding over the East River at night. Fireworks also preceded the celebration, and these came from the Irish societies of New York City. May 24 happened to be Queen Victoria's birthday, and every loyal Irishman was enraged at the coincidence. The Irish feared that opening the Brooklyn Bridge on the queen's birthday would be construed elsewhere as a subtle tribute to Ireland's oppressor, but their protests went unheeded.

Many said it was a bad omen for the bridge, that contemporary marvel of American technology. Their apprehensions were soon justified. Six days later, on Decoration (now Memorial) Day, thousands of people came from all parts of the city to make a holiday excursion out of viewing and crossing the bridge. Al Smith would never forget that day. "My father, mother and sister and I crossed over to Brooklyn on the bridge. We came back by the Fulton Street ferry. Late in the afternoon of Decoration Day, there was an immense crowd on the bridge crossing in both directions. I seem to remember that somebody in the crowd at the New York end yelled that the bridge was falling."

Actually someone had slipped on the promenade, somebody else shouted that the bridge was collapsing, and the utmost panic ensued. Looking up from the street below, Al and his sister could see hats, coats, parasols, and purses raining down over the cobbles of South Street. A dozen persons were trampled to death, and scores were injured in the witless stampede. "Some of us boys from the waterfront," Al would remember, "hurried to Park Row. . . . It was growing dark. We crowded as close as the police would let us. They were taking away wounded people, and policemen were piling up quantities of hats and clothing taken from the victims. That was my first view of a great calamity. I did not sleep for nights."

* * *

Nothing defines a New Yorker so accurately as what he calls, in boyhood, his turf, the neighborhood, street, and block in which he was born. A boy born on Delancey Street is as proud of his native turf as one raised on Park Avenue. The Grand Street Boys—many of them wealthy or famous and long since departed from the Lower East Side—revel in their memories at their annual banquets, but there is no similar organization of Park Avenue Boys. To an outlander it would seem that the sheer triumph of having survived a childhood on the narrow, crowded sidewalks of Manhattan contributes justifiably to that feeling of pride.

Although born on South Street, Al Smith was accounted "one of the Oliver Street families," and for many years, until he moved to a Fifth Avenue apartment house, he lived on that street with his own family. The street in which his father was born was regarded as one of the lace-curtain streets of the Lower East Side; it was quieter, cleaner, more respectable than most, and for that matter it still retains traces of gentility.

His neighborhood was the Battery section of the Fourth Ward, extending from the East River westward to the Bowery and Park Row, from South Street to East Broadway. It was covered with tenements, shacks and shanties, warehouses, saloons, and rooming houses. It was not a slum. Poor and shabby, yes, and bounded by the lurid resorts of the Bowery, with its thousands of prostitutes and such deadfalls as McGurk's Suicide Hall; but its 18,000 residents maintained their standards of morality, largely inculcated by the church, in their wedge of streets between the hell raising of the waterfront and the commercial degradations of the Bowery. The people who lived there were knit closely to their families and the church, as they had been in the old country. The district had acquired its character from the successive waves of immigration that rolled across the Atlantic from 1840 until the Civil War. These were largely composed of the Irish driven from their homeland by the potato famines and the Germans fleeing from hunger and political oppression in the south German states. Most of those who settled in Al Smith's neighborhood were Irish, but there was an admixture of Germans and a few Jews and Italians. The first lesson of his life, observed on the streets, in Morganweck's barbershop and other local institutions, was that people of all kinds could get along together if they were willing to make the slightest effort.

For young Al Smith, as with most of those who lived in the district, the unifying and dominating force was St. James' Roman Catholic Church and its parochial school. When he was five years old, the parish was taken over by a tall, vigorous, and handsome young priest named Father John J. Kean. Under his dynamic administration the parish was revitalized and a complex of church societies built up to engage every parishioner in its activities most of his waking hours. Father Kean was a strong and direct influence on Al Smith's boyhood. "When I was a boy," he later recalled, "I was a member of what was known as St. James's Union. . . . The pastor of the church was the spiritual director of the Union, and the constitution of the Union contained a provision to the effect that no boy could become a member or remain a member after the pastor's expressed wish to the contrary. Nobody wanted to have the stigma of being taken out of the Union. A strange thing about it was that it became known in the neighborhood, and businessmen and trades people recruited their employees from the Union because they were sure that the boy was leading the kind of life that met with the approval of the pastor, and if he wasn't, he wouldn't be in the Union."

And Father Kean knew what his young parishioners were up to. Soon after dark he patrolled the streets of his parish, like many priests in the tenement districts, and ordered the kids off the streets. To keep them busy and out of mischief, he organized fifteen different societies, among them the Rifle Guard, the Longshoreman's Protective Society, the Ladies' Sodality, the Free School Society, a choir of twenty girls, as well as the St. James' Union. He never permitted an advertisement for a saloon to be published in the church program. He conducted a

five-year campaign against a saloonkeeper in the neighborhood who permitted women to be served in the back room and
finally drove him out of business.

From his earliest years, Al Smith's life was bound to the
daily routine of the parish. From the age of seven to fourteen he
served as one of Father Kean's altar boys, getting up at six in
the morning to serve at the seven o'clock mass, and for years he
pumped the organ for Annie Rush. He also attended the parish
school, operated by the Christian Brothers, during all eight
years of his formal education.

His mother hoped he would become a priest—the undying
dream of most Irish mothers—but Al had other ambitions
from his earliest boyhood. At first he wanted to be a fireman,
emulating his much-admired maternal uncle, Peter Mulvehill,
who drove Hook and Ladder No. 10 for Engine Company 32
on Fulton Street. Al spent most of his free time at the fire station, running errands for the firemen and helping them polish
the brass on their engines. To him, then and later, the proudest uniform in the world was the blue shirt of the New York
fireman. He was a buff all his life, and one of his greatest hon-
ors came when he was made honorary deputy chief of the New
York Fire Department.

Much as he looked up to his brawny father and his dashing
Uncle Peter, and much as he was held in awe of Father Kean,
the strongest influence on his life by far was his mother. It is
apparent that she had all the virtues of the Irishwoman—not
least the strength of character required in dealing with the
whims of the Irishman. She was intelligent, resourceful, strict
with her son and daughter without being harsh, and until the
end of her long life she was always the one to whom Al looked
for approval of whatever he did. Those who knew the family
well remarked, in later years, "the speed and ardor with which
he sought her out when he entered the house, the way he knelt
to receive her blessing, the pride with which he saw that she was
in the best seat at functions marking his success in life. . . ."

Something of the firmness of Catherine Smith's character

was conveyed by Henry Moskowitz, whose wife, Belle, was one of her son's closest associates. "In later years," he wrote, "Mrs. Smith lived with her daughter [Mary], the wife of John J. Glynn, long a member of the New York police force. To the very end, habits of supervision persisted in her, although she was able to toss them off with sufficient lightness to avoid making a problem with a generation she little understood. During the years she lived with Mrs. Glynn, she used to keep awake until the grown-up grandsons came in at night. She could see under her door the light which was put out when the last member of the family went to bed. She would then flash a light, look at her watch, and make note of the time. In the morning she was likely to make some remark about the hour. Nobody took it seriously, and once Mrs. Glynn asked her mother why she bothered about the grandchildren as long as she had no part in that responsibility, whereupon the old lady laughed and passed it off with a remark that she liked to know what was going on."

There is no doubt that she knew what was "going on" in every moment of her own son's young life. If he escaped the violence, the corruption, the pervasive immorality of the Bowery and the waterfront, later of his political education as one of the sons of St. Tammany and his years in Albany, when the uncorrupted legislator was odd man out, and a curious specimen indeed, it must be credited to Mrs. Smith's influence, as well as Father Kean's vigilance.

Smith was far from a prudish man, earthy enough for the bull sessions of his fellow politicians, always puffing on a cigar and rarely averse to a glass of beer, but there was always a definable space between him and his companions. Not exactly an aloofness, but a certain knowledge that Alfred E. Smith was marked out for something different, if not better than his fellows. That was inculcated by his mother. The several available photographs of him as a boy—the existence of those photographs in itself was significant in a day when a person was photographed only on his wedding day or posed involuntarily for the police—show a well-scrubbed, neatly dressed child with his father's dark-blond hair and blue eyes, his Uncle Peter's cast of features. There were many elements of a Horatio Alger tale in his boyhood, particularly after his father died, but many more of the self-respecting, lower-middle-class, lace-curtain Irish. He was brought up to be something better than a truckman, or even a fireman, and he was never allowed to run with the boy gangs of his neighborhood.

Whatever aspirations were stirring in the boy were not, however, greatly evident in his schooling. He was an indifferent pupil, though well behaved, and showed signs of talent only in his elocution class. Later he would say, almost boastfully, that he could find little of interest in books, that "Life furnishes me with all the thrills." He did not inherit the Irish love of language, of literature, but he did inherit more than his share of the Irish way with the spoken word. The one distinction of his boyhood was the oratorical contest he won among parochial schoolboys for his recitation on the death of Robespierre, the reward for which was a silver medal inscribed "Alfred E. Smith for Elocution," which his mother kept until her death.

Another trait which marked his boyhood, and with equal definition his manhood, was a passionate love of animals, rather unusual in a city-bred boy. It verged on zoophilia. All his life, to the extent dictated by circumstances, he kept himself surrounded by pets of all kinds. Any home of Al Smith's rapidly became part zoo. Something of a lesson in human relations was driven home, perhaps, by his observation that the most diverse creatures could be induced to live together peacefully.

"For a time," he would recall, "I had a West Indian goat, four dogs, a parrot and a monkey, all living in peace and harmony in the garret of the South Street house." Most of his animals were "brought to port by sailors as pets, and when a sailor was short of funds and ready to ship again, it was easy to drive a sharp bargain with him for his pet monkey. . . . Sailors' boarding houses located on the streets adjacent to the waterfront were small menageries. . . . There were no dog-catchers. Dogs of all kinds and varieties were allowed the absolute freedom of the city, and one of the hobbies of the small boy was collecting dogs. At one time, in company with half a dozen companions, I had gathered together as many as seven dogs. Being unable to take them home at night, we left them in the shed of a warehouse in Front Street near Dover, and each member of the firm was charged with bringing his share of food from home to take care of the dogs. My familiarity, in later years, with various breeds of dogs makes me realize that this early collection in which I had an interest was probably just dogs."

In 1884, when Al was eleven years old, the family was forced to move from its cold-water flat on South Street because the building was to be torn down. The family took up new quarters at 316 Pearl Street, and from then on, whatever was carefree in his boyhood seemed to be rapidly evaporating. His father's health suddenly declined, though he was only in his mid-forties. It was a common enough working-class tragedy. For years a man would do the heaviest sort of labor, six days a week, twelve hours or more a day, and then suddenly his body, perhaps his psyche, too, would rebel, and the whole mechanism would fall apart. The exact nature of the elder Smith's illness was not disclosed, but it was some wasting sickness that made him unable to continue handling a heavy freight wagon. For about a year he worked as a night watchman; then he couldn't work at all, and the family was forced to move to poorer quarters at 12 Dover Street.

In November, 1886, when Al was just a month short of his thirteenth birthday, his father died. Medical expenses had taken practically the last dollar in the family treasury, and money for his funeral had to be raised among the men he entertained with his storytelling in Morganweck's barbershop. "The evening of the funeral," Al would recall, "my aunt— my mother's sister, who lived with us—my sister, my mother and myself returned to the little flat. It was cold and cheerless.

I made the fire in the kitchen stove and we ate a hurriedly prepared dinner. . . ."

Immediately after that hasty meal, only hours after her husband was buried, Catherine Smith hurried over to the Madison Street house where the forewoman of an umbrella factory, in which Mrs. Smith had been employed before her marriage, lived and asked for her old job back. That was a measure of Catherine Smith's character, along with the fact that she took work home at night to make enough money so that Al and his sister at least would be able to finish the eighth grade at St. James' school.

Mrs. Smith also supplemented the family's income by buying the stock and fixtures of the candy and grocery store in the basement at 12 Dover Street and operating it with the help of her daughter, while Al went into the newspaper business on the retail side. He bustled about establishing a delivery route along Beekman Street, part of South Street, the lower end of Fulton Street, and the lower part of Peck Slip, along which he delivered the *Daily News*, the *Evening Sun*, the *World*, the *Evening Post*, the *Commercial*, the *Telegram*, and the *Mail & Express*. He also worked in his mother's store from suppertime to bedtime. When his father died, Al had tried to comfort his mother, as his Aunt Mamie later recalled, by saying (with the solemnity of his twelve years), "I'm here, I can take care of you," and he did his best to live up to that promise.

On March 12, 1888, that disastrous late-season storm ever afterward known as the Blizzard struck New York with a fury that shut down the city for days. Like most of its survivors, Al Smith had his own story of that shattering event. The night before the blizzard struck with the unpredictability which makes New York weather forecasting an almost masochistic profession, a gentle rain was falling, and there was only a breath of wind off the bay. The next day the entrance to the candy store in the basement was buried under the snow. "I distinctly remember that I was not very much concerned with the inconvenience of our customers or the fear for the perishable quality of the merchandise, but I was very deeply concerned about the welfare of a Scotch terrier dog with four puppies to which I wanted to get food." He finally managed to dig out the entrance and feed the Scottie and her pups the next day. He and other neighborhood boys also slid down the side of a pier to the ice-covered East River, solidly frozen for the first time in anyone's memory. The schools were closed for days, so Al along with other members of the Buffaloes, a boys' auxiliary attached to the various Manhattan firehouses, reported to Engine Company 32 for duty. The streets were so covered with snow that the engine company borrowed four sleighs from a leather store, loaded them with hoses, and answered fire calls with gleeful Buffaloes clinging to the runners.

Several months later his schooling ended with a diploma from the eighth grade, which was about as far as most boys got; a high-school education then was as difficult to obtain for those from poor families as college is today. For the next seven years he drifted from one poorly paid job to another. There was little to distinguish him from the thousands of other youths struggling for a foothold. He was a late starter, one of those amiable fellows who need marriage or some other stimulus to awaken ambition, and he came from the class that raised up that subsequent antihero of the urban Irish-American, Studs Lonigan.

2

A Diploma from the Fish Market

YEARS after Al Smith struggled up from the Lower East Side and the competitive process of ward politics, he was serving as an assemblyman in Albany. The chamber was holding a night session when another young assemblyman burst in shouting the news that Cornell had just won an important boat race and insisting that the victory be commemorated on the record.

After the hubbub subsided, Assemblyman Smith rose and announced, to the surprise of all who knew him, "I too hold a degree."

"What is your Alma Mater?" the Cornell man inquired.

"I'm an FFM."

"I don't believe I've heard of such a degree."

"Fulton Fish Market," Smith replied with a grin.

Before he went to work at the fish market, he tried out a variety of jobs on the teen-age slave market. His first wages, $3 a week, were earned as a "chaser" for a trucker named William J. Redmond. His job was to race up and down the waterfront finding orders for his employer's wagons. A better one turned up shortly at the oil supply concern of Clarkson & Ford near Peck Slip, where he was employed as an assistant shipping clerk and "handy boy" at $8 a week. Nights he scouted around for odd jobs to supplement the family's income. One such, more in line with his public-speaking talent, was calling out the telegraphic, blow-by-blow account of the heavyweight championship fight in New Orleans between John L. Sullivan and James J. Corbett, on the night of September 7, 1892, for a Lower East Side throng.

That same year, when he was nineteen, he began his career in the Fulton Fish Market. The commission house of John Feeney & Company hired him at $12 a week with the title of assistant bookkeeper. He was also allowed to take home as much fish as he wanted for the family table. The added income came in handily, because by then his mother's health had forced her to give up working at the umbrella factory, poor business had forced them to close the candy store in the basement (the United States was foundering in the worst depression it would know until that of the thirties), and the only other money coming into the house was his Aunt Mamie's $6.50 a week she earned addressing envelopes for a firm on Vesey Street.

He earned his pay at the market. The day's work began at four o'clock in the morning (three o'clock on Fridays) and ended late in the afternoon. Part of his job—his "assistant bookkeeper's" title was euphemistic—consisted of trundling barrels of fish from one place to another, through a market crowded with other men moving their merchandise around, bawling offers, and negotiating at the top of their lungs over the day's catch.

A more important part of his job was as the firm's spotter. On his guesswork depended the prices to be charged that day by Feeney & Company and, to a great extent, the day's profits. In those days the fish could be kept, on ice, only the day they were caught; there were no cold-storage warehouses. It was the spotter's job to climb up on one of the market's roofs, equipped with a pair of marine glasses, and watch for his firm's fishing smacks as they came up New York Harbor and into the East River, via Buttermilk Channel between Governors Island and the Brooklyn shore. From the way the smacks rode in the water, he had to estimate how big the day's catch was. If the boats were low in the water, it meant a big catch and lower prices; if high, a light catch and higher prices. Advance knowledge of the size of the catch gave the firm's salesmen a bargaining edge even before the smacks tied up at the wharves of the fish market.

From the two years he served in the Fulton Market came many of the homely similes that sprinkled his speech in the days of political glory ahead. In describing someone he didn't like, he would say the man had "an eye as glassy as a dead cod," or of another, "He shakes hands like a frozen mackerel."

Even after twelve or more hours a day plunged into the turmoil of the Fulton Market, the young man had enough energy to devote himself to the neighborhood's busy social life. When he grew up, he would deplore the "absolute disappearance of neighborhood spirit." In his youth he rarely wandered far from the lower Manhattan streets in which he was raised. Uptown was for the nabobs, sports, and swells; Yorkville and Harlem were then suburban areas, and Longacre (later Times) Square was the outpost of urban civilization. Anything north of Forty-Second Street was rated as an excursion. "We used to have a picnic in the summer," he recalled, "up at Jones Woods, at the foot of East Sixtieth Street, where we saw the familiar picture of the goat licking the label off a tomato can. . . ."

In the summer he swam in the East River and on Sundays made the long trek to Coney Island by boat from the foot of Fulton Street, Brooklyn, to Sixty-Fifth Street, South Brooklyn, where a train ran along the old Sea Beach route to the western tip of Coney Island.

More absorbing, however, was the flair for acting he had discovered in himself. For many years, until he was dissuaded by the family of the young woman he married, his overriding ambition was to go on the stage. Dramatic aspirations are anything but rare in the early lives of politicians. From boy orator to youthful amateur actor to the theater of politics is a natural enough progression, currently to be noted in the mellifluent performances of Senator Everett M. Dirksen on and off the floor of Congress.

"Deprived" as his circumstances were, he dressed up to the role of embryonic actor and always carried himself with a notable self-assurance partly founded in successes as a parlor entertainer—with "Cohen on the Telephone" and "The Face on the Barroom Floor" among his set pieces—and partly to displays of extroversion and mouth-to-mouth combat required of a salesman in the Fulton Fish Market. On summer evenings he would loiter with his peers on the front stoops, tell stories, and flirt with the girls until one of the priests in the St. James' parish house across the way would rap on the window and send everyone—except possibly a few stray Lutherans—home to bed.

One of the girls who lived in the Fourth Ward remembered him well as one of the sportier youths and recalled for a reporter: "He used to wear fancy vests, a red necktie and tight trousers. I can't remember whether he wore a brown derby or not. Probably he did; one of those funny ones with a narrow brim and a high crown that you see now only on the vaudeville stage. But I do remember that when he was nineteen or twenty, maybe a little older, he was quite pleased with himself.

"He was talking all the time, at parties, or reciting or dancing. He was quite a boy at jigs and *he* thought he could sing, too. One day some of us girls were making plans for a picnic. For some reason we hadn't invited Alfred—no one called him Al in those days—but while we were talking it over he happened along and chimed in. 'You haven't been asked to go,' one of us said. 'Oh, you'll ask me,' he answered. 'You won't be able to get along without the talent.' "

He was self-assertive enough to consider himself indispensable to any affair at which entertainment would be required, and he started performing, singing, jigging, hurling one-liners at his audience, at the first opportunity. There never was any doubt in his mind that he was born to bind spells or weave magic, one way or another. He felt himself warmed by what he took to be a receptive glow—though, often, undoubtedly, it was merely a shrugging tolerance—whenever he found himself in front of an audience. The theatrical bug nipped him at an early age when he climbed the gallery at Niblo's Garden on Prince Street and saw his first play, *The Arkansas Traveler.* Thereafter whatever money he could spare from the family budget and buying red neckties clinked—a quarter a time, for gallery seats—into the box offices on Fourteenth Street. He worshiped at the shrines of the reigning theatrical stars—David Warfield, Sam Bernard, Pat Rooney, Sr., Maggie Kline, Weber and Fields, Fanny Davenport, and above all the Irish comedy team of Harrigan and Hart, whose hit song, "The Mulligan Guard," Al often rendered, with or without request, in his booming baritone:

> We shouldered arms, and march'd and march'd away,
> From Baxter Street we marched to Avenue A.

His own theatrical debut had occurred, with little notice, in the garret of the South Street house when he and his sister and a few of their playmates appeared in homemade dramas. On making his mark as an elocutionist, however, it was evident to him that his talent deserved a wider display. He joined the St. James Dramatic Society, which produced two plays a year, and at the same time hired himself out as a super, or extra, for crowd scenes at the Windsor Theater on the Bowery when such extravaganzas as *The Fall of Rome* and *The Last Days of Pompeii* were staged. As a spearcarrier, he was enabled to study professional actors up close and envy the broad style with which they hurled their lines at the farthest reaches of the second balcony.

The glamor of being able to boast that he rubbed shoulders with real actors and was allowed to join in shouts of "Off with his head" raised his standing in amateur theatrical circles. He was given a speaking part in *May Blossom,* a sentimental drama then running at the Madison Square Theater, and exhibited so forceful a presence that in the next production, *The Confederate Spy,* he was given a leading role. Eight hundred persons could jam their way into the auditorium in the basement of St. James', and their laughter and applause, the way they hung on his words, provided a heady sensation he would never tire of experiencing.

His greatest successes were playing the villains in Dion Boucicault's *The Shaughraun* and the farce *The Mighty Dollar* which had brought fame to the Irish comedian Billy Florence. The latter made an especially deep impression on him because the central character was Congressman Bardwell Slote, a homespun but slightly corrupt gentleman who was fond of saying, "I'd like to have a contract to supply society with all the powder and paint it uses. It would beat a government contract by a large majority"—a rather daring attack on the mores of the establishment for those Victorian years. The amateurs of St. James' parish presented *The Shaughraun* with such success that it was given a two-night run at the London Theater on the Bowery. Many years later, in 1916, the parish needed money, and the play was revived with Al Smith, then sheriff of New York County, again playing Cory Kinchella, the villain. The hero was portrayed by James J. Walker, future mayor of New York. Political historians would later judge their roles should have been reversed.

The young man turned twenty-one with nothing more weighty on his mind than earning a living by day in the fish market and displaying his talents as an entertainer, whenever and wherever possible, by night. His sister, Mary, married John Glynn, the policeman on the beat, and moved to the Bronx, which seemed the outer edge of the earth to Lower East Siders. She missed her family and familiar surroundings so much that they soon moved back to the old neighborhood.

Al got a better job across the river in Brooklyn as receiving clerk at the Davison Pump Works, but he was beginning to see that his life would be limited to a variety of low-paying jobs,

enlivened only by occasional dreams of theatrical success, unless he tackled a more ambitious program for himself. He had
begun courting a girl from the "old neighborhood" whose
family had moved to the Bronx, and her family, lace-curtain
verging on cut-glass Irish, was not inclined to look favorably
on a fellow with day-labor prospects. Also, there had been
slowly growing in him an appetite for a political career. It was
the only reasonably accessible avenue opening out of the waterfront streets to a world where men wore silk hats and
smoked two-bit cigars and were looked up to as the natural leaders of men.

3

Running with the Tiger

No one has described more succinctly the firm hold Tammany Hall exercised on the political loyalty of the New York Irish than Daniel P. Moynihan in his section of *Beyond the Melting Pot* (written in collaboration with Nathan Glazer): "The Irish village was a place of stable, predictable social relations in which almost everyone had a role to play, under the surveillance of a stern oligarchy of elders, and in which, on the whole, a person's position was likely to improve with time. Transferred to Manhattan, these were the essentials of Tammany Hall."

The Sons of St. Tammany had been named for an Indian chief, but from 1817 on it was a thoroughly Celtic institution with the Irish holding the positions of power from county leader to block captains. The party bureaucracy, which extended its influence into every tenement house, numbered 32,000 at its peak. Madison Square Garden had to be engaged for its meetings. And while a backslapping, have-another-drink-me-boy joviality prevailed in the district clubhouses and ward bosses' saloons in the lower echelons, the hierarchy was dominated by sober-minded, stern, and businesslike men with a sharp eye for profit; neither Kelly nor Croker nor Murphy, who presided over Tammany Hall for half a century, were anything but cold-eyed manipulators of power and influence. The ward and district leaders presented themselves to their followers as benign and jovial dispensers of "chowders," picnics, balls, bail money, buckets of coal, and baskets of food for the needy and wore the public face of Tammany.

Their chiefs, however, were granite-faced men who permitted themselves little show of emotion even in moments of victory. In William L. Riordan's *Plunkitt of Tammany Hall*, George Washington Plunkitt, Tammany district leader, provides as a sharp insight into their self-contained character on the night of the election victory of 1897, when the whole town went wild celebrating the downfall of the reformers:

> Up to 10 P.M. Croker, John F. Carroll, Tim Sullivan, Charlie Murphy and myself sat in the committee-room receiving returns. When nearly all the city was heard from and we saw that Van Wyck was elected by a big majority, I invited the crowd to go across the street for a little celebration. A lot of small politicians followed us, expectin' to see magnums of champagne opened. The waiters in the restaurant expected it, too, and you never saw a more disgusted lot of waiters when they got our orders. Here's the orders: Croker, Vichy and bicarbonate of soda; Carroll, seltzer lemonade; Sullivan, Apollinaris water; Murphy, Vichy; Plunkitt, ditto. Before midnight we were all in bed, and next mornin' we were up bright and early attendin' to business while other men were nursin' swelled heads. Is there anything the matter with temperance as a pure business proposition?

Everywhere Al Smith went in his youth there was talk of politics, Tammany politics; it was the center of life in the Fourth Ward. The struggles for power among the ward and district leaders engrossed everyone, none more than the Irish, for whom politics were the Olympic Games, the World Series, the heavyweight championship of the world. They permeated the daily life in a way never equaled. Such orators as Bourke Cochran and State Senator Tom Grady were the heroes, as much as John L. Sullivan or James J. Corbett, of Al Smith and his friends.

Inevitably, the principles taught by the church and those practiced at street level by Tammany Hall came into conflict. Even as a boy, Al Smith knew that Tammany was not just the defender of the poor; no honest biographer could acquit him of not knowing from the beginning, though perhaps to an extent limited by the secrecy with which its leaders clothed their actions, that the organization to which he linked his fortunes and which for a long time he served with the utmost loyalty was basically corrupt.

But for him and others of his class it was the only game in town—Tammany or nothing. You made good in and with the system or resigned yourself to being one of its patronized followers. He could no more have risen through the ranks of the bluestocking, middle- and upper-class-oriented Republican Party than he could have gained admission to Yale, entered the Union League Club through the front door, or led a cotillion.

Smith was never tainted with any of the periodic charges of corruption which spattered Tammany Hall; he was as personally honest as his mother could have wished and probably would have tossed all his ambitions aside if they had required that he do something squarely opposed to his conscience. He also had the corner boys' cynicism, the wisdom about human motives acquired from his earliest years in the waterfront streets. He had started reading about politics when he took up peddling newspapers and (according to his autobiography) reading leftover copies of Henry George's reform-minded daily *Leader*. In the columns of George's anti-Tammany organ, he surely read of the recurring scandals that demonstrated Tammany Hall's leadership for what it was.

In 1884, when he was eleven years old, twenty of twenty-one of New York City's aldermen took bribes of $22,000 each in return for granting a streetcar franchise. This was during the administration of Mayor William R. Grace, an immigrant Irish lad who made a shipping fortune and was elected as an anti-Tammany Democrat (and who served as Smith's forerunner, as Smith served as that of the Kennedys). Mayor Grace vetoed the franchise, and the bribed aldermen promptly passed the measure over his veto. The one alderman who had refused to accept a bribe, Hugh J. Grant, was elected mayor in 1888 and 1890 under the halo of supposed incorruptibility. Later it was revealed that Grant had given five "presents" of $10,000 each to Richard Croker, the Grand Sachem of Tammany Hall. Grant explained that they were an "expression of affection" for Croker's goddaughter, and went down in municipal history as the most generous friend of a friend's goddaughter. After a decent interval, Grant had been nominated for sheriff of New York County, the most lucrative office under Croker's patronage.

In 1889 the Grand Sachem of Tammany himself was sent to prison for fraud against the courts. A year later, when Al was seventeen and just beginning to feel the stirrings of political interest, it was disclosed that the wiskinkie (doorkeeper) of Tammany Hall was collecting 5 to 10 percent of the salaries paid City Hall employees for the organization's treasury.

With that knowledge in his background, it was not entirely surprising that he made his first plunge into politics as a supporter of a schismatic movement in the local Democratic Party, which was expressing the dissatisfaction of Lower East Side voters with the dictates handed down by the Wigwam on Fourteenth Street. Tammany had decided to junk Congressman Timothy J. Campbell in favor of the proprietor of Miner's Bowery Theater. Although he wasn't yet old enough to vote in that election of 1894, Al Smith made a number of speeches and worked vigorously on Campbell's behalf, "beginning my political career," as he would later write, "as an opponent of Tammany Hall and as violently opposed to carpetbagging and the importation into our neighborhood of candidates for office not known to the people they were supposed to represent." The effort failed, and Henry C. Miner went to Congress. It served, perhaps, as a lesson in party regularity and the sanctity of decisions made by the Grand Sachem and his medicine men.

Soon Al became a member of the Seymour Club of the Fourth Ward of the Second Assembly District and a regular member of the forum at Tom Foley's saloon on the corner of Oliver and Water streets. Foley, the coming man in the district's political life, had migrated from Ireland in 1872 and worked as a blacksmith. With his savings he soon opened a saloon, which in that time and place meant he was going into politics in a serious way. Saloons were the "nodal points" of Tammany's district organization, as Daniel Moynihan has put it. The only way to break up a meeting of Tammany's executive committee, it was said, was to stick your head in the door and shout, "Your saloon's on fire!"

Foley, though not greatly interested in public office for himself, soon became a power in the neighborhood through the tested process of "doing favors," "saying a word" for someone whose son was in trouble, presiding at picnics and "chowders" for the faithful. Al Smith had known him since childhood, and would recall, "My earliest recollection of him is of an enormous big man with a jet-black mustache, known to all the children of the neighborhood for his extreme generosity. In those days a penny looked big, but when you got a nickel you thought it was Sunday."

When Al was old enough to belly up to a bar and call for a glass of beer without being jeered at, he naturally gravitated to the openhanded friend of his boyhood. Tom Foley's became his hangout, though he didn't have the money to cut much of a figure in drinking circles. Here he would meet Henry Campbell, an older man who owned real estate and operated a wholesale grocery business and who, like Tom Foley, became one of Smith's early patrons.

Soon he was well known throughout the Lower East Side as a powerfully earnest young orator, always ready to give a speech on the glories of the Democratic Party. He began keeping a scrapbook of newspaper items relating these early triumphs: "A number of prominent young Democrats of the Second Assembly District will spend Saturday and Sunday at the

Lenox Hotel, Far Rockaway. They will be under the leadership of Alfred E. Smith, one of the most prominent Democrats of the district, an amateur actor of no mean ability and the leading man of the St. James company. . . . Alfred E. Smith, the orator of the Seymour Club of the Second Assembly District, was a hard worker during the last two campaigns. He has announced that he will take the stump for Timothy J. Campbell next year if he is not engaged in a personal canvass. . . . Friends of Alfred Emanuel Smith, Secretary of the Seymour Club of the Second Assembly District, are quietly nursing his boom for the nomination for the Assembly."

Shortly after he turned twenty-one, through the influence of Foley and Henry Campbell, he was awarded his first political plum, a rather small one, paying $800 a year. His new job was that of an investigator in the office of the commissioner of jurors. It was easier than manhandling iron pipes at the pump works in Brooklyn—white-collar work for the first time in his life. His assignment was to serve summonses for jury duty all over New York County. Many businessmen loathed receiving such calls to civic duty and used every possible excuse to evade it. It was part of Smith's job, in which he took a certain amount of sardonic delight, to investigate the alibis offered and, if necessary, prove them false. His immediate superior, Frederick O'Byrne, later recollected that Smith was quick as a falcon to pounce on those who tried to dodge jury service.

O'Byrne, in fact, was so impressed by Smith's ardor that he preserved the memos the latter wrote in the course of his investigations of the malingerers. One more or less artful dodger was a member of the Stock Exchange who claimed that he was too hard of hearing to serve as a juror. Smith sneaked up to him on the floor of the Stock Exchange, explained that he had a cold and had to talk in a whisper, and asked several questions about buying securities. The broker heard him without difficulty, upon which Smith reported to his superiors: "Found his claim was of no use and put him back on the wheel. His attorney called and threatened to mandamus myself and O'Byrne to show cause why we should go behind a doctor's certificate. The Commissioner allowed the exemption—that put the boots to us."

Another of his pungently phrased reports told of tracking down a talesman who claimed he was too impoverished to spare the time for jury duty. "Swore he was not worth $250," Smith noted. "Investigated at house and found a swell apartment furnished in luxury. His wife admitted that he was the owner of everything in there and when I showed her the affidavit her husband swore to she said they were all wedding presents to her and he had nothing to do with them. They must of talked it over that night as he appeared a little later and brought a judge of the District Court and asked as a favor of O'Byrne the return of the affidavit. We put him on the District Court list."

About the time he was making a career of tracking down jury dodgers, he met and fell in love with a girl born in the old neighborhood who now lived in the Bronx, a girl who might have stepped out of the pages of a Kathleen Norris novel, sweetly domestic yet with a firmness of character that made it quite certain, along with his mother's influence, that Alfred E. Smith would always be known as a model family man. It was the first and last real romance of his life. He had "called on" or briefly courted other girls. In his autobiography he recalled that he made a New Year's call on the older sister of Jimmy Walker way over on St. Luke's Place, and that was the first time he met Beau James. About all he could remember of that meeting was that young Jimmy was sent to bed early, which was the last time Smith would ever remember Jimmy Walker docilely following orders.

It was Smith's misfortune that the girl he fell in love with, Catherine Dunn, lived on Third Avenue near 170th Street. He was so powerfully attracted to the slender, blue-eyed, dark-haired girl, however, that he braved what he called the "wilderness" of the Bronx in the days when the Bronx Park and Zoo was farmland and the whole area was "sparsely settled." To a Lower East Side boy it was like venturing into Indian country.

The transportation that far north was so uncertain that he often showed up for work at the commissioner of jurors' office with only a few hours' sleep and barely enough energy to amuse his fellow workers by sticking a feather duster in his hat and bellowing the Toreador song from *Carmen*. He had to take the Third Avenue Elevated uptown, change to the Bronx line with its steam locomotive at the Harlem Bridge, then a trolley the rest of the way. Often it was 2 A.M. before he got home. He would fall asleep on the homeward journey and once had his umbrella stolen on the trolley car, after which he always tied his umbrella to his suspenders with a piece of twine before falling asleep.

Something of the lost, shy innocence of that late Victorian courtship of Katie Dunn was conveyed in the recollections many years later of Claude Bowers, the journalist who served as Ambassador to Spain during the Roosevelt administration. Bowers and the Smiths were among the guests at a dinner given by Ed Flynn, the party leader in the Bronx. "During the cocktail interval he [Smith] held forth with boyish enthusiasm on the Bronx of their courtship days, when she had lived there and, when, he said, 'it was a wilderness,' " Bowers wrote in his autobiography (*My Life*). "He had had a job which called for the delivery of summonses, and no one relished an assignment to the Bronx, since the houses were widely scattered. On a Thursday young Smith offered to deliver all the Bronx summonses on condition that he would not be called upon to report until the task was finished. . . . That night the young lover appeared at the home of Katie's family, and when it grew late a gentle hint was given. 'But I'm staying all night,' he said, and he explained the bargain. . . . 'The next morning,' he continued, 'I got on Katie's brother's bicycle and by Friday noon the job was finished and I had two and a half days to wander with Katie on the commons and along the riverbank.' He recalled the strategy with all the gusto of a mischievous boy, while Katie smiled. . . ."

To the elder Dunns, young Mr. Smith appeared to be a decent, respectable young man, if a little too easygoing and amiable to make a great success of himself. They were concerned by his theatrical ambitions; no family with any pride could bear the thought of having an actor even for an in-law. Al finally made headway against their objections to his marrying Katie when he foreswore any further hopes of becoming a professional actor.

Probably because of the doubtfulness of the Dunns, the courtship was prolonged and carefully supervised. It went on, in fact, for half a dozen years until the Dunns finally yielded. On May 6, 1900, the marriage took place at the Church of St. Augustine, 167th Street and Franklin Avenue, with Father Kean coming up from the St. James' parish to perform the ceremony. They spent their honeymoon and the rest of the summer at Bath Beach, Brooklyn.

That fall the young couple moved back to the "old neighborhood" and into a flat at 83 Madison Street, a few blocks from St. James' Church, and there the first child was born, Alfred, Jr. Next came their first daughter, Emily, who would always be her father's favorite and confidante. In fairly short order they were followed by Catherine, Arthur, and Walter.

Smith was in his late twenties, with a growing family to support, and it was evident that there was no great future in the commissioner of jurors' office. His political activity had obtained that minor post for him, so why shouldn't redoubled efforts as a Fourth Ward party worker reward him with a more substantial office?

The time was ripe for an ambitious young man to make his way upward in the Tammany organization. That structure was in considerable disarray, discredited even with the masses who had supported it for almost a century. During the early nineties the Reverend Charles H. Parkhurst had launched his famous crusade against the vicious, police-protected, and therefore Tammany-protected prostitution in the Tenderloin uptown and the Bowery downtown. The *Mail & Express* had followed it up with an exposé that listed 250 faro banks, 720 policy games (now known as the numbers racket), hundreds of houses of prostitution, and 600 saloons which were violating the 1 A.M. closing law. The result was the state legislature's Lexow Committee investigation into the New York Police Department.

Almost 6,000 pages of testimony were taken on how crime and vice had been organized on a businesslike basis. Captain Max Schmittberger of the Tenderloin precinct admitted that he collected $1,000 a month from brothels, gambling houses, and saloons, and Inspector Alexander "Clubber" Williams was revealed to be the owner of a seventeen-room mansion in Connecticut, a racing stable, and a sizable yacht. Police Superintendent Thomas F. Byrnes owned up to a net worth of $350,000. All these gentlemen had bought their promotions from the politicians—Tammany Hall. Of greater importance to the people living in the Fourth Ward and other tenement districts was the public revelation of how the daughters of the poor were lured, tricked, or forced into the life of a prostitute, often with the connivance of the police and, farther up the line, with the approval of their patrons in Tammany. People began to see that the degradation of their daughters was a rather high price to pay for picnic excursions and an occasional handout from a ward boss or district leader.

"Not an Irishman in New York will vote again for Tammany Hall," Father Ducey of St. Leo's Church shouted at an anti-Tammany rally during the mayoralty election of 1894. The reformers coalesced around a Fusion ticket, their candidate (Colonel William L. Strong) was elected over Tammany's Hugh Grant, and the New York *Times* exulted that "The Tammany tiger has been flayed alive."

Al Smith, as a member of the dissident faction in the Fourth Ward, rebelling against the imposition of "outsiders" by Tammany headquarters, worked for Strong's election. There was a vigorous cleanup led by such men as William Travers Jerome, the combative lawyer who would devote much of a spectacular career to fighting Tammany and who was named to the Special Sessions bench, and the young Theodore Roosevelt,

who was appointed to head the Police Commission. Boss Croker
fled to England until the town cooled off. New York, however,
can stand just so much of reformist politics, and the working
people strongly resented the ordinance against selling beer and
liquor on Sunday. Dick Croker came back home in the fall of
1897, just in time to preside over Tammany's comeback at the
polls. Asa Bird Gardiner, the Tammany candidate for district
attorney, was swept into office on his blunt slogan, "To Hell
with reform!" and Tammany's candidate for mayor, Judge
Robert A. Van Wyck, was also elected.

As though to make up for its hiatus in power, the Tammany
tiger immediately went on the prowl again for boodle. The
Tenderloin began operating at full blast. Even more damag-
ing to Boss Croker and his associates was the investigation conducted by the Mazet Committee of the State Assembly, which
uncovered the monopoly held by the ice trust. Iceboxes then,
in those prerefrigerator days, were needed to keep children's
milk from spoiling, and the cost of ice was a matter of constant
concern to every tenement family. The American Ice Company,
through Boss Croker and Mayor Van Wyck, was enabled to
obtain a monopoly over the sale of ice in New York City. The
monopoly did away with the custom of selling ice in five-cent
chunks and forced the people, rich and poor alike, to buy
it in hundred-pound cakes. It was revealed by the Mazet Committee that Mayor Van Wyck had acquired half a million dollars' worth of stock in the American Ice Company and was unable to prove that he had paid for a single share. The ordinary
New Yorker now realized the price he had to pay for beer on
Sunday: spoiled milk for his children. Once again reform became fashionable, and in 1901 its candidates, Seth Low for
mayor, Judge Jerome for district attorney, were swept into office.

It was about this time that Al Smith's political ambitions were
reawakened under the necessity of providing for his family
and undoubtedly under the prod of his own honest revulsion
against the Tammany high command. Destruction of so ancient

an institution was unthinkable to an Irishman—it was still shield and buckler against a hostile world dominated by the Anglo-Saxon majority—but reform from within was certainly indicated. In the Fourth Ward, under Tom Foley's leadership, there was a stirring of revolt against the district leader, Patrick Divver, who was especially resented because he insisted on nominating the same old faces, mostly those of fellow saloon-keepers, for the Board of Aldermen and the State Assembly. Tom Foley now owned two saloons himself, but he promised that if he gained the district leadership, he would throw his weight behind new and younger faces. Naturally Al Smith joined in Foley's campaign, which was successful. Foley then moved to the district leader's headquarters, the Downtown Tammany Club. He was an honest man, within the limits prescribed for a Tammany leader, and imbued Smith with his personal philosophy: "If you make a promise, keep it; and if you tell anything, tell the truth." Implicit in this pragmatic philosophy, of course, was the suggestion that it was best to make as few promises as possible and tell nothing to the electorate if it could be avoided.

For several years Smith had been nursing an ambition to be nominated for the Assembly. With Tom Foley installed as district leader in 1901, and Charles Francis Murphy taking command of Tammany headquarters on Fourteenth Street, similarly promising that new and more youthful men would be nominated in place of the old Croker boodlers, it must have seemed that his time had come. Foley, however, nominated Joseph P. Bourke, who had attended St. James' school with Smith and was a very popular and personable young man in the neighborhood. Bourke was elected, then reelected the following year. He had dismayed Foley and others in the Downtown Tammany Club, however, by spending as much time as possible in Albany and away from the old neighborhood. This was fiercely resented. The word went around that Joe Bourke was getting above himself, thought he was too good for his old friends—

the kiss of death for an assemblyman, who had to show constantly that he was unaffected by success and keep mending his fences, who was under the tightest possible control by the electorate.

In 1903, Foley decided to dump Bourke and nominate another man for the Second Assembly District seat. Once again Smith was passed over as the district leader's first choice, even though he had been working diligently for club and party and had never made any demands in exchange for his loyalty. Why? Well, Al was eminently a good fellow, very popular on the sidewalks and in the backrooms, always ready to break out in a song, dance, or speech. He was a happy warrior, all right, maybe a little too happy. People wondered whether he wasn't a lightweight, with his happy-go-lucky disposition, his ineffable high spirits, and his fascination with the theater. A political officeholder was expected to be solemn, dignified, even pompous, to show he was burdened with the concerns of the voters. Al was too chipper, too actorish, too much the cock o' the walk.

Aside from ward politics, he had taken little serious interest in the science of government or the process of lawmaking; no one ever caught him with a book in hand or heard him expound on the workings of the state government. Joe Bourke's chief fault, from Foley's viewpoint, was that with his eupeptic personality he had fallen into the social whirligig and, when Foley had remonstrated with him, had replied, "Why should I have to spend all my time around here? You know where to find me when you want me." With something like the same sociable disposition, Al Smith might turn out the same way.

So Foley approached another Second District candidate named Pat Whalen, who was working as a clerk in District Attorney William Travers Jerome's office. Whalen asked for time to think about the offer of the nomination and used it to confer with Jerome. "If you take my advice," District Attorney Jerome told Whalen, "you will stay where you are. There is no future in being an assemblyman. Look around and you'll see a lot of former assemblymen walking the streets looking for a job. Let Foley get somebody else."

Whalen took Jerome's advice and turned down Foley's offer. The latter, having run out of promising young men, was in a receptive mood when Smith's old friend and patron, Henry Campbell, suggested that Smith be given the chance. About all that would be expected of him, after all, was that he vote as instructed by the organization. You didn't have to be a statesman to stand up and be counted at roll call. And Smith didn't seem to be the type who would start flaming with civic ardor and political independence the moment he got out of sight of the boys at the clubhouse.

Legend says that Smith got the word he was going to be given his first boost up the political ladder from a heeler from Tammany headquarters, who came up to him on the street and asked, "Is that the only suit you've got?" Smith nodded. "Well, hurry home and get it pressed," the other man is supposed to have told him, "because tonight you're going to be nominated for the Assembly."

By Smith's own account the news was brought to him by Henry Campbell, who looked him up at the commissioner of jurors' office late in the afternoon of the night the Assembly convention was held. First, Smith consulted with his superior for the past eight years, Judge Allison, who gave him almost the same advice District Attorney Jerome had given Pat Whalen. "He said that a man who went to the legislature who was not a lawyer had very little chance, and that there were blocks and blocks of ex-aldermen and ex-assemblymen walking the streets of New York; a great many of whom seemed to have done nothing for the rest of their lives, after they had once served in the legislature." With his ebullient self-confidence, Smith disregarded the advice, certain that he could make the State Assembly a stepping-stone, not a dead end.

Rejoicing, he hurried over to Brooklyn Heights, where his mother was living with his sister and her family. Like any good

Irishman, he knew it was his duty to tell his mother the good news first. Then he hurried back over the East River and gave Katie the news. Al Smith was on his way. Few others may have thought so, outside his family and Henry Campbell.

There were certain niceties to be observed before Smith could spread the news through the neighborhood. A small drama had to be made out of the process of nomination. That process had already taken place inside Tom Foley's head, but the Assembly convention had to go through the motions of formally nominating. The surprised nominee would then be sought out by a committee of two and escorted to the clubhouse, where he had to pretend to be overwhelmed by the news that he had been tapped for the honor. It was a ponderous bit of nonsense that might have been plagiarized from a Japanese *no* play, but Smith was enough of an actor to recognize the disciplines of the political theater. "It was accordingly arranged that I should be found to be notified at St. James' Union, the parish club on Oliver Street," a piece of symbolism that would not be lost on the decent, churchgoing voters of the district. "The demands of the family purse of those days did not permit of a very extensive wardrobe, and my winter suit was in camphor, so that while comtemplating my coming nomination, I was in the kitchen . . . wearing my wife's apron while I pressed my summer blue serge in order to be presentable to the convention."

He was wildly cheered that night and believed, he later recalled, that "I had reached the very zenith of my political fortunes."

The occasion was marred, in fact, only by the sullen face of Joe Bourke, who had been his friend since their school days. Bourke somehow had convinced himself that Smith had undercut him with Tom Foley; hot words were exchanged, and a friendship ended. Smith learned that night that politics makes not only strange bedfellows but strange enemies. Political humiliation, no matter that it should have been foreseen, arouses the bitterest feelings of rejection and seeks an object of retaliation. The lesson of that triumphant autumn evening in 1903 was forgotten, however, when Smith experienced his own replacement by a friend almost thirty years later. And Smith would take it with just as much bad grace as Joe Bourke when the prize was the Presidency and the supposed betrayer was Franklin D. Roosevelt.

Winning the Democratic nomination, of course, made his election a cinch in the Second Assembly District. Nevertheless, as a matter of form, he campaigned vigorously all through the district, speaking to his prospective constituents from the tail of a truck. He was always rather proud of the fact that, whatever the content of his addresses to the electorate, he could be heard a block away "over the rattle of the horse cars on Madison Street."

On election night his mother and sister and her family came over from Brooklyn Heights to celebrate the anticipated victory. The voters did not let them down. He received twice as many votes as the combined totals of his three opponents. The tallies were 4,942 for Smith, 1,472 for his Republican opponent, Paul M. Kaminsky, 106 for the Socialist, and 5 for the Prohibitionist.

That first electoral triumph in the career of Alfred E. Smith was merely noted in passing by the city's newspapers, with the exception of the *Morning Telegraph,* the racy theatrical and sporting sheet, which sent a man down to interview Smith, apparently because of his slender connection with the theater. Smith obliged with a discourse that reflected both his lingering fascination with the stage and his chestiness over winning the election.

"You see it's this way," he was quoted as saying. "Acting is a lot harder work than helping make the laws. That's why I'm booked for Albany for the season. The footlights for your Irvings and Mansfields, but the comfortable and cozy seats of the State Capitol for mine.

"The fact is, politics pays better than the wig-paste profession, and, if I'm not exactly a star in the House as yet, this is my first venture, I guess I'll get the center of the stage and bask in the political limelight before I get through.

"Yes, I'm dead stuck on acting. Always have been, and my friends say I'm a corker at the game. There are lots of comedy men with big names now acting who might not be able to hold a candle to me, and if I hadn't been elected to a seat in the Assembly, some of the top-liners in the Broadway bills might have been occupying a back seat. But it's all over now.

"I'm a politician now, and it would not be good form to brag, but you can just mention in that respect that I defeated Kaminsky, my opponent, by 3,500 votes—more than twice as many as he got. It was like rolling off a log. I could have sat home and been elected, but I took the stump and did a bit of talking. I like it, you see."

Tom Foley must have pursed his lips on reading that half-column of bluster (though there was an excellent chance that the reporter had touched up Smith's remarks); the organization elected a man and did not like the man to forget it.

Smith had to hang onto his jury-chasing job in the county offices because he could not afford a two-month layoff between the election and the start of his assemblyman's salary the first of January, 1904. His patron, Henry Campbell, took him up to Brooks Brothers and had him fitted for his first dress clothes, a cutaway (better known as a claw-hammer) for wear on the floor of the Assembly and a spiketail evening suit for ceremonial functions. "The old neighborhood," declared Campbell, "is going to have as well dressed an assemblyman as the uptown folks have."

4

A Freshman in Albany

On the first Tuesday in January, 1904, Al Smith set out for Albany and the opening of the state legislature. That night would be the first he ever spent more than a few miles from the Lower East Side, and he began suffering from homesickness before the train passed through suburban Harlem. He and another freshman, Tom Caughlan, who was "Battery Dan" Finn's protégé in the neighboring assembly district, made the trip together, clinging to each other for mutual support and comfort. There is nothing lonelier or more forlorn than a native New Yorker leaving the city for the first time. And Albany was known to be a hellhole, full of temptations for innocents from the big city; the days of the Black Horse Cavalry, as the corrupt legislators were known, were not long past, and the impression still lingered that a man sent to the state legislature would have to ward off lobbyists and bagmen offering sex, cash, and booze from the moment he stepped off the New York Central train in the Albany station.

The representatives of the First and Second Districts, clutching their luggage, climbed down from their train at dusk and set out on foot to find a place to stay. It would have to be inexpensive, because both men had to support themselves and their families back in New York City on the assemblyman's annual salary of $1,500.

Smith would never forget that first, cold, homesick night away from his family. He and Caughlan trudged through the snow drifts in the fifteen-below-zero temperature until they came to the ramshackle old Keeler's Hotel on Broadway at Maiden Lane. Icy winds sweeping down from Capitol Hill to the Hudson pierced the clapboards of the room they shared, which was heated only by a wood-burning stove. Still wrapped in his overcoat against the freezing drafts, Smith settled down to read the evening newspaper. The front page was almost as cheerless as their surroundings: A number of people had just lost their lives in a Chicago hotel fire.

Smith got up and surveyed the possibilities in case a fire broke out at Keeler's. Their room was on the seventh floor. He looked out the window to see if it opened onto a fire escape; there was none, and they would have to hope the local hook and ladder was efficient. He then recalled that on their way upstairs the men down in the lobby had been piling wood into the fireplace so that the fire roared up the chimney. He hadn't been a member of the Buffaloes for nothing, and it was easy to visualize Keeler's burning down in the middle of the night.

Caughlan had already gone to bed, but his nervous room-mate woke him up and insisted that they play pinochle. They stayed up until 5 A.M. over the cards, then took turns sleeping an hour or so each until breakfast time.

Later that day, after attending a caucus of the Democratic minority in the Assembly parlor and taking the oath of office, they found a furnished room on Broadway with something less than a seven-story drop to the ground.

Then he plunged into the business of being a legislator. For a young man with only an eighth-grade schooling and a passing acquaintance with legal terminology, it seemed an over-whelmingly complex task to digest and understand all the bills presented for passage. He realized, of course, that he wasn't required to understand anything he voted for, merely to go along with the party, but that didn't satisfy him.

Nobody could ever say Al Smith hadn't done his best at whatever job he was assigned, whether it was peddling papers, man-handling barrels of fish, or tracking down jury-service dodgers. He had come to Albany with the solemn intention of mastering the work, learning the processes of state government, and comprehending just how laws were created, debated, and enacted into the state codes. A freshman who took himself and his responsibilities so seriously ran the risk of being considered something of a clown. As a member of the minority party, even more as one serving his first term, he was expected to sit back in the rear row and speak when spoken to.

But in addition to the solemn purpose he brought to Albany, he somehow fell in love with the whole place, its atmosphere and tradition. Albany is far from the loveliest of state capitals. Its architectural ambience is about par with its long history of corruption, dating back to the days when one political historian wrote: "Men who were fit to be ushers at minstrel shows were made State Senators, and the keepers of gin-shops were manufactured into legislators for the great state of New York." The Capitol itself, however, seemed to possess a majesty unequaled by any structure in New York City. Crowning a hilltop, it appeared to have been designed, as the late Gene Fowler wrote, by "some desperate fellow who during a nightmare envisioned haunted chateaus and then proceeded to spend twenty-three million dollars of public money duplicating his dream." It was a garish mixture of styles in the Victorian wedding-cake tradition. Furthermore, after walking up the hill, one still had to surmount a two-story flight of steps to the main entrance. According to the tale later told by Jimmy Walker, Smith trudged up that plateau for two weeks after coming to Albany before learning there was an elevator operating at one side of the grand staircase.

Smith stood in awe of all that pile represented and of the lawmaking processes that were initiated in the marble-paneled, granite-pillared Assembly chamber. He was determined to make good there. Let the elders jeer at a "greenie" from the

Lower East Side. Let the cynics and sybarites spend their nights down in the Gut, a section of saloons and parlor houses where a drunken legislator was anything but a shocking sight. Alfred E. Smith would make himself a credit to the "old neighborhood," which had regarded him highly enough to send him here as their representative.

He had been brought up in a fairly tough neighborhood, but he declined to join in the occasional rowdyism that broke out on the Assembly floor during Smith's service there. During a debate on direct primaries, for instance, one enraged legislator fired a statute book at a colleague across the floor and knocked the hat off a woman in the gallery. On another combative occasion, a number of Tammany men, not including Smith, bombarded a minister who had come to the Capitol to plead for a racetrack reform bill with books and pamphlets.

Instead of joining in after-session revelry, Smith later testified (and his colleagues sustained him, some of them rather scornfully), "I brought all the pending bills to the little furnished room off Broadway, occupied by Tom Caughlan and myself, in an attempt to study them and understand what it was all about. On several occasions I spoke to him of my discouragement with the whole situation and my apparent inability to get a proper understanding of it. I was reading amendments to laws that I had never heard of before. In fact, I never knew there was so much law. My early school training under the Christian Brothers made me familiar with the Commandments and, consequently, familiar with the Penal Code, but all the rest was Greek, and appeared to be too much for me."

He was also made to feel his unimportance as a rear-row member of the Assembly when he introduced a number of bills on behalf of constituents, and every one of them disappeared into the hopper, was kicked around various committees, and never surfaced for consideration by the Assembly. He was appointed, for some mysterious reason, to the committees on banking and state forests, even though he complained that the only time he'd ever entered a bank was to serve a jury summons and that he'd never seen a forest except from the window of the train which brought him to Albany.

Once he waved a handful of bills in Tom Caughlan's face after an evening's study in their room and almost shouted in his exasperation, "I can tell a haddock from a hake by the look in its eye, but in two hundred years I could not tell these things from a bale of hay."

His insignificance was further impressed on him when Governor Benjamin B. Odell, Jr., gave a reception for the legislature. Elated at the prospect of rubbing elbows and exchanging ideas with his presumed betters, he got into his white tie and tails for the first time and clapped a silk hat on his head. He was under the mistaken impression that only members of the legislature attended the legislative reception. He and four other assemblymen hired a sleigh to take them to the Governor's Mansion in style.

Smith and his companions found themselves involved in an occasion about as festive as a Bureau of Health lineup for smallpox vaccinations. They were herded to the rear door of the mansion by a uniformed soldier, shaped up like longshoremen and passed along the reception line for a handshake with Governor Odell, an introduction to Mrs. Odell, and a nod to and from the secretary of state and various other officials and their wives. Then they were firmly guided to the cloakroom and ushered out the front door. The whole joyous occasion had taken up about three minutes of the evening. He then learned that 5,000 others had been invited to the reception. With his companions, he went on to a party at the Ten Eyck Hotel, where "I casually observed"—probably to the unconcealed amusement of his friends—"that if I was ever governor and gave a reception to the legislature, it would be for members and their families only, so that they might receive the full attention of their host."

After that first bewildering session, Smith was ready to give up his legislative career. He was certain that he would never be able to master the complexities of lawmaking or rise above his fellows in the rear rows enough to make an impression on the legislative process. Voting aye or nay as required by the party whip, poring over endless reams of bills he couldn't understand, was even less interesting than serving jury notices. One morning he breakfasted with the district leader, Tom Foley, in a Broadway restaurant and brought up the matter of his disaffection. Right then his political career might have been short-circuited. Foley, as it happened, had the post of superintendent of buildings available under his patronage. Smith could have that job if he wanted it. It was decided that Smith would take a few weeks to think it over. Second thoughts about quitting the legislature—giving up on a job simply because it was too difficult—fortunately dissuaded him. He decided to run for the Assembly again.

As it turned out, that was a wise move. When he returned to Albany for the next session, still a rear bencher, things began to work out better for him.

That he found life in Albany more pleasant—and his work more understandable—was largely due to the fact that a young man named Robert F. Wagner had just been elected to the Assembly, as a Tammany man, from an Upper East Side district. They took a room together and became the closest of friends and collaborators throughout their years in Albany.

Superficially it would have seemed that the two men had little in common. Smith was a gregarious, easygoing, quick-witted Irishman. Wagner was the son of immigrants and had himself been born in Germany. He was a trifle ponderous, slow-moving, but thorough in his mental processes. He had graduated from City College and the New York Law School. The fact that he was a Lutheran was not likely to endear him, right off, to a devout Catholic.*

Yet the two men hit it off. The qualities of one com-

---

* Wagner later married an Irish Catholic girl. Their son, Robert F. Wagner, Jr., was mayor of New York for many years and is still a major influence in the state Democratic Party.

plemented those of the other. Wagner understood the process of lawmaking and was willing to pass his knowledge along to the untutored Smith. The latter, on the other hand, was street-wise and party-wise, with an instinctive grasp of how to influence human affairs. A College of One was instituted in their room over a shabby tavern on State Street, with Wagner as instructor in the art of comprehending the language of the legislature.

Smith slowly and painfully caught up on his education, and once he had absorbed a short course in law, the work of an assemblyman became more understandable and therefore more enjoyable to him. He began to believe that he might be able to make a career for himself in state government after all.

Just as Wagner taught him how to cope with legislative verbiage, Smith acquired some of the social graces from another new assemblyman, a rather unlikely candidate for friendship, but it indicated some of Smith's ability to transcend class differences without resentment or self-consciousness. James W. Wadsworth, Jr., like Robert Wagner a future United States Senator, came from a wealthy Mount Morris family. His seat in the Assembly was just across the dividing line from Wagner's. When Wadsworth and Wagner became friendly despite political differences, they drew Smith, who sat next to Wagner, into their discussions. Soon the three young men were dining together. Wadsworth, the upstate patrician, had even less in common with them than Smith with Wagner, but in a way they represented the national triumvirate which had been running the country and still seems to be doing so: the Anglo-Saxon majority reinforced by the millions of upward-striving Germans and Irish who migrated to the United States during the nineteenth century.

Wadsworth later confessed that he was fascinated by the Tammany Hall mentality, its peculiar metropolitan brand of provincialism, which Wagner and Smith represented in both its uptown and downtown variations. An upstate Republican, as the record of the New York state legislature shows, usually is as opposed in every fundamental outlook to a downstate Democrat as if they had come from different planets. The history of that legislature has been one of a long, unremitting combat between the city and its hinterland; the interests of one rarely coincide with those of the other.

"I learned a lot from Al," Wadsworth said later. "In fact, I learned a lot from a number of the City members. They had a point of view I had never encountered. They interested me. Even then Al was a man of great charm, who was soon fraternizing with both sides of the house. He was a really talented storyteller and all of us looked forward to hearing the new jokes he picked up."

A Yale graduate and a star athlete, Wadsworth was elected speaker of the house after only one term as an apprentice legislator. Although a Republican, he was convinced of the necessity of promoting the younger members with political talent and enthusiasm, regardless of their party, to more important roles. One of the comers, he believed, was Al Smith. As Smith put it, Wadsworth gave him committee assignments that placed him in "a position to understand better just what was going on."

One such assignment was to the Committee on Insurance. It became an important committee during the 1906 session because a mass of insurance-reform measures was being considered by the legislature. The previous year the great insurance companies had been rocked by scandal and recrimination, charged with using their huge funds to speculate in securities without profit to their policyholders, bribing state legislatures and Congress to prevent the passage of laws that would hamper their uncontrolled methods of doing business. The state legislature's Armstrong Committee, with Charles Evans Hughes as its counsel, conducted hearings in the fall of 1905 which disclosed how the insurance companies were governed by interlocking directorates, had formed secret security-buying syndicates, and diverted corporate funds with the efficiency of a cream separator. One insurance company, it was disclosed, had spent $2,000,000 from 1898 to 1904 in Albany alone, providing, among other things, a "House of Mirth" at which the legislators were entertained, with a plentiful supply of liquor and women, a few doors from the Capitol. The Armstrong Committee concluded that the insurance companies had "systematically attempted to control legislation" in New York and that something had better be done about it. Eager to prove that they had not been clients of the House of Mirth, the legislators responded with a rash of bills designed to control the companies' political activity and regulate their use of corporate funds.

The account of how the big insurance companies rooked their policyholders, using the pennies of the poor to enrich their major stockholders through Wall Street speculations, fascinated Smith. It showed that Tammany Hall wasn't the only institution that fattened itself at the expense of the poor and helpless. Furthermore, the insurance companies had operated in their freebooting way largely through their influence over the Republicans. Smith studied the means of curbing such practices night and day and made himself an authority on the subject. "I went back to the Capitol at night," he related, "and devoted every minute to a study of what was taking place."

At the same time he was making friends on both sides of the aisle in the Assembly. Already, perhaps, there was dimly forming the idea that one day he would acquire larger powers; perhaps he could attain the speaker's chair if and when the Democrats won a majority of the seats. To be effective as his party's leader, he would have to be able to influence Republicans, as well as Democrats. Smith early began laying pipelines to the opposition. He had acquired the patience, the longer vision that political ambition requires.

Thus he realized that part of his program was social. It wasn't enough to do his homework, as few other members did, or simply to master the legislative process. Back in his home district, in the councils of Tom Foley's Downtown Tammany Club and increasingly even at the Tammany headquarters on Fourteenth Street, he was assured of solid support. Now he had to win over his fellow legislators, who would help him up the next rung of the ladder.

Despite his slender means, he began giving small, inexpensive dinners at the less elegant Albany restaurants—corned beef, cabbage, and beer usually made up the menu—for members of the legislature, Republican as well as Democrat. From upstate members he learned something of rural problems and the small-town outlook. Politics was mostly give-and-take, at the practical level, and at those corned beef and beer feasts Smith began to learn how the cow-county representatives and the equally parochial men of Tammany Hall might work together with a little goodwill on both sides. He became almost as popular with the Republicans as with members of his own party, and when Tammany had a measure it urgently wanted to be passed, it looked to Smith to work out a compromise with the Republicans across the aisle. After 1907, he wrote, "I felt my influence in the legislature growing year by year."

The reformist Citizens' Union of New York, which rarely looked with favor on any Tammany man, examined Smith's record and somewhat condescendingly pronounced him "intelligent and active, somewhat above average of machine men"; the following year it reported that he had shown "increased ability." Some of the bills he introduced were a reflection of his interest in bettering conditions for the ordinary people— one to lower telephone rates, another requiring air brakes on all trains, another for the admission to the bar of justices of the peace without further schooling.

He was notorious among his lazier colleagues for reading and comprehending the most complex bills, thick with technical verbiage, and rooting out the stealage, the juice that would be extracted by the corporations or persons for whose benefit they were presented. He even mastered the intricacies of the annual appropriations bill, a document running hundreds of pages long.

All this, and the prestige it brought, allowed him to relax

occasionally and join in the horseplay with which the Assembly enlivened its transactions. Once he sent a Chinese laundry bill to the speaker's desk for passage; it was regarded as such a hilarious joke that the chamber cheered him. Another time two young women from the Fourth Ward came to Albany on an excursion and missed their train back to New York. They looked up Assemblyman Smith and explained that none of the respectable hotels would risk their reputations by sheltering two unescorted females. Would Mr. Smith help them find a place to stay that night? Of course; Mr. Smith was always at the disposal of his constituents, even if they hadn't yet been given the right to vote. Smith found them a room. Hours later the young women were awakened by a noise outside their door and later swore they heard Assemblyman Smith chuckling to himself. In the morning they found that he had dumped a collection of old (men's) shoes at their door. Such pranks may not have won him any place in the annals of American humor, but they rounded out his image with his colleagues as a rough-and-ready good fellow; it was important not to be suspected of being a stuffed shirt.

By 1908, when he was thirty-five, he had compiled such an impressive record as a man able to work both sides of the house and charm even the most moss-backed rural representatives that the top echelon at Tammany Hall began to take notice of him. The Grand Sachem himself, Charles F. Murphy, the dour and self-contained "Silent Charlie," decided that Smith was a man on the rise and wanted to look him over.

Murphy had taken over the Wigwam in 1902, when the ripeness of local corruption forced Boss Croker to decide it was time to retire to an estate in Ireland. He was born in the old gashouse district just north of Smith's Fourth Ward and first came to notice as the star catcher of the gashouse baseball team. He saved his money as a driver on the horsecar lines and opened a saloon at Nineteenth Street and Avenue A, which became known as the headquarters of the Sylvan Social Club, though the neighborhood was anything but sylvan and the club's activities more political than social. By 1890 Murphy was a four-saloon man and a power in district politics. He profited enormously through municipal contracting, his connection being the firm of James Gaffney and John J. Murphy (known as Brother Jack), which displayed considerable success at obtaining railroad construction work and controlled valuable pier facilities. When Smith met him, Silent Charlie Murphy was just fifty years old and already a millionaire.

Murphy was then trying to fit himself into the unfamiliar role of Long Island country gentleman and invited Smith down to his estate, Good Ground. Apparently he was impressed by Smith and considered him a reliable conduit for legislation in which Tammany was interested. Tammany, responding to the demands of the electorate, had suddenly become more favorably inclined to rudimentary social legislation, such as stricter regulation of the utilities and lower gas rates. Smith seemed to have a grasp of such matters. If Tammany could clamber onto that bandwagon and pose again as the champion of the downtrodden, it might rehabilitate itself after the turn-of-the-century investigations showed it to be the instrument by which the daughters of the tenements were inducted into prostitution and the sons became graft-collecting cops. Murphy needed a man like Smith, who could help refurbish Tammany Hall's reputation, almost as much as Smith needed the top man in the organization to further his own ambitions.

Later Smith would write somewhat disingenuously of Murphy as "a man who himself had come up from lowly surroundings"—only rarely a guarantee of interest in social reform—who gave such measures his "unfailing and enthusiastic support," supposedly out of the warmth of his millionaire's heart. At any rate Smith was soon invited to attend lunches at Delmonico's at which Murphy met with Robert F. Wagner, now a state senator; Martin Littleton, the celebrated criminal lawyer and a Democratic bigwig, and Congressman Tom Smith. Soon this was a regular weekend conference, and Smith's attendance certified him as Tammany's chief representative at the

State Assembly. Smith would later insist that he was not given his marching orders at those weekly meetings, that "Mr. Murphy was not what is commonly called The Boss." Murphy's role, as Smith pictured it, was that of a benign, big-brotherly counselor engrossed by the urgency of promoting legislation for the benefit of the people. "He was a good adviser, and if he placed his confidence in a man he allowed that man to make the decision. The Democratic attitude in all major proposals was determined by the group of men he called around him. They being usually leading lawyers and well-trained business men, his familiar expression was, 'If these men do not understand this thing, who does?' "

Smith's standing as a man of responsibility was indicated when the frolicsome young James J. Walker was sent to Albany with Tammany's highest hopes. In 1910, Walker was twenty-nine years old and known mainly as the author of the lyrics of "Goodbye Eyes of Blue." He was a thin, nattily dressed, quick-witted fellow, who had adopted the song-and-dance-man style of George M. Cohan and was inclined to look on life as an extension of the musical comedy stage. The Tammany bigwigs believed that when "Jimmy matured a little" he would make a great vote catcher, and the maturing process was entrusted to Al Smith. They were to be roommates at the Ten Eyck Hotel during sessions of the legislature, part of the Tammany buddy system, just as Smith himself had been teamed up with Tom Caughlan.

Regarding Smith's performance as his guardian, Walker later remarked that "he did it thoroughly. . . . My father went with me to Grand Central the day I was leaving, and Al was there to meet us. He practically took me aboard the train by the hand, and our rooms were there in readiness for us when we reached Albany. He introduced me to all the people he thought I should know—and kept me away from those he thought I shouldn't. It was a wonderful break for me and I never forgot his kindness."

When he first saw Jimmy Walker in his red-and-white pajamas—Smith was an old-fashioned nightshirt man himself—Smith remarked that Walker looked "exactly like a peppermint stick." He also marveled at the young man's quick and easy entry into the affairs of the legislature, which it had taken Smith years to accomplish. Walker had been graduated from the New York Law School, and he plunged into the Assembly debates with complete self-assurance. His command of parliamentary tactics caused Smith to comment, "This boy is a greater strategist than General Sheridan, and he rides twice as fast."

Beau James did not stay Smith's roommate or pupil for long. He was quickly advanced to the Senate, where he soon became the Democratic floor leader. With his blithe charm, effortlessly exercised on both the voters and the party leadership, his career took off like a skyrocket. His fortunes and those of Al Smith would be closely linked, and the latter was always exasperatedly fond of him (like almost everyone else), but there was a vast difference in style and attitude. Walker was a cigarette, Scotch-and-soda, night-prowling man constantly strewing wisecracks. Smith preferred a cigar, a glass of beer, and the company of his wife and children, and his humor was expressed in an occasional, rather unimaginative practical joke. It was to be a vexed relationship.

5

Turning Point

THE first turning point in Smith's career had come when he determined to stick it out in Albany and master the craft of lawmaking, but an even more important pivot was that formed in 1911 by an event over which he had no control —the mass tragedy of a Lower East Side fire which had such enormous consequences that, more than anything else, it was the start of social welfare legislation in the United States and the inception of what its enemies would call the welfare state. The year was 1911. By then Smith had been elected majority leader in the Assembly, and his career was continuing its steady progress; there was a little more money coming into the family budget now, and the Smiths had taken over half of the red-brick row house at 23 Oliver Street.*

The legislature was in session, and Smith was in Albany on that Saturday afternoon of March 26, 1911, when the disaster occurred.

It was 4:45 P.M., and the 600 workers at the Triangle Shirt-waist Factory, which occupied the eighth, ninth, and tenth floors of the ten-story building on Washington Place near Greene Street, were getting ready to quit work for the weekend. Ninety-five percent of the employees were girls, needleworkers,

---

* The house still stands, now serving as the rectory of St. James' Church, across from the parochial school.

buttonhole makers, operators, finishers, who worked nine and a half hours a day, six days a week, for an average weekly wage of $15.40. There were only five lavatories for the 600 workers. The heavy iron rear exit door on the ninth floor was locked because there had been charges of pilfering of materials and the management insisted that all employees had to be searched at the front door at quitting time.

On the eighth floor several male employees were laying out fabrics on the huge cutting tables in preparation for a Monday that would never come for the Triangle Shirtwaist Company. One of the tables had just been saturated with a cleaning fluid and was highly inflammable. One of the men piling fabrics on the table lit a cigarette, tossed away the match, and it landed on a pile of scraps on the floor. At first it appeared to be a minor blaze which could be quickly extinguished. The men tried to stamp it out, but it spread to boxes of finished goods and bolts of crepe de Chine. They rushed out to the standpipe in the hallway, but the hose was rotten and fell apart in their hands. In desperation, they tried to turn on the standpipe and flood the whole floor, but the valve was stuck and couldn't be opened.

In a few minutes roaring flames spread through the three floors occupied by the sweatshop, and the girls panicked. Some of those on the tenth floor hurried up to the roof and jumped to that of an adjoining building with the assistance of students at the New York University Law School next door. Flames were shooting out the windows, up the stairways. On the ninth floor three girls jumped arm in arm to the firemen's net 110 feet down, plunged through the netting and were killed. Others climbed out the windows and clung to the cornices, fearful of the drop to the street below, and finally jumped or were pushed off the ledge by the screaming throng behind them. Forty plunged to their deaths on the sidewalks. The elevator man had fled a few moments after the fire broke out, but a passerby came in from the street, took over the elevator, and brought about 220 girls down to safety before the flames reached the elevator shaft. After the elevator stopped running, 19 girls tried to slide down the cables; their bodies were found on top of the cage below. Many other girls were trampled to death at the rear exit on the ninth floor, which they found locked, and in trying to get out the front door leading to the elevator. Thirty-four bodies were found in front of the locked iron door at the rear of the ninth-floor workroom. By the time the fire was extinguished the death toll stood at 146.

All over the Lower East Side, from which most of the victims came, a cry of anguish went up that Saturday night. It was followed by a roar of outrage all over the city and nation, which were awakened to the inhuman conditions of the sweatshops only when it was too late for those who had worked at the Triangle factory.

Succeeding events convinced the politicians, particularly those in the Wigwam, that something had better be done quickly to damp down the public temper. Nearly 100,000 persons marched in the funeral procession for five hours through a cold spring rain, "claiming," as one funeral orator said, "the seven unidentified dead as their brothers and sisters." The bodies were buried in a single mass grave provided by the *Arbeiter Ring* (Workmen's Circle). Although the proprietors of the Triangle Shirtwaist Factory were no worse than hundreds of other sweatshop owners, and paid higher wages than many, they were quickly indicted on manslaughter charges. They won an acquittal, however, when the famous criminal lawyer, Max D. Steuer, managed to show that the chief prosecution witness had been thoroughly drilled by the district attorney's office on how to tell her story.

The public demanded that such a tragedy never be permitted to happen again in the teeming loft workshops downtown. Banker Jacob H. Schiff and Rabbi Stephen S. Wise addressed a mass meeting at the Metropolitan Opera House, called for the relief of the victims' families and urged that laws be passed to prevent other such disasters. Several of the speakers pointed out that the Triangle fire was related to the general degradation of working people in the city. A year or two before the fire, it was also disclosed, the Triangle firm had opposed a shirtwaist makers' strike. Some of their girl employees had complained that they were locked in at night and forced to finish work on rush orders. Those who struck against Triangle were fired and replaced by girls who had recently come to this country, mostly Russian-Jewish or Italian, because they were more docile. The real responsibility lay in the attitude of employers toward their employees, the fiery young Rose Schneiderman of the Women's Trade Union League told the mass meeting at the opera house. "The life of men and women is so cheap and property is so sacred, there are so many of us for one job," she declared, "that it matters little if one hundred and forty-six of us are burned to death." Thus the issue was made, not of sterner fire prevention laws but of the relation of labor to society.

About the same time a Committee of Public Safety was formed with Henry L. Stimson, George W. Perkins, R. Bayard Cutting, Anne Morgan, and Henry Morgenthau, Sr., among its members. It urged that the state government appoint a commission to investigate the need for new fire prevention laws, specifically, and in a broader way to seek ways of improving labor relations. On June 30 the Factory Commission accordingly was appointed. The president of the Senate named Senators Robert F. Wagner and Charles M. Hamilton; the speaker of the Assembly nominated Smith and two other assemblymen, Edward D. Jackson and Cyrus W. Phillips; and the governor selected Simon Brentano, Robert E. Dowling, Samuel Gompers (head of the American Federation of Labor), and Miss Mary E. Dreier. Wagner was to be chairman of the commission, Smith vice-chairman. Its chief counsel was Abram I. Elkus. One of its attachés was Dr. Henry Moskowitz, who was a member of the Ethical Culture Society and had worked in the Madison Street settlement house, as was Mrs. Belle Israel, a member of the staff of the Educational Alliance, who later married him.

During the session of the legislature just ending as the commission began its work, Smith had acquired considerably more influence in the Assembly. As majority leader he had been named chairman of the Ways and Means Committee and single-handedly had succeeded in trimming $11,000,000 out of the state's budget. The post taught him a lot about the laxness of legislative methods, the lazy-mindedness of his fellow legislators. To them the appropriations they mechanically voted for or against were a hazy blur of boring figures. "I am convinced," he told a friend, "that even to this day there are not more than ten men who could answer such questions as 'How much money is appropriated for the building, maintenance and repair of state highways?' There are not ten men who could give you an intelligent reason for the increase in the amounts appropriated. When I was working on this committee, I would see the majority perfectly willing to appropriate $35,000,000 on quick rollcall without knowing what it was all about."

As majority leader and surgeon on the state budget, he had quickly learned much about how the state government operated in the business sense. The workings of the political parties, arriving at compromises that greased the machinery of human affairs, also had become familiar to him; better than any other man who operated on the floors of the New York legislature he soft-talked the upstate legislators into working with the city members, one hand washing the other. Now his College of One was convened, with suitable instructors, to educate him in modern sociology. The keynote of the Factory Commission's report, contained in three weighty volumes, was to serve as his own guide when he was a governor who pioneered in social reform:

> Health is the principal asset of the working man and the working woman. The State is bound to do everything in its power to preserve the health of the workers, who contribute so materially to its economic wealth and its industrial prosperity. . . . Indifference to these matters reflects grossly upon present-day civilization, and it is regrettable that our state and national legislation upon the subject of industrial hygiene compares so unfavorably with that of other countries.

The Factory Commission began its four-year inquiry into

working conditions with hearings on the Triangle fire, suitably enough, and then broadened the scope of its investigation to take in almost every factory town in the state. From the beginning, Smith and his fellow commissioners were presented with three conditions common to workers everywhere in the state, from the large factories in Manhattan and Brooklyn to the smallest in towns upstate which generated power from a mill-race: low pay; long hours; abject fear of the absolute power of the boss. None of this could have shocked Al Smith. His widowed mother had trudged out on the evening of his father's funeral to get work in an umbrella factory and had to take piece-work home at night to keep her family together. His father literally had worked himself to death as truck-wagon driver. Smith himself had started working for $3 a week.

The commission's hearings made him realize the generality of the conditions in which he was raised, rubbed his nose in the fact that a handout from the ward boss—a bag of coal or a basket of groceries—wasn't much good in healing deep social wounds. They made him think less like a Tammany man, stirred doubts that what was good for the boys on Fourteenth Street was good for the people whose votes bought them estates on Long Island.

It would be exaggerating to say that Smith was struck by visions of social good, Paul on the road to Tarsus, as he sat through those long recitals of injustice and hopelessness, but he was one commission member to whom the case histories presented were more than names and statistics; he could feel the pain and misery behind them at his own nerve ends because he himself had experienced them, in a lesser degree perhaps. No doubt he was able to clothe with flesh and feeling the bare bones of the case histories of the Triangle fire victims as they were presented to the commission. Case No. 210, an Italian girl, eighteen years old, the sole support of her parents. Case No. 120, male, aged thirty, had a wife and three children who arrived in the United States three months before the fire; they were left without means of support. Case No. 85, a thirty-three-year-old widow with her five small children, her parents and a sixteen-year-old brother dependent on her. There was no legal provision for the survivors of any of those people, no compensation for those who had been injured in the fire.

From investigating the Triangle disaster, the Factory Commission turned to probing industrial conditions throughout the state with the help of a force of ten inspectors. More than 200 witnesses testified and 3,489 pages of testimony were taken. Such manufacturing industries as printing, tobacco, chemicals, baking, meat-packing, paper boxes, textiles, artificial flowers, cleaning and dyeing, and canning were investigated on the spot. Smith and his fellow commissioners saw whole families upstate, including young children, working from first light to dusk, seven days a week, for the canneries.

The canneries, run by shrewd, tightfisted country-slicker types, were especially adept at marshaling opposition to any regulations of their use of the laboring force. Attempting to prove that they should be exempted from any general provisions of an industrial relations act that would cut into their tidy profits, they sent a delegation of clergymen to plead their case. Smith was unimpressed by the intervention of the clergy and bluntly remarked: "If these distinguished champions of women and children were to rewrite the divine law I have no doubt they would change it to read, 'Remember the Sabbath day to keep it holy—except in the canneries.' "

He knew enough of the child-labor practices in certain industries to insist, while making a personal inspection, on being led to the elevator. Often the elevator was halted between floors and crammed with children who had been working at their machines a few minutes before Smith and his investigators appeared.

"He was a pleasant boss," Henry Moskowitz of the commission's staff later described him, "but not an easy one. He knew his people, and his rough determination gave no offense. As he sat in his chair, banging his gavel, or shouting at some speaker to hurry along, he made on many observers the impression of being much taller than his five feet seven inches. His face might be in repose or it might be lighted with expression, but it always showed that the mind behind it was active and intent upon its duties. The mild blue eyes were easily aroused, and when they did begin to shine, they were like a fire fed both by intense thought and by emotion."

The young social workers engaged as investigators by the commission, among them Frances Perkins, made certain that both Smith and Wagner were brought face to face with the conditions under which women and children were employed. They took Smith, as Miss Perkins related, to "see the women, thousands of them, coming off the ten-hour night shift on the rope walks in Auburn. We made sure that Robert Wagner personally crawled through the tiny hole in the wall that gave egress to a steep iron ladder covered with ice and ending twelve feet from the ground, which was euphemistically labelled 'Fire Escape' in many factories. We saw to it that the austere legislative members of the Commission got up at dawn and drove with us for an unannounced visit to a Cattaraugus County cannery and that they saw with their own eyes the little children, not adolescents, but five-, six- and seven-year-olds, snipping beans and shelling peas. . . . We made sure that they saw the machinery which would scalp a girl or cut off a man's arm. Hours so long that both men and women were depleted and exhausted became realities to them through seeing for themselves the dirty little factories. . . ."

Smith and other members of the commission also were introduced to several enlightened employers who had voluntarily improved working conditions and found that there was profit to themselves in enabling their employees to produce more work under safer and more healthful conditions.

Without any great shock, Chairman Wagner and Vice-Chairman Smith learned that people who pretended to be bleeding-heart liberals in their political and public life privately could be as conservative as Mr. Scrooge. Thomas Mott Osborne was the leader of the reformist group known as Progressive Democrats, yet in his Auburn factory the commission reported finding "the vilest and most uncivilized conditions of labor in the state."

On completing its investigation, the Factory Commission recommended a number of bills which would protect labor against the employers. In the 1912 session of the legislature, Smith began introducing the legislation which would embody those recommendations. A Bureau of Fire Prevention was to be established to make certain there were easily opened exits, fire-proofing, fire drills, automatic sprinkler systems in factories. Workrooms were to be adequately ventilated; the employment of women after childbirth was to be limited; female employees were to be given rest periods; working children were to be examined for physical fitness. The hours women and children could work were to be regulated. People injured on the job were to be compensated—that measure later ruled out by the courts, but in 1913 placed in effect through a constitutional amendment.

Throughout 1912, as Democratic floor leader, he pleaded for passage of those bills and bulldozed their path through the legislative maze. Many of the upstate members, trying to protect farmers and canneries from laws governing their use of labor, were bitterly opposed. One particular gadfly was an assemblyman named Pratt, who insisted on referring to Smith as "Mr. Tammany Leader" whenever he addressed the opposition.

During a wearying night session, Assemblyman Pratt jumped up from his seat and demanded, "Mr. Tammany Leader, what good is the Workmen's Compensation Act to the 350,000 men who are out of work in this state?"

Smith sighed windily and turned to the speaker, remarking, "As I was walking down Park Row one morning, a friend of mine tapped me on the shoulder and said, 'Al, which would you rather be, a cellar full of stepladders, a basketful of door-knobs or a piece of cracked ice?' and I replied I would rather be a fish because you can always break a pane of plate glass with a hammer."

Assemblyman Pratt's jaw dropped in bewilderment at the double-talk. Finally, sputtering, he addressed the chair: "Mr. Speaker, I certainly do not get the point to the Tammany Leader's answer."

"You don't get the point to my answer?" Smith roared across the floor. "Well, let me say to you that there is just as much point to my answer as there is to your question. This bill is a meritorious measure, and its passage should not be impeded by unnecessary delay, due to the propounding of silly questions and foolish answers. I move the previous question."

Smith needed all his comparative youth to push the compensation laws through the legislature. They were opposed by a powerful lobby of special (industrial) interests and their high-priced legal talent, determined to prevent the establishment of the principle that the employer is responsible for on-the-job injuries to his workmen. They even argued that a laborer might deliberately lose his arm or leg to collect compensation. Thanks to Smith in the Assembly and Wagner in the Senate, such arguments were beaten down. For the next fifteen years, both in the legislature and the Governor's Mansion, Smith worked to tighten the provisions of laws protecting the working people.

Admittedly, that crusade was good politics—his political base on the Lower East Side was changing with Jews and Italians, almost all working people, moving in beside the Irish and Germans in greater numbers every year—but undoubtedly it was also a reflection of his background and deepest sympathies.

The election of 1912 not only put Woodrow Wilson in the White House but resulted in a Democratic sweep in New York. The legislature was overwhelmingly Democratic, controlling 105 of the 150 seats in the State Assembly. Thus the electoral tide swept Smith, as Democratic leader in the Assembly, into the speaker's chair, while his close associate Robert F. Wagner assumed the presidency of the State Senate. It also produced a phenomenon named William Sulzer as governor, whom Max Eastman described as a "gaunt Andrew Jackson of a man with a ten-gallon black hat and a madly glittering eye."

Sulzer had been nominated for the governorship under a reluctant agreement between Tammany and the Progressive Democrats, who sponsored him. Tammany soon regretted the bargain, which Smith had opposed at the convention and which placed a maverick exhibitionist in control of the state government.

Katie and their five children came up to Albany to watch from the spectators' seats the proud occasion when the thirty-eight-year-old Al Smith mounted the rostrum as speaker of the Assembly. He then proceeded to rule that house with a firm hand. The anti-Tammany New York *Times,* in a series titled "Our Honorable Legislators," provided a close-up of Smith in action. The writer was careless about details in Smith's background but managed to convey a vivid impression of an earthy, energetic master of legislation:

> Speaker Smith, who I am told was once a barker at Coney Island and a vaudeville performer, yells with hoarse, raucous voice from the Speaker's table as if he were at Coney, and pounds his gavel as if he were pounding on one of those sledge-hammer affairs at Coney which are supposed to show how strong you are. He ate luncheon during the session and at times talked with food in his mouth. There is a complete lack of dignity. At times bills on the calendar are rushed through at the rate of eight a minute by a process of antiphonal mumbling by the clerk and Bull-of-Bashan-like roars from the throne behind, "Read the last section," "Call the roll," "The bill is passed." The roll is not called—just a name or two and the clerk says so many ayes and noes none. I timed the work and found that when running full speed the bills were enacted at the rate of eight a minute.

The *Knickerbocker Press* of Albany also had noted the emphatic manner with which Smith had taken control of the Assembly. "Speaker Smith is running the Assembly and nobody else. He is conducting it on a business basis. There is no dilly-dallying. Nobody has to put their hands to their [sic] ears to hear what he is saying. His powerful voice is at times almost sinister."

The anti-Democratic press professed to find something even more sinister than his bullish voice in the frequent visits to Albany that session of Boss Murphy and his conferences at the Ten Eyck Hotel with Smith and Wagner. Even the New York *World*, fascinated at the moment by the possibilities of Progressive Democracy led by Governor Sulzer, declared that the legislature was being run that session by "Charles F. Murphy at one end of a telephone wire and the Democratic leader at the other." The reformist Citizens' Union, in its watchdog role, reported that Smith was showing "not the slightest evidence of independence."

Boss Murphy's and Tammany's concern over events in Albany was triggered by the flamboyant independence of Governor Sulzer, who had decided that he needed no further assistance from the Wigwam. Almost from the moment of his inauguration Governor Sulzer had indicated that, by assuming a folksy persona, he could appeal directly to the electorate without the barrier of any political organization. A former Congressman, he had come to Albany insisting he would do away with the pomp and folderol of high office. "Sulzer insisted that business clothes were formal enough for the inaugural ceremonies," the journalist Henry Pringle observed. "The quality of his democracy was studied. He expectorated frequently, but without the spontanteity with which Al Smith does the same thing. One of his first acts was to inform the newspaper correspondents that they were the most important persons at Albany and that he would interrupt any conference to talk with them. He granted one important interview at the Executive Mansion in his nightshirt. The reporters thought him very much of an ass. . . ."

At first Smith tried to get along with the new governor, fearful of a party split which could only benefit the Republicans. In a special message, Sulzer proposed laws to control the New York Stock Exchange. Smith publicly allowed that the legislation made "good sense," but probably he knew that, with Wall Street bringing all possible pressure to bear on both parties, it would never emerge from committee consideration. In April, 1913, the governor began agitating on a subject much closer to the heart of all organization men. He proposed a direct-primary bill, a measure that would have threatened Tammany's control over the nomination of candidates for public office. A Tammany-backed bill with watered-down provisions was denounced by the governor as "a betrayal of the people, a fraud and a sham."

Tammany couldn't take such charges lying down, and before that session ended, it had mustered all its forces to remove Sulzer from the Executive Mansion as quickly as possible. Smith deployed his well-drilled battalion and killed the Stock Exchange bill and others of Sulzer's pet projects. The governor retaliated by withholding patronage from Tammany Hall.

Tammany's reply to that unkindest of cuts was impeachment proceedings. Sulzer was charged with violating the Corrupt Practices Act during the 1912 campaign. He had the maverick's courage, at least, and fought back by claiming that Smith and other minions of the Tammany machine were rigging a frame-up. Actually Smith went along with the impeachment with the greatest reluctance, believing that it might succeed in destroying Sulzer's political career but also bring down the party in the process, a view which was sustained by the results of the next state elections. Sulzer was placed on trial before a Court of Impeachment formed by the judges of the State Court of Appeals and members of the State Senate and found guilty of diverting campaign funds to his own use. The Assembly voted for his removal by a vote of 79 to 45, with Smith obeying the dictates of Tammany Hall and voting aye. Sulzer was replaced by Lieutenant Governor Martin H. Glynn and Glynn by Robert F. Wagner.* As it turned out, that was almost as bad

---

* In a mood for vengeance, Sulzer ran for the Assembly in the Sixth District and was elected. He also invaded Smith's district in a foolhardy effort to persuade the voters to reject Smith. Speaking at a Fourth Ward rally, he was

a bargain as the one which gave Sulzer the governorship in the first place.

In looking back on that hectic 1913 session of the legislature, with all its Tammany-dictated skulduggery, Smith in his autobiography preferred to dwell not on "a year of turmoil," as he phrased it, but on the fact that "during that year some of the most comprehensive reform legislation in the history of the state was enacted." It was no empty boast. Years after his death Warren Moscow (*Politics in the Empire State*), a veteran Albany correspondent, would write that Smith "more than any other one man, set the tone for the government the people get in New York State . . . politicians of both parties still run on his record."

During that session, in addition to completing the passage of bills recommended by the Factory Commission, he was proudest of having initiated the Child Welfare Act, which provided pensions for widowed mothers to enable them to keep their children at home rather than having them turned over to institutions. The measure was proposed by Mrs. William Einstein, Sophie Irene Loeb, and other women interested in progressive legislation—the sort of women, pioneer social workers, who would soon be closely allied with the cigar-chewing Fourth Ward politician with the carny barker's voice. A strange alliance, but one which endured and was strengthened. Their widowed mothers' pension plan touched him personally. "Had my mother not been in the enjoyment of good physical health," he reflected, "I would probably have found myself in the same position" as those children sent to orphanages. It took him two more legislative sessions to secure enough support on both sides of the house and in both houses of the legislature, but he persisted until the bill was passed.

interrupted by a group of young women screaming with laughter on a nearby fire escape, by a fife and drum corps parading by, fire engines summoned by a false alarm, and finally firecrackers thrown by a gang of ruffians. Finally, he had to flee the scene with Smith partisans on his heels.

6

Accumulations of Prestige

THERE were two supreme ironies connected with Alfred E. Smith's career. Perhaps the greater was that the natural father of the New Deal, which was conceived in Albany years before it was born in Washington, later renounced his paternity. Of almost equally sardonic importance was the fact that Smith, a loyal servant of machine politics for most of his career, was the man who unwittingly executed its death warrant. More than any other man, perhaps, he was responsible for the disintegration of Tammany Hall and the other big-city political organizations. Until Smith introduced social welfare programs in New York State, Tammany and the other political machines functioned, more effectively than may now be credited, as all-under-one-roof welfare agencies. This primary function, providing such an intimate relationship with the tenement masses, was eliminated by the state government. After that the big-city machines slowly lost their effectiveness.

Even such a progressive social thinker as Daniel P. Moynihan now has his doubts about the total efficacy of that shift in power from the political machines to the welfare bureaucracy. The latter has instituted such rigid rules for the distribution of welfare, Moynihan believes, that the fiber of family life in the slums is being destroyed. "Having destroyed the power of the local bosses," he stated in the 1968 commencement address at the New School for Social Research, "we learn that the people feel powerless. Having put an end to patronage and established merit systems in the civil service, we learn that the poor and unqualified are without jobs. Having banished felons from public employment, we find enormous numbers of men who need jobs have criminal records."

Undoubtedly Smith did not foresee that result or indeed the disestablishment of Tammany, which he regarded with all the loyalty which men of superior advantages bestowed on their Alma Mater, their college fraternity, and their yacht club's pennant. He was particularly devoted, in an almost filial way, to the man he always called "Mr. Murphy," the Grand Sachem of Tammany until his death in 1924. He was less devoted to Murphy's successor and in his last years in public office would make himself almost completely independent of Tammany, but he was always its defender.

Smith's crusading for social reform was undertaken, however, with at best lukewarm approval from Murphy. The Tammany leader's attitude toward social legislation was indicated in the recollections of Frances Perkins, who had started out in public life as an investigator for the Factory Committee. Miss Perkins went to see him at the Tammany headquarters on Fourteenth Street to appeal for his support of legislation to make factories safer. She approached him in "a good deal of trepidation" because of his "sinister reputation" but was received in a "reserved but courteous way."

Murphy listened to her arguments on behalf of the legislation, then leaned forward and said, "You are the young lady who managed to get the fifty-four hour [workweek] bill passed?"

Miss Perkins admitted it, and Murphy reminded her that he had been opposed to the bill.

"Yes," she said, "I so gathered, Mr. Murphy."

"It is my observation," he told her no less sternly, "that that bill made us many votes. I will tell the boys to give all the help they can to this new bill. Goodbye."

In her dispassionate way, Miss Perkins believed that the social welfare causes she worked for in Albany were implemented by the politicians, Al Smith foremost among them, because of the "pull of social forces" rather than "vote-getting considerations." Nor was it entirely true that such programs succeeded because the politicians allowed their hearts to rule their heads. "It was not because some Democrats were poor boys and many of the Republicans were well-to-do in their youth that the Democrats were more responsive to social reform. I think it was purely chance that the Democrats were in office when the opportunities and necessities to move in this direction came. Thousands of people became Democrats or voted that ticket when the Democrats espoused these ideas. There was nothing social minded about the upstate Democrats who boasted they were Jeffersonians, whatever that means. In my experience it meant they were for the farmers and the canneries and regarded labor laws as interfering with the liberty of individuals."

The session of 1914 was marked by incessant bickering between the Democratic-controlled Senate and the Republican-controlled Assembly. Once again the minority leader, Smith devoted much of his energy to pressing for passage of the Widows' Pension Act, a cause he also pursued through the next legislative session—his last—in the early months of 1915. Thanks in large part to his cajolery in the cloakroom and eloquence on the Assembly floor, it was finally passed. One of his more stirring speeches was delivered on March 24, 1915, on the third reading of the bill.

What happened, he asked, when the head of a family died? First, the widow and her children were separated. "The mother stands in the police court," he continued, the usual rasp in his voice smoothed down. "She witnesses the separation of herself and her children. They are torn away from her and given over to the custody of an institution, and nothing is left for her but to go out into the world and make her own living. What must be her feelings? What must be her idea of the State's policy when she sees these children separated from her by due process of law, particularly when she must remember that for every one of them she went down into the valley of death that a new pair of eyes might look out upon the world? . . ."

Under the bill Smith was pleading for, he said, the state would be saying to the widow and her children, "We recognize in you a resource to the State and we propose to take care of you, not as a matter of charity, but as a matter of government and public duty." (This, apparently, was an echo of the ideas being circulated by the social reformers' lobby in Albany, following the theory of Simon Patten of the Wharton School of Finance and Commerce. Patten had coined the phrases "surplus civilization" and "deficit civilization." The latter was represented by the old America, dominated by the Puritan ethic, which stressed the values of thrift and individual effort. The United States had become a "surplus civilization," Patten believed, which had the resources and the will to devote part of them to the social betterment of the underprivileged classes.)

It was time, Smith declared, to consider the conservation of human as well as natural resources. "We are pledged to conserve the natural resources of the State. Millions of dollars of the taxpayers' money, untold and uncounted millions have been poured into that channel. We have been in a great hurry to legislate for the interests. We have been in a great hurry to conserve that which means to the State dollars and cents. We have been slow to legislate along the direction that means thanksgiving to the poorest man recorded in history—to Him who was born in the stable at Bethlehem."

The speech constituted a stirring farewell to the Assembly in which he had served for fourteen years. In that long service as apprentice and journeyman he had built a solid reputation, along with Robert Wagner, as both a champion of social progress and a devoted legate of Tammany Hall. Few could believe the roles were compatible, but Smith continued to prove they weren't mutually exclusive that spring when he was named as a delegate to the Constitutional Convention.

The convention sat for five long verbose months in the spring and summer of 1915, charged with updating the state constitution. Al Smith took his place among some of the most distinguished citizens of the state and emerged as a statesmanlike leader of his party respected by the dignitaries of the opposition. His ability to cut through legal terminology and express himself with a pungent simplicity greatly impressed such men as Elihu Root, Henry L. Stimson, Louis Marshall, Seth Low, James Wadsworth, George W. Wickersham, and John Lord O'Brian, all of whom represented the Republican contingent. Because of Democratic reverses in the recent election, which saw Charles S. Whitman elevating himself from district attorney of New York to governor and Republican majorities sent to both the Assembly and the State Senate, the Democrats held only 32 seats at the Constitutional Convention to the Republicans' 133.

Against an array of celebrated lawyers and public servants, Smith stood out for his knowledge of how the state governmental machinery worked, of practical politics and the give-and-take of the committee rooms. The conservative George Wickersham nominated Smith as "the most useful man at the convention." Elihu Root, the former Cabinet member and international lawyer, who was chairman of the convention, later said he was "the best informed on the business of the state of New York." The glacial Charles Evans Hughes was inclined to qualify his verdict on Smith's performance when he remarked, "I distrust Tammany Hall even in its most amiable aspect."

That bouquet of compliments was bestowed even after, in the heat of debate, Smith attacked the "ironclad nerve" and "galvanized gall" of the Republican grandees with whom he deliberated. The reputation he gained at the convention, in fact, was the most important result of those deliberations; the constitutional changes they recommended were turned down by the voters in the referendum later that year.

Smith summoned all his parliamentary talent in an attempt to beat down a home-rule proposal for New York City which he denounced as fraudulent and which he claimed would give New Yorkers less self-government than the federal government had just awarded the Filipinos, "a half-civilized bunch of half-dressed men that we got by accident." (Not an instance of his emerging statesmanship.) In passing, he also denounced those prosperous ex-New Yorkers who had fled to the suburbs, where they had "hot and cold folding doors." Men who lived two to a house had to try to understand the masses who lived forty to a house. They must disabuse themselves of the idea that rural wisdom was superior to metropolitan. "The man who comes from a farm, after battling with the handles of a plow," didn't necessarily know what was best for the whole state. He suggested that legislative debates be published as "a kind of automatic valve" because "if there is anything needed in this room, it is said valve." The city masses could and should be trusted with the privileges of democracy. For this proposition, he performed in his familiar role as a barroom Aesop and offered an illustration.

He told of a Socialist sent to the Assembly from Schenectady and how he was tamed by the democratic process. "When he found the debate was open, free and unrestricted and he was enabled to participate absolutely freely, and when he found that 76 votes and 76 only did anything in this chamber, he went immediately down to the Ten Eyck barbershop and got a haircut."

The rights of the majority were denied as far as New York City was concerned, Smith declared. Because of the manner in which legislative seats were apportioned, the more sparsely settled rural counties upstate outbalanced the millions in the city in exerting governmental influence. "The minute we assemble to build a basic law," he argued before the convention, "one of the first declarations of principle is that the rule of the majority is right, except when the majority is in New York City. And yet the commonwealth will look into the tenement for a defense of itself, just as it will look to the farm, and may receive it more readily from the city than from the country." He was voicing the outrage being felt in the metropolis over the fact that the Republican-controlled legislature was trying to raise taxes for New York City, which was already contributing more than 70 percent of the funds collected by the state government, also by a bill providing $3,400,000 for the highway department, even though the Republican governor had asked for only $2,000-000. The money, of course, would be spent to improve roads in the upstate counties.

He displayed a surprising expertise in the political history of the state and of his native city in arguing for a greater share of legislative power for the metropolis. "Going back as far as you can in political history," he told the convention, "apportionments have always spelled politics. In 1894 the Constitutional Convention erected this Senatorial district on Manhattan Island. . . ." He reeled off the limits from Fourteenth to Fortieth Street, from Lexington Avenue to Eighth Avenue, which any New Yorker could recognize as a jigsaw section carved out of the center of the island. "That was done," he continued, "so that the candidate for senator from the political Senatorial district could on registration days and election days just walk up Fifth Avenue, look up and down the streets, and look around and see if the election district captains and the poll clerks and workers were absolutely Republican and thereby assure to them at least one senator on Manhattan Island."

Smith pleaded for an amendment giving the city the right to apportion its own aldermanic districts, but it was denied by the majority. So was amendment after amendment he offered in that field. Finally, he cried out in desperation: "I desire to offer one final amendment. The Good Book says, 'While the light holds out to burn, the vilest sinner may return.' "

That amendment, too, was defeated by the convention.

Smith fought hardest, and most eloquently, against the amendment offered by Walter Barnes, Jr., an archconservative and the state leader of the Republican Party. Barnes was outraged by the social-welfare laws passed by the legislature during the recent years of Democratic domination and was determined to block any further such legislation in the future. His amendment would have provided that the legislature "shall not grant any privilege or immunity not granted equally to all members of the State."

Smith and Barnes locked horns in committee and on the convention floor. Politically they stood at opposite poles, and their debate, to a considerable extent, set the tone for an acrimonious dialogue that has continued for more than half a century over the limits of responsibility the government has for its less fortunate citizens. Smith considered his opponent "a man of unusual ability, a good talker with a broad knowledge of affairs, but he was probably as reactionary a man as I ever met."

With the war in Europe then raging with a bloody futility, Barnes seized on imperial Germany as the example of what happened when the state concerned itself too directly with the social welfare of the people. Germany under Bismarck, of course, had instituted the first national welfare system. Barnes shrewdly seized upon the Bismarckian model of State Socialism as an instrument to bludgeon the New York welfare laws. The German system, he said, forced the people to believe that they existed for the government, made them mindless automatons serving the state. He quoted Bismarck as telling the Reichstag in 1873, "Take care of the widowed mother; provide insurance against sickness and old age, and they [the Socialists] will have sung their swan song."

Many of Barnes' fellow Republicans disagreed with him on the issue, though less forcefully than Smith. Thus when Smith rose to reply to Barnes on the convention floor, George Wickersham, who had been Attorney General in the Taft administration, yielded to Smith twenty minutes of his speaking time, so that Smith would have a half hour in which to present his carefully reasoned defense of the welfare laws he had helped coax through the legislature. And Smith rose to the occasion with one of the best speeches of his career.

He opened by asserting that Barnes' preachments for "a return to the American ideal" would actually drive us farther away from it.

In his opening paragraph, he compressed the thinking that would guide his political career during its sunniest and most successful stages:

"The gentlemen around this chamber would lead us to believe that law in a democracy is the expression of some divine or eternal right. I am unable to see it that way. My idea of law and democracy is the expression of what is best, what fits the present needs of society, what goes the farthest to do the greatest good for the greatest number. And, after all, is not that the reason for the existence of the great political parties? Has it not been conceded time and time again that the only question at issue between them is how to reach it in the safest, the surest, and the quickest way?"

Workmen's compensation, he insisted, was not a "privilege" or "immunity." It was "an indirect tax upon the industry of the State for the purpose of relieving the shoulders of all the people from carrying the burden of the men injured or destroyed in the upbuilding of an industry." The state was not only "green fields and rivers and lakes and mountains and cities" but people, and "anything that tends to make the members of the State strong and vigorous in turn helps to make the State so. . . ."

He suggested that the convention "get down to business and stop all this constitutional talk. . . . Let us get right down to the hardpan." The essential question, he said, was: "Is it prudent for this convention to do what it can to reduce the basic law to the level of the cave-man's law, the law of the sharpest tooth, the angriest brow, and the greediest maw?"

Women and children must be protected by a minimum wage. The suggestion that it might be extended to cover men too "can be dissipated into thin air by a wave of the hand," he declared, because men were protected by unions. Women and children, however, were unorganized. "No woman goes to work . . . with the intention of working forever in the department store or shirt factory or shirtwaist manufactory. She goes there for a start in life. Her ultimate desire is the desire of all women, that she have her own home and her own family. Consequently women never organize. Consequently they are without the power to present their claims. . . ."

He appealed to the moral sense of the delegates in declaring the need for better pay for young women, quoting one of the investigators for the Factory Commission: "I do not think the problem ever presented itself to a girl, 'Shall I sell myself in order to make more than six dollars a week?' But the absence of amusement, the barrenness and ugliness of life, the whole thing combined with unemployment, does tend powerfully in that direction. Low wages put too severe a strain on the moral strength of the individual."

He concluded by urging that the convention consult its collective conscience before deciding to bar further social legislation and "see if you can excuse yourself at some future time, when its necessity may be much more apparent, upon the ground that you are afraid to trust this great question to the elected representatives of the people in the Senate and Assembly."

Eventually the Barnes resolution was defeated by a coalition of Democrats, solidly arrayed behind Smith, and a number of liberal Republicans like Root and Wickersham.

Those five hot months ending in late summer, 1915, comprised "the hardest work I have ever done," Smith wrote later. His reward was the recognition that he was "the greatest master of government in the whole state," as Norman Hapgood and Henry Moscowitz observed. Even Charles Evans Hughes came to reluctant agreement with that verdict, when he observed, regarding the Constitutional Convention, that "Root planted the crop and Smith watered it."

7

A Tin Star Worth $105,000

ON his return to the old neighborhood Al Smith
wore his new laurels lightly. Everyone on Oliver Street knew
that he was regarded as the state Democratic Party's coming
man, that some people were even talking of him for the governorship in due time. Al, however, appeared to be still the same
old hail-fellow, tipping his derby to cries of "You know me,
Al!" from the stoops as he sailed down the street.

He and Katie and their five children had moved to slightly
roomier quarters at 25 Oliver, a three-story red-brick row house
like its neighbors. (It still stands, much as when the Smith family occupied it for more than a dozen years, between stays in
Albany, until they moved up to Fifth Avenue. The house—
with its small dark rooms, tiled hallways, and cramped stair-
cases lighted by stained-glass windows on the landings—is now
occupied by a physician. There is no marker to show that it
was Smith's residence for many years.) He was more distinguished, perhaps, with a touch of gray in his hair, but he
was still willing to step through the swinging doors of the near-
est saloon for a glass of beer. Not the slightest sign of "going
high hat" could be detected by ever-watchful Irish eyes quick to
notice such signs of deterioration. On Sundays, after mass at St.
James', he still walked across the Brooklyn Bridge to visit his
mother. He still insisted that he was "one of Tom Foley's boys"

and showed up at the beery annual picnics at Harlem River Park.

But that return from Albany was unlike the others in preceding years. He had been notified while at the Constitutional Convention that the district leaders of Tammany had decided to nominate him for the office of sheriff of New York County. In any other locality, that would have seemed like a comedown for a man who had won great distinction in the state legislature, but not in New York. The sheriff's office was not only the cushiest reward Tammany could have backed him for, not only a springboard to higher office, but a test of his vote-getting ability on a wider basis than the Fourth Ward, which had so regularly sent him to the Assembly.

The sheriff of New York County is not a man hunter or a law enforcement officer in the sense that prevails elsewhere. It was a sinecure, concerned mostly with writ serving and above all with fee collecting. The wearer of the tin star in New York could count on an annual take of $50,000 to $60,000 a year—his salary of $12,000, plus half of all fees collected. In Smith's case it would amount to a $105,000 bonanza for two years in office—a considerable jump in income from his $1,500 salary, plus "lulus," the time-honored payments "in lieu of," which he had received as an assemblyman.

Smith was frankly astonished by the news that he had been awarded Tammany's support for that juiciest of local plums. He had believed that it would go to Big Bill Edwards, a former Princeton football captain and later the street-cleaning commissioner.

And his joy was matched by that of his Oliver Street neighbors, who threw an Old Home Night in his honor. All the windows in the neighborhood were decorated with Chinese lanterns. There was a fireworks display and bands marching up and down the street. A solemn procession of Chinese came over from Mott Street. The Irish first families rubbed elbows with Greeks, Italians, Jews in the congregation that gathered in front of the stoop to the Smith house. The changing composition of the neighborhood was indicated by the names of the delegation made up by the neighborhood mothers with the largest families: Mrs. Michael Santangelo, with eleven children; Mrs. Louis Lehan, seven; Mrs. Jacob Cohen, fourteen; Mrs. Charles McDermott, eight; Mrs. Charles Napoli, eight.

There was considerable joshing when that delegation toddled into view, and a friend called from the crowd, "It must make you feel sort of lonesome, Al, all these members of the Anti-Race-Suicide Club and you with only five kids."

"Don't blame me," Smith roared back. "Remember for twelve years I have been a member of the Legislature and had to spend my winters in Albany."

For hours Al and Katie sat on their steps and received their old friends. The dozen saloons nearby did a roaring business. "For those of the men whose thirsts returned with them," the New York *Tribune* reporter wrote of men who had moved away from the neighborhood but came back to honor Smith that night, "the doors of the Pan-Hellenic cafe swung easily. Displayed in one of its windows was a portrait of Premier Venizelos and a no-less austere one of Mr. Smith."

With that block party as a send-off, his campaign for sheriff zoomed away in high-spirited fashion. In his first speech he admitted, "I don't know much about the office of sheriff, as I haven't been there ever since Tom Foley held the job." Referring to the Republican incumbent, he added, "If I am elected in November, I will know more about the sheriff's office by January 1 than Sheriff Grifenhagen does, and by January 15 I will know all about it."

His nonpartisan stature, even among reformist, ordinarily anti-Tammany groups, could be measured by the endorsements attracted by his candidacy. The Citizens' Union no longer regarded him as a simple machine politician, but declared:

"Alfred E. Smith is endorsed for Sheriff of New York County. As to his qualifications for this office there can be no question. The service to the State rendered by Mr. Smith in the Constitutional Convention this year entitles him to special consideration.

"Although a party leader, Mr. Smith has in recent years been instrumental in obtaining much desirable and important legislation. We are endorsing Mr. Smith in the expectation that he will improve conditions in the Sheriff's office."

The New York *World* gave him a backhanded compliment in commenting on the Citizens' Union endorsement which, a *World* editorial noted, "has always been part of the honest graft of Republican candidates for main offices. . . . It is a scandal that Charles F. Murphy should pander to the moral sentiment of the community and permit a respectable candidate to be nominated for Sheriff." Ogden Reid's conservative Republican organ, the *Tribune,* rather surprisingly endorsed him as a man of "ability, integrity, industry." A few days later the *Tribune* editorial page analyzed his political merits at considerable length:

> The City of New York could well afford to pay Alfred E. Smith all the prospective emoluments of the Sheriff's office as a consideration for his continuing to represent a local Assembly district at Albany. In the past ten years there has been no Republican, Progressive or Democrat in the State Legislature who has rendered as effective, useful, downright valuable service to this town as ex-Speaker Smith.
>
> The limitations of the Tammany candidate for Sheriff are the limitations of the machine politician. At Albany Mr. Smith has "taken orders." He is one of Murphy's "boys." But he has not hesitated to oppose Tammany proposals in conference, and he has never lacked the courage to tell Murphy to his face what other Democrats of far greater pretensions to independence and influence hesitated to whisper around the corner.
>
> The trouble with most Republican representatives at Albany has been that they have been Republicans before they were New Yorkers, that they have given attention to what was desired by a party having its headquarters up the state instead of in the city. As a consequence the city has been

plundered and despoiled and the local Republican representative has been without honor at home or elsewhere.

With no such handicap to carry, Assemblyman Smith has given his whole attention to city interests. A true leader, a genuine compeller of men, a man of wit and force and an instinctive grasp on legislative practice, he has made a real reputation for himself at the Capitol and has deserved well of the large constituency which is his own town.

The *Sun* and *Times* also backed him for sheriff.

As a measure of his growing stature, he was invited to address such organizations as the Real Estate Owners' Association and the Taxpayers' Alliance, but most of his stumping took place before street crowds and clubhouse rallies. At one mass meeting before which he appeared with Judge Edward Swann, the Democratic candidate for district attorney, he was momentarily embarrassed by the chairman, who introduced him as "the next man who will get you when you go wrong," apparently ignorant of the fact that the sheriff of New York no longer went around clapping people into jail. Smith rose from his chair on the platform, looking annoyed by the suggestion that he would ever put the arm on any of the loyal Democrats in the assemblage, and gracefully replied, "The chairman, I fear, has touched on the most unpleasant of my duties as Sheriff. But I give you my word of honor that no personal act of mine will bring the blush of shame to the cheek of any one of you."

As the campaign progressed, it became apparent to Tammany's observers that Smith possessed the broad appeal, crossing racial and religious lines, that a successful politician needed in New York, particularly any Tammany candidate hopeful of capturing the allegiance of the immigrants. Professor David Burner in a recent analysis of Smith's career has observed that it "represents in microcosm the politics of the ghetto," even though he was "often forced to subordinate his own progressive instincts to the will of Charles Murphy, who supported reform only when it seemed likely to pass anyway or was dictated by political expediency." Smith's appeal, Burner adds, was largely that of an outgoing, easily projected personality. "The other ethnic and racial minorities easily identified with Al Smith, who radiated warmth and genial impulsiveness. Hitherto, immigrants of different nationalities had often quarreled more strenuously among themselves than against the nativists; but Smith's affability, his stand on prohibition, and the urban-rural tensions of the day molded the city immigrant Democracy into a force of unprecedented cohesion."

Smith defeated his Republican opponent for sheriff, Frank K. Bowers, by a robust margin, 113,791 to 72,590. On taking office on January 1, 1916, he posed for the newspaper photographers in his flower-decked office, flanked by his wife and mother and his five children. That had become a tradition on all ceremonial occasions: Al with his mother on one side and his wife on the other. It was good image making, of course, but there was nothing phony about his devotion to the elder Mrs. Smith. He would always see to it that his mother was included whenever honor came to the family.

Smith also followed tradition on taking over the sheriff's office and kicking out all the Republicans, replacing them with worthy, usually Irish, Democrats. Two of the best jobs in the office, paying $6,000 a year, went to his friend since boyhood, John F. Gilchrist, and to George W. Olvany. Gilchrist became undersheriff, and Olvany the sheriff's counsel. The latter, on the death of Charles Murphy, assumed the leadership of Tammany Hall.

At times Smith grew restless in the sheriff's office. It was a governmental backwater, almost an anachronism in New York City. Later he would recall that he spent most of his time "looking for something to do."

During those two years the country slipped closer and closer to involvement in the European war, and finally, midway through his last year in the sheriff's office, it declared war on Germany and her allies. Many Irish-Americans, particularly in New York, were bitterly opposed to American entry as an ally of

imperial Britain. Ever since the Easter Rebellion, Irish agitators
had been stirring up trouble, particularly along the New York
waterfront, and trying to sabotage American aid to the Allies.
Probably a majority of the American Irish, like the German-
Americans, were against joining the Allies in Europe. It was a
very ticklish political question for an Irish Democrat. His own
party occupied the White House when the United States
entered the war, and he was torn between party loyalty and
older, but more vivid in many cases, memories of what England had done to Ireland. Al Smith apparently stayed neutral
on the question; as sheriff of New York his opinions on the
war were not of critical importance, and both Tammany and
the church went along with the Wilson administration, just as
thousands of young Irishmen went along with the AEF. At
any rate there is nothing of record to show where his sympathies
lay; his interests were too parochial to be much engaged by
events so far away—as H. L. Mencken would observe in a few
years, "his world begins at Coney Island and ends at Buffalo."
At the age of forty-four, of course, he was too old for military
service.

On his $50,000 a year income as sheriff he was able to buy
his first automobile, take his family to a summer home, and invest a good share of it in war bonds. For the first time in his life
he experienced a period of financial security.

But that wasn't good enough for a man still feeling the itch
of ambition, conscious that his ability, his appeal as a vote getter could carry him farther than a picturesque county office.

It was amazing how he could attract his social and intellectual opposites, convince them of his sincerity and ability, and
win them to his cause. He never enlisted a more fervent and
enduring admirer than the young man he met in 1917—Robert
Moses, Yale '09, Oxford '13, then twenty-eight years old and
the offspring of a wealthy mercantile family. Moses had returned from Oxford with his master's degree and worked in a
reform group; now he yearned to make a career in public service.

He first met Smith on the street one day while walking along with Charles F. Kerrigan, the Albany correspondent of the Brooklyn *Eagle* and later Mayor Walker's secretary. Kerrigan introduced him to Sheriff Smith, and Moses was not initially impressed. "He is a typical Tammany politician," he told a friend. "What can you expect from a man who wears a brown derby on the side of his head and always has a big cigar in the corner of his mouth?"

Moses soon became better acquainted with Smith, and his friend Ernest Willvonseder would recall, "Moses came in one day and declared, with mingled surprise and enthusiasm, 'Ernest, Al Smith *listens* to me.' "

Listening was a rare quality in a politician, and undoubtedly it helped Smith enormously with people like Moses, outside the orbit of most politicians, whose loyalties and services would be invaluable to him. Coupled with his talent for receptivity, and even rarer, was his lack of resentment of those who were better educated and socially superior. He withstood any feelings of inferiority, and instead of resenting them, he picked their brains, enlisted their help, and made them his supporters. Instinctively he seemed to grasp that the new complexities of government—its growth and extension into fields hitherto ignored—would require the talents of better educated and less parochial people than the old-line politicians and time-serving officeholders. It needed young blood, new ideas, a quality of venturesomeness. Thus he made himself the indispensable link between the old politics and the new. Essentially he would always be the practical politician, at home in the back rooms, but in a time when a college professor could be elected and re-elected President of the United States he was aware of the new realities.

In the summer of 1917 the sachems of Tammany decided to move Smith up another notch. They would run him for President of the Board of Aldermen, a position next in importance to the mayor. The big question at Tammany was the mayoralty candidate. William Randolph Hearst, as the most powerful of newspaper publishers, with unquenched political ambitions, wanted the Democratic nomination. Among those opposed to Tammany's backing Hearst were Tom Foley, still one of the most influential district leaders, and his protégé, Al Smith. Finally, both Tammany and Hearst compromised on John F. Hylan, a rather dull-witted fellow who had started out as a manufacturer of bicycle whistles. Hylan, also known as Red Mike (for his red hair, not his political coloration), was Hearst's man as much as Tammany's. One of his first official acts in the mayor's office was to appoint as a city magistrate one Bernard J. Douras, who happened to be the father of Marion Davies, a young blonde who danced in the chorus of the 1917 *Ziegfeld Follies*, and who was, to say the least, Mr. Hearst's protégé.

Smith's opponent in the 1917 election was Robert Adamson, a former newspaperman who had been secretary to Mayor William J. Gaynor. Adamson was a quick-witted young man, but no match for Smith as a political campaigner. He made the mistake of challenging Smith to meet him in a debate at a Brooklyn political club. At the end of his speech Adamson turned to Smith and demanded: "What are your qualifications for the office of the President of the Board of Aldermen?"

Smith bounded forward, only too happy to reply. "My qualifications are twelve years as a member of the New York Legislature and four years Democratic floor leader there. I was for one year Speaker of the Assembly. I was six years on its Cities Committee, which revised the New York City charter. As chairman of the Ways and Means Committee I personally prepared the state budget. It cut down expenses by $15,000,000 as compared with the last of Governor Hughes's administrations.

"I was vice-chairman of the committee which obtained the enactment of our existing excellent factory fire prevention laws. I was a member of all the important committees of the last Constitutional Convention.

"If there is any man in the city with the same legislative experience, let him speak. I will be glad to surrender my nomination to him and go back to the Fulton Market."

With that indiscreet question, and the reply widely quoted in the press, Adamson practically handed the election to his opponent. The Hylan-Smith ticket won by a comfortable margin.

As president of the Board of Aldermen, Smith's most important function was sitting on the Board of Estimate, which draws up the city budget and in effect rules the city government. The chairman of that board is the mayor. From their association on the Board of Estimate, Smith formed a rather unflattering opinion of Mayor Hylan. Hylan slavishly filled the municipal offices with Tammany appointees and at the same time carried out the policies advocated by the *Journal* and the *American,* the Hearst newspapers in New York. A friend later wrote that Smith decided "Hylan was entirely lacking in intelligence." In his pragmatic way, Smith tried to get all the facts concerning some proposed measure or appropriation, while Hylan was "incapable of such research, or such thought, and tried to solve everything by the application of some moral law."

He had been elected to serve a four-year term as Red Mike's chief collaborator but was spared that ordeal before his first year as president of the Board of Aldermen ended. Tammany had decided that summer of 1918 that the biggest prize in its grabbag should be Al Smith's for the taking.

There were several avowed candidates for the Democratic nomination for the governorship. The Republican incumbent, Charles S. Whitman, had not lived up to expectations either in his own party or in the electorate, and it appeared that a strong candidate from the opposition could defeat him in a campaign for reelection. William Randolph Hearst, as on so many previous occasions, gallantly offered himself for the role of Whitman slayer, and he had the firm support of Boss John McCooey's Brooklyn machine, as well as that of many German-Americans who approved his antiwar efforts. The reformist and independent Democrats were offering William Church Osborn, a high-minded upstater.

To settle on a candidate who would be presented to the Saratoga convention as the choice of the party's regulars, a meeting of the more prominent county leaders was held in Syracuse. At a secret session in the home of William F. Kelly, the Onondaga County leader, the Tammany representatives maneuvered skillfully to obtain the backing for Murphy's choice—Al Smith. They didn't want to give the appearance of cramming their nominee down the upstate leaders' throats, so they waited while Osborn was eliminated as impossible and Hearst, with all the enemies he had made, as unacceptable. The Tammany men then announced that they would prefer Smith, but only if he were completely acceptable to the upstaters. Fortunately, as an assemblyman, Smith had always tended his upstate fences. It was agreed that Smith would be the choice of the regulars.

His nomination was ratified at Saratoga, and in the primary he easily defeated Osborn, whose name had been placed on the ballot as the nominee of the upstate independents.

Now it was Smith vs. Whitman. Smith organized his campaign as though he had been running for governor all his life, drawing together many disparate elements in support of his candidacy. Assured of Tammany's most vigorous efforts on his behalf, he delicately moved to deemphasize that primary association of his political career. His leading campaigners and visible advisers bore no Tammany stripes. They included Abram I. Elkus, who had been the counsel for the Factory Commission and Ambassador to Turkey and now headed the Independent Citizens' Committee for Smith; his law partner, Judge Joseph M. Proskauer, who was to become an intimate associate throughout the rest of Smith's political career; the O'Connell clan of Albany, just building the foundations of its overlordship in the capital; Bob Moses and others of the Young Turk stripe. Undersheriff Gilchrist undertook the role of liaison man between Elkus' citizens' committee and Tammany. He devoted three weeks of the campaign to stumping county fairs and other outdoor gatherings upstate and spoke to large assemblages only in Buffalo, Ithaca, and Albany. The fourth week he spent touring political meetings in New York City, the suburbs, and Long Island.

It would be a close race, both Smith and his advisers believed. There was a certain amount of anti-Wilsonian backlash to be confronted, and Governor Whitman and his campaigners hit hard on the issue of Smith's anti-Prohibition stance. Women were voting for the first time, and the opposition counted on their abhorrence of the liquor traffic to weigh heavily against Smith. Nothing, of course, could be done to efface the fairly accurate picture of Smith as a man who liked to put a foot on a bar rail and a hand around a glass. Religion was also inserted as an issue, the Ku Klux Klan was just below the horizon, and Smith's Catholicism worked against him in the rural sections upstate. He could only hope that a large turnout at the polls in the big cities would tip the balance against those handicaps.

In the closing days of the campaign, a transit disaster, tragically enough, gave him the break he needed. On Friday evening, November 1, he was scheduled to make a windup speech in Brooklyn, where the vote was crucial. A large turnout might give him the election. He had been hammering away at Governor Whitman's administration with the charge that it had turned the Public Service Commission into a Republican fief, with its offices filled with incompetents. Shortly before he was to appear that evening at the Brooklyn Academy of Music, a Brighton train on the BMT roared through its signals and crashed in the Malbone Street tunnel. Ninety persons were killed, 100 injured.

Smith seized on the incident while the ink on the headlines was still damp and charged the regulatory agency, the Public Service Commission, was "the mostly costly fiasco in the history of our government. . . . Politics controlling the appointments has made itself felt down through the minor employes, and even positions undoubtedly requiring technical knowledge because of their character were filled by Republican district leaders.

. . . What has Governor Whitman to say about all this? Does he really believe it to be entirely necessary that he make any explanation? What can be his conception of this State?"

Election day, 1918, he later said, was "probably the longest day of my life up to that time." Even his most optimistic supporters knew the two candidates were neck and neck; the Brooklyn transit disaster, bringing out a larger vote in that borough, might give Smith the edge. Smith and his closest associates spent the day at the Hotel Biltmore, opposite Grand Central, sweating, fretting, knowing that it might be twenty-four to forty-eight hours before they could be sure of the result. Collecting all the returns throughout the state was still a slow process.

One vote he could be sure of was his mother's. Mrs. Smith had been violently opposed to women's suffrage, as many older women were. When suffrage was granted, she declared repeatedly she would never vote. Then Al was nominated for the governorship. She put on her best hat and was among the first five to register at her polling place in Brooklyn.

The big-city returns came in early that night and gave Smith the lead, particularly the plurality of 90,000 provided by Brooklyn. The issue was still in doubt even at midnight because many of the upstate returns weren't in and a heavy turnout in the Republican counties could reverse the verdict of the cities. At dawn Smith still held the lead by a slender margin, but returns still weren't available from many counties in the central and upper tier. At 8:30 A.M. Smith and some of his equally sleepless associates, including Senator Jimmy Walker, caught the Empire State Express from Grand Central and headed for the upstate headquarters of the party in Syracuse. Smith's followers were convinced that knavish Republican county leaders were holding back upstate returns. As soon as they arrived in Syracuse, they stationed themselves at a battery of telephones and began calling Democratic election commissioners to be alert for ballot-box tampering, bad arithmetic in the counting process, and other naughtiness attributed to desperate Republicans.

By Thursday night Smith was still out in front with a majority of about 7,500 votes, but Governor Whitman was refusing to concede the election. Smith, however, announced that he had won. The absentee ballots cast by servicemen—it was still a few days short of the armistice—had not yet been counted. When they were several days later, the final results showed that Smith had won with a majority of almost 15,000 votes. A squeaker.

With the vote that close Governor Whitman demanded a recount in certain New York City election districts. He and his supporters were particularly suspicious of the tally announced for Smith's district, which was Smith 387, Whitman 2. On his part Smith was surprised that even two voters in the old neighborhood would mark their ballots for his opponent and was even more irked by the two backsliders than Whitman's demand for a recount. In any case, the new count showed no significant irregularities. The new Smith address would be the Executive Mansion, Albany.

8

Smith Takes on Hearst

ON December 30, 1918, his forty-fifth birthday,
Governor-Elect Smith, his mother, wife, and all their children
took the train to Albany. They celebrated his birthday—also,
at a distance, his sister's—in the Governor's Mansion.

Along with them went the family's outsize pet, a Great Dane
named Caesar. The dog-loving Smith would not consider leaving
Caesar behind, despite his huge size and his conviction that he
was a small puppy entitled to sit on laps and chairs. When they
arrived in Albany, Smith's oldest son, Alfred, Jr., was assigned
to lead Caesar to the mansion on foot while the rest of the family
proceeded there by automobile.

As soon as Caesar was led into the mansion, he sniffed around
for his master, then broke loose from the boy with one
eager bound, and began coursing through the corridors. In a
reception room upstairs he found Smith and his predecessor,
Governor Whitman, and the latter's military aide, exchanging
formal courtesies. Caesar broke the ice. He leaped into the
room, scaring the wits out of Whitman and his aide.

"Don't worry, gentlemen," Smith assured them. "That's
only the Tammany tiger come to take possession of the Executive Mansion."

That was not the only homely touch to the inauguration of
the new administration. The next evening the inaugural ball

was held in the State Armory, and it must have appeared to the Albany elite, mostly survivors of the old Dutch aristocracy, that a band of Visigoths had breached the walls and taken possession of the city.

When the governor-elect and his family appeared in their box, the military band played the traditional "Hail to the Chief." After that, the proceedings took on some of the flavor of a Lower East Side block party. The band began playing "The Sidewalks of New York" and other jigtime melodies. The armory was crowded with hundreds of old friends of the Smith family from the Fourth Ward. Many wore evening clothes for the first time, the dress suits rented for the occasion from the gents' haberdasheries on Canal Street. The old Knickerbocker families, smiling bravely, painfully, rubbed elbows with Mr. and Mrs. James Colombo, Solly Bernstein, Jimmy Kelly, Michael Kuku, and Dr. Paul Sarrubbi—all prominent and respected names in the Fourth Ward but unknown to the *Social Register*. Mrs. William Bayard Van Rensselaer was introduced to Mr. and Mrs. Charles Murphy and their daughter Mabel. Tom Foley, the new governor's political discoverer, went around pumping limp blue-veined hands whether extended or not.

Up in the Smith family box, his mother shyly displayed a picture postcard Al had sent her from Albany in 1904. It was a view of the Executive Mansion, and on the back Al had written, "Dear Mother: This is a picture of the Governor's residence. I'm going to work hard and stick to the ideals you taught me and some day—maybe—I'll occupy this house."

The next day he took the oath of office as cannon boomed from Capitol Hill. Within a few weeks, it was apparent that something more resounding than the firing of salute guns could be expected from the new governor. The state government, he believed, would have to function more vigorously and responsively to solve the social and economic problems growing out of the World War. One of his first moves was to assign Frances Perkins, whom he had appointed to the board of the Industrial Commission, to intervene in the violent and lengthy strike at the Rome Brass and Copper Company. She went to Rome and immediately sat down with a committee of the striking workers and their employers, although the latter had balked at the idea of settling a labor problem with the mediation of a woman. The strike was settled, and one of the company officials sent a message to Governor Smith: "Do us a favor and tell us where you found that woman." There were appeals from various cities to send in state police and national guardsmen to halt strike violence, but Smith declined on the grounds that "the civilized world had been treated to such an exhibition of military force and power" during the recent war that he would use the state's police power only in an emergency.

Having lambasted the Whitman administration for stuffing the Public Service Commission with deserving Republicans, he leaned backward to avoid the same sort of charges against himself. Mr. Charles Murphy installed himself at the Ten Eyck and presented him with a list of suggestions for appointees, but he was anything but slavish in accepting them. He often told the story of an old St. James' parochial schoolmate who approached him while he was president of the Board of Aldermen and asked him for a job as elevator starter at the Municipal Building.

"Don't you know about civil service?" Smith asked. "There's a stiff examination for that job."

"Examination in what?"

"Hydraulics," Smith replied, "and a lot of other things you don't know anything about."

"Listen, Al," his old friend snorted, "save that stuff for the Eyetalians and the Poles. I went to school with you."

Thus when he undertook the first major action of his administration, within days after taking office, he saw to it that its complexion was impeccably nonpartisan. This was the creation of the Reconstruction Commission, which was charged with building a new and more efficient structure for the state government and implementing the recommendations, though they had been turned down in the state referendum, of the 1915 Constitutional Convention. All that spelled reform, as well as increased government efficiency.

To make certain that the commission's program would be widely acceptable, he named such figures as Charles H. Sabin, president of the Guaranty Trust; Bernard Baruch, who had headed the War Industries Board; Gerrit Y. Lansing, an Albany banker; Charles P. Steinmetz, General Electric's "wizard of Schenectady"; Dr. Felix Adler, president of the New York Society for Ethical Culture; William M. I. Olcott, former Republican district attorney of New York; Otto B. Schulhof, a New York manufacturer; Michael Friedsam, president of B. Altman & Company; Mortimer L. Schiff of the private banking family; and Arthur Williams of New York Edison. Its chairman was Abram Elkus. Belle Moskowitz was named secretary of the commission, and Robert Moses its chief of staff. Most of the hard work, predictably, fell to Mrs. Moskowitz and young Mr. Moses.

After many sessions, the commission approved a document largely composed by Moses, certainly bearing the benchmarks of his vigorous personality, sternly critical of the jumble of 187 offices, commissions, boards, and other agencies constituting the administrative branch as organized under a constitution adopted in 1777. It read in part:

"The existing system of administration stands condemned by its obvious objectionable features. . . . The Constitution says that the executive power shall be vested in the Governor, but at the same time the Constitution and the laws strip him of the instruments for executing that power. . . . If New York wants retrenchment and efficient government it must make someone responsible who can be held to account and give him power commensurate with his obligations. There is no other way. . . .

"Democracy does not merely mean periodical elections. It means a government held accountable to the people between elections. . . . In order that the people may hold their government to account they must have a government they can understand. . . .

"No citizen can hope to understand the present collection of departments, offices, boards and commissions. A Governor with a cabinet of reasonable size, responsible for proposing a program in the annual budget and for administering the program as modified by the Legislature, may be brought daily under public scrutiny, held accountable to the Legislature and public opinion, and be turned out of office if he fails to measure up to the public requirements. If this is not democracy then it is difficult to imagine what it is."

More concretely, the Reconstruction Commission proposed the enlargement of the system of state employment agencies, the establishment of compulsory continuation schools for working boys and girls, new housing, and other solutions to the problems of the postwar world. Some of the recommendations required changes in the state constitution, which had to be passed by two successive legislatures and a referendum; they could not be made effective until 1922 at the earliest. Other changes could be induced only by legislative action and statutory revision.

Putting the program into effect would require a long and patient campaign of educating and persuading the legislature and the public, but that was an art in which Smith was adept, an unrivaled master. Less than two months after he took office, in February, 1919, President Wilson wrote a friend that he believed Smith "feels in an unusual degree the impulses and compulsions of the changed order of the nation's and the world's affairs." In addition to that understanding, Smith possessed the ability to influence, to make people understand what he was trying to do. Supreme Court Justice Felix Frankfurter believed that the reason for his success as a governor could be traced to "his extraordinary talent for accomplishing great reforms not merely *with* popular assent, but *because* he is able to awaken public interest in his aims and to enlist popular understanding of the technical means by which alone social policies can be realized."

The program recommended by his commission and made part of his continuing campaign for improving the quality of life for all of the state's citizens was "one of the best things Smith ever did," Frances Perkins wrote long after her service in his administration and as Franklin D. Roosevelt's Secretary of Labor.

For all the earnestness of his administration, Smith had not entirely lost the prankishness of his youth. He detested anything that was stuffy or pompous, particularly any such tendencies he noted in himsef. When he closeted himself with his closest advisers, who called themselves the Governor's Court of Appeals, to consider the bills sent up by the legislature and winnow out the worthy from the unworthy, he delighted in passing out trick cigars and cigarettes filled with rubber bands. Presiding over this "court," with his shrewd insight into the motives behind the bills forwarded for his signature or veto, he would bellow, "Grabenheimer vs. People," when a measure that served some special interest came up for consideration. "Baskets of doorknobs," he would rasp at other self-serving bills, "fur coats for elephants," or "left-handed monkey wrenches" for measures that would prove costly but contribute little social good. Sometimes when he got bored with the stream of legislative phrases he would get up from his chair, dance a jig, or sing "Kathleen Mavourneen" in his bathtub baritone.

He could, however, smite with a vengeance any of his juniors who did not seem to uphold the dignity of the governor's establishment. Two of the frolicsome young men whose activities came to his attention were Major A. J. Glynn, his military secretary, who not at all coincidentally was his sister's son, and Edward J. Flynn, just starting a political career that included his long and powerful reign as the Democratic leader of Bronx County. Flynn was then the assemblyman from a Bronx district. As Flynn has recalled, he and his friend Glynn "believed in alleviating the monotony of our residence in Albany with social relaxation. Our little escapades, mild enough in them-selves, soon came to the attention of the Governor."

Smith decided it was time to break up the fun-making firm of Glynn & Flynn and summoned Flynn to his office. "I went in fear and trembling," he recalled. "When I finally en-tered the great room, Governor Smith, in his usual rasping voice, gave me as stiff a dressing down as I have ever gotten. It ended with a dire prophecy that no good would ever come, either to his nephew or myself. I determined then and there to surprise him."

During the first four months of his administration, Smith was pleasantly surprised by the approving tone in the Hearst news-papers. In those years, when the press was the unrivaled me-dium of communications, the power of the Hearst papers was considerable, especially since they circulated among and catered to the same classes that made up the bulk of Smith's political following. In New York State, Hearst published newspapers in Albany, Rochester, and Syracuse in addition to his two mass-circulated dailies in New York City. His support was important, though not crucial.

After Smith had won the nomination for governor over him, Hearst appeared to be cordial, even helpful. His papers backed Smith. The two men were on close enough terms during the campaign, in fact, for the Smith children to be brought up to the publisher's residence on Riverside Drive to play with the Hearst children.

Then a cloud no larger than a copy of the New York *Ameri-can* appeared on the horizon to the south. The Hearst papers suddenly began to find fault with Governor Smith, and on May 8 they carried an editorial criticizing him for having ap-pointed Robert L. Luce to serve on the State Supreme Court. Luce, they declared, was a "tool of the interests" who had served as attorney for the New York Central Railroad. The following day the New York *Times* published a report that Hearst was angered by the Luce appointment because, through an intermediary, he had asked Smith to name his own attorney,

William De Ford, to the judicial post. Hearst entered an angry denial, saying, "I have been particularly careful never to ask any appointment or any other political favor of Governor Smith, for I have never been quite convinced of the sincerity of his professions of progressive principles. He has always been too close to Tammany, and too close to certain public service corporations to make an ideal public official from my point of view."

It appeared that Hearst had hoped that Smith, in return for the campaign support of the Hearst newspapers, would prove as compliant as Mayor Hylan. There was also the possibility that the publisher saw in the governor an obstacle to his own political ambitions. Smith had beat him out for the nomination for governor, which was forgivable, but he had given no indication that he would support Hearst for governor or U.S. Senator in the future, which was not.

Hearst needed an issue with which to belabor Smith, and he found it easily enough in the milk-price situation. For the past half century New York had been stirred up by milk scandals; the price of milk and of ice and the five-cent subway fare were always reliable political issues. Milk was then selling for eighteen cents a quart in New York City. The price had gone up during a dairymen's strike, and it had stayed at that level even after the strike was settled.

There was nothing Governor Smith could do about that; it was beyond his jurisdiction. All a powerless governor was able to think of was to appoint an equally powerless Fair Milk Price Committee. Smith's enemies, of course, did not point out that the authority rested with the Department of Farms and Markets, an agency controlled by the state legislature, which was then Republican-dominated—another instance, in fact, of the divided executive powers which the Reconstruction Commission was trying to reapportion.

Hearst, believing the governor was vulnerable, proceeded to attack him relentlessly on that issue during the summer of 1919. It was a characteristic Hearst campaign, with tomtoms

beating and assegais brandished in both the news and editorial-
page columns. His papers throughout the state charged that
"Governor Smith is whimpering and whining, but babies in
New York are dying for lack of milk." Smith was "in league
with the milk trust."

Day after day, the Hearst papers published cartoons showing mothers pleading, children dying of starvation in the slums,
while Smith stood by in silk-hatted indifference.

At first Smith ignored the campaign against him, apparently
in hope that Hearst and his editors, with their notoriously
short attention span, would fretfully turn to some other "crusade" and he would be spared the necessity of counter-at-
tacking a fellow Democrat. But the Hearst drums were still
beating well into autumn, and it was obvious that Smith would
have to reply, and hit hard, or his credibility as a liberal, humanitarian leader would suffer.

When he did fight back, it was with all the compressed outrage of a man who loved children, was the father of five, and
prided himself on his reputation as a defender of the poor.
Indignation, in fact, overpowered him. Instead of coolly replying that the milk prices could be regulated only by a state
agency responsible to a Republican-controlled legislature, he
responded in highly emotional terms. He let it be known that
his mother was dangerously ill and in her delirium had mur-
mured, "My son did not kill the babies." On October 18, 1919,
he issued his challenge to Hearst: they would meet in a public debate and let the people decide who was at fault. "He
can get up on the platform," Smith told his press conference,
"and he can ask me any question he likes about my public or
private life, if he will let me do the same."

In the next few days Smith followed that up by condemning
Hearst in the harshest printable terms as a "mean" and "particularly low type" of man, the "greatest living enemy of the
people," the "greatest autocrat the country has ever known."
His newspapers, Smith added, reaching back to his Fulton

Market days for a homely simile, were "like a cuttlefish that emits black ink."

Doubtless Hearst was taken aback when he heard of the challenge out in California. While complaining editorially about the sufferings of the poor because of eighteen-cent milk prices, the publisher had been busy all summer supervising the construction of the castle to be called San Simeon, a rococo project which the unhinged Ludwig of Bavaria would have drooled over. It would never have occurred to "the Chief" that he might have used some of those millions he spent on castle building to establish free-milk depots in the slums.

Hearst, with his high-pitched, almost falsetto voice, his rather furtive manner on the platform, knew that he would be no match for Al Smith in the rough-and-tumble of a debate. He must also have wondered whether Smith's suggestion that they poke into each other's "private lives" was not a concealed threat to expose his relations with Marion Davies.

So he replied to Smith's challenge with a lofty seigneurial contempt—but the answer was no.

"I do not have to meet him," the Hearst reply read, "as I am not running for office, and I certainly do not want to meet him for the pleasure of the association, as I find no satisfaction in the company of crooked politicians.

"Neither have I the time or inclination to debate with every public plunderer or faithless public servant whom my papers have exposed, for the reason that every pilloried rascal in every city where my papers are published aways tries to divert attention from the real issue of his political crookedness by making some sort of blatherskite onslaught upon me.

"I have no explanations to make for attacking the Milk Trust and the Traction Trust and the politicians who have surrendered to these rich and powerful plundering corporations and are committed to twenty-cent milk and ten-cent streetcar fares.

"The only apology I would have to make would be for having supported Governor Smith. . . ."

Hearst concluded by suggesting that "if they are going to hire Carnegie Hall every time my papers expose rascally politicians, you would better take a long-term lease on the property."

On the night of October 29, 1919, Al Smith appeared on the platform at Carnegie Hall, before an audience that overflowed onto the street, and gave William Randolph Hearst what has been described as the most searing tongue-lashing in political history.

Reporters covering that public execution—which is what it was, so far as Hearst's political aspirations were concerned—observed that Smith was boiling mad when he strode to the lectern. His Irish was up and running away with him, his normally red face was purplish red, and sweat was soon pouring down. He spoke off the cuff, without the prepared speech any present-day politician would consider essential on such an occasion. Yet with all the outrage and indignation he vented at high pressure, his speech was grounded on the facts of the milk-price situation, which he presented with a cold logic before proceeding to demolish Hearst as a man, a politician and a newspaper publisher.

"I am going to ask for your absolute silence and attention," he began. "I feel that I am here tonight upon a mission as important not only to myself, but to this city, to this state and to this country, as I could possibly perform. Of course, I am here alone . . . but I knew that I would, and I felt that I would, because I know the man to whom I issued the challenge, and I know that he has not got a drop of good, clean, pure red blood in his whole body. And I know the color of his liver, and it is whiter, if that could be, than the driven snow. . . ."

He then launched into the background of the milk strike, using his two characteristic forensic gestures, the stabbing and accusatory forefinger, the fist crashing for emphasis on the lectern. "Under the law of the State I had no power to command any man to do anything I thought he ought to do, but I undertook to settle the strike. . . .

"Throughout this whole campaign it was attempted to fix in the minds of the people that there existed some place in the statute law of this state the power on the part of the Governor to fix the price of milk, and in Hearst's desperation after a nomination he didn't like, that was put into his paper in so many words, and he knew that it is not so. His lawyers knew that it is not so, and I defy him—and he has the best legal advice in this city, because he never utters a word until it is well scrutinized by an array of lawyers to keep him away from libel suits—I defy him or his lawyers to challenge that cold, straightforward statement of mine, that no power exists in my hands or in the hands of any other agency of this government, to fix the price at which anybody can sell anything in this state, whether it is milk or shoes or clothing or houses or anything else.

"By insinuation and, at times, in his desperation, by direct declaration, the public has been given to believe that the Governor has some power of removal over the officials of the Department of Agriculture and the Department of Farms and Markets. He knows that I have not. . . . He knows that they are all appointed by a Council of Farms and Markets, and he knows that the Council is elected by the legislature, and in 1917 the agricultural, farming, and marketing interests of this state, to the minutest detail, were removed away from the control of the Governor, in order that they may be a regency, as are the educational affairs of the state. . . .

"Now, he flares out a headline that Smith appointed a representative of the milk trust to office. That is a lie. I never appointed the man whose name he mentioned in the paper in my life, and every appointment that is made by the Governor, even to a notary public, has to be recorded in a book that is public property in the Executive Chamber in Albany, and he can go up and look at that book. . . .

"Another flare headline, 'Why don't the Governor bring the milk trust into court and make them show up their books?' Why, the answer to that is just this: We have in this state a government of laws, not men. I am not a czar, I am not a despot; I am just a plain ordinary man, picked out by a majority of the people in this state to administer the law as it is in the statute books. . . . absolutely ridiculous, but a play to the poor, and a play to the man that does not understand the orderly legal procedure of the state. The man that does that, making you think he is your friend, is the greatest enemy you can find. . . ."

No political figure was safe from Hearst's smearing, Smith declared. "Follow back the history of this man's newspapers since he came to this part of the country, and you will have to read out of his newspapers this remarkable fact: That in this great democracy—there has never been a man elected to office yet that has not been tainted in some way. If the Hearst newspapers were the textbooks for the children of our schools, they would have to spell out of its every line that no man can be trusted in this country after he is put into public office . . . no public man in this state, from Grover Cleveland right down to today, has ever escaped this fellow. . . ."

He asserted that he had received 5,000 letters supporting his stand against Hearst and only one condemning him. From that one letter Smith read quotations charging him with being a "Judas" and with sharing in the $5,000,000 in excessive profits reaped by the milk distributors. He would have ignored the letter, he explained, except that on rereading, he discovered "it contains almost verbatim a number of headlines from the Hearst papers." Journalistic demagoguery of that type was dangerously inflammatory when there was a "condition of unrest throughout this whole country," when "I was called out of bed at an early hour this morning because of striking and rioting and murder that was being committed in one of the Upstate cities." He sketched in a vivid picture of Hearst lurching around a powder magazine with a lighted match, a man who would incite the gravest disorders to avenge himself on a political enemy.

Worse, yet, perhaps, Hearst was a largely absentee observer of the New York scene, a *rentier* with little personal involvement in the miseries he clamored about in the columns of his newspapers. "Why, the man is entirely lacking in any understanding of the situation," Smith scornfully pointed out. "He doesn't spend any time in New York, to know what is going on here; he is in Palm Beach all winter, and in California all summer." Yet at safe remove, he said, Hearst was "the man that is sowing in their minds and in their hearts the seeds of disorder and discontent to suit his own selfish purpose."

Smith wound up his oration by attempting what was admittedly impossible: to determine the source of Hearstian bitterness and malice. (That deep wellspring, it might be divined, was Hearst's frustration over being constantly rejected as the voluntary savior of the nation, if only the stupid electorate would put him in the White House.) He cited the facts of his own career, how he had worked hard for everything he got, how he had entered the Executive Mansion with the gravest sense of responsibility—yet Hearst was determined to ruin him.

"What can it be?" he cried out. "It has got to be envy, it has got to be hatred or it has got to be something that nobody understands. . . ." He urged his audience to "organize in this city to stay the danger that comes from these papers. . . ." The only way to ensure the welfare of the state and its people was to "get rid of this pestilence that walks in the darkness."

It was an expert job of demolition. Hearst, labeled as "the pestilence that walks in the darkness," was left for dead on the platform of Carnegie Hall. But the reverberations of the Smith-Hearst vendetta shook the state and national parties at a time of Republican resurgence. For both men the feud was a bad thing. It was fatal to Hearst's personal ambitions, and ultimately to Smith's. It was "one of those phenomena," as the ablest of Hearst's biographers has written, "fit to make philosophers ponder the consequences of human prejudice. It was fated to make history. . . . It would reach out over the years to give an incidental boost to a younger New York politician, Franklin Delano Roosevelt, and elevate him to the post both

Hearst and Smith longed for and failed to achieve—the Presidency."

It would have been far wiser for Smith to have replied to Hearst coolly, on legalistic grounds which made Hearst's charges ridiculous and indefensible, without engaging in personalities, without deepening an enmity that could only harm him, but then he wouldn't have been much of an Irishman if he'd kept that shillelagh behind his back.

The Smiths celebrated the first of many Christmases in the Executive Mansion. There was a huge tree in one of the reception rooms, and the area around it looked like the toy section of a department store; "a sharp contrast to the small, cramped apartment in Oliver Street," Smith thought in remembering Christmases Past. Even his Great Dane, Caesar, was remembered with "a new shining brass collar that, when hanging on the Christmas tree, looked as though it could surround the smokestack of the *Leviathan*."

The holiday festivities, no doubt, braced him for a second year in office, a second round of combat with a Republican-dominated state legislature, that would require a continuing display of political courage—more than it took, in fact, to face down William Randolph Hearst.

One of the first confrontations of the new year developed between Smith and his liberal conscience. In 1920 there was an anti-Communist crusade still sweeping the land so encompassingly that federal agents were assigned to keep an eye on the general who had commanded the Siberian Expeditionary Force on his return to the United States, simply because it was believed the Bolshevik virus could be transmitted to practically anybody exposed to it long enough. All forms of radicalism were having a bad time of it; the mood of the nation was one of longing for what Warren G. Harding would call normalcy. Smith himself had no great urge to join the crusade, though he did inveigh on one occasion, at a Cornell University convocation in June, 1919, against the dangers of political extremism.

He could only feel repugnance, however, for the witch-hunting atmosphere largely created by the much-headlined Red Raids of Attorney General A. Mitchell Palmer and the resultant hysteria. Thousands of suspected Communists and anarchists were imprisoned or deported.

The New York legislature early in its 1920 session decided to join the anti-Marxist pogrom. Five Socialists had been elected to serve in that legislature. The Assembly, however, reared up and announced that it had the constitutional right to sit in judgment on who should or should not be seated among them. It then voted to exclude the five Socialists.

It would have been the easy, momentarily popular thing for Governor Smith to go along with that drumhead verdict. During the war and under the Wilson administration, after all, two of the country's leading Socialists, Eugene Debs and Congressman Victor Berger, had been sent to prison on charges of sedition. Smith, however, would not allow himself to be pushed along by the current of public hysteria. He invited the expelled Socialists to attend a reception at the Executive Mansion. And on the night the Assembly voted for expulsion, he attended a dinner of the Amen Corner, an organization made up largely of newspaper correspondents, and flung his political grenade in the form of a short statement on the subject:

"Although I am unalterably opposed to the fundamental principles of the Socialist party, it is inconceivable that a minority party . . . should be deprived of its right to expression . . . unless the chosen representatives are unfit as individuals. . . . If the majority party at present in control of the Assembly possesses information that leads them to believe that these men are hostile to our form of government and would overthrow it by processes subversive of law and order, these charges in due form should have been presented to the legislature and these men tried by orderly processes. . . .

"Our faith in American democracy is confirmed not only by its results but by its methods and organs of free expression. They are the safeguards against revolution. To discard the

THE FIRST HURRAH   118

method of representative government leads to misdeeds of the very extremists we denounce and serves to increase the number of enemies of orderly, free government."

Perhaps that statement should have cooled the feverish anti-Bolshevik passions of the legislature, but it did not. On the contrary, the legislators ignored Smith's pleas that it consider social reform and took upon itself the mission of stamping on Reds wherever they might raise their heads; they found time only to pass pork-barrel and other appropriations bills in their preoccupation with what the Hearst papers called the Red Menace. The Lusk Committee of the Assembly urged the passage of an amendment requiring public schoolteachers to take loyalty tests; another bill hammered out by the committee would require private schools to submit their courses of study to state officials for approval. A third would have given the state attorney general the authority to take any radical political party before the appellate division of the State Supreme Court and have it ruled off the ballot.

Governor Smith promptly vetoed all three bills, submitting definitive proof of their constitutional absurdity, in language which libertarians should, perhaps, have cherished with greater devotion than they did. His veto messages still stand, in fact, as commonsense antidotes to antiextremist extremism, in whatever time.

Regarding the bill to provide the appellate court with the power to rule a party off the ballot, he wrote that the justices would be given "despotic power," that they would, "of necessity," apply "not legal but political tests" of the accused party's loyalty to American principles. "The bill would confer upon this small body of men, perhaps of one political faith, the absolute power in effect to disenfranchise hundreds of thousands of voters. . . . If unpopular minorities are to be deprived of their basic rights to representation upon the ballot they will, indeed, have conferred upon them a just claim to political martyrdom." And he said it all when he concluded his indictment of the bill with: "It is a confession of the weakness of our own faith in the righteousness of our cause when we attempt to suppress by law those who do not agree with us."

Regarding the teachers' loyalty tests, he declared: "No man is so omniscient or wise as to have entrusted to him such arbitrary power not only to condemn any individual teacher but to decree what belief or opinion is opposed to what he deems to be the institutions of the country." On state supervision of the curriculum of private, but not parochial, schools, he asserted that it was "unthinkable" that "any body of men" should have the "absolute power to prohibit the teaching of any subject of which it may disapprove. . . . The clash of conflicting opinions, from which progress arises more than any other source, would be abolished by law; tolerance and intellectual freedom destroyed and an intellectual autocracy imposed upon the people. . . . The safety of this government and its institutions rests upon the reasoned and devoted loyalty of its people."

Looking back on those several postwar years when the most repressive measures were taken by the federal and state governments against a suspected conspiracy directed from Moscow— when a man speaking in a foreign accent could be thrown into jail on the theory that he might be a menace to the Republic— it is possible to discern in the governor of New York State one of the few public men with the courage to stand against the prevailing hysteria. He held to his libertarian principles at a time when it was difficult to defend them, and lonely besides. Lesser men who felt as he did simply stayed under cover until the psychological storm passed over.

If he needed a gadfly during that first term in the Executive Mansion, which he didn't with a Republican majority in both houses of the legislature, Senator Jimmy Walker on occasion took on the role. By now Walker was minority leader in the Senate, a responsibility which had not noticeably tamed his frisky disposition. Smith had always regarded himself as a combination of godfather, Dutch uncle, philosopher, moralist, and friend, with an overriding mission to help Jimmy "grow up." Jimmy was close to his fortieth birthday, but he was still a blithe and occasionally irresponsible spirit. He insisted on calling the governor "Algie" for some elfin reason, and refused to take either himself or "Algie" very seriously.

One cause of disagreement between them was the Walker bill to permit prizefights in the state under an unsalaried boxing commission, which would license everyone from seconds to promoters, managers, and fighters. Boxing had been legalized several times, and each time it had had to be banned because its participants turned it into a malodorous racket. Now Senator Walker had organized enough support for the measure to jockey it through the legislature; Mr. Murphy and the boys at Tammany predictably approved it, and it had the enthusiastic sponsorship of the wealthy socialite-sportsman Major Anthony J. Drexel Biddle, who was equally interested in the manly art and in his Bible Society.

The bill went up to Governor Smith's desk, and there it stayed. Smith neither signed it nor vetoed it. Finally, Senator Walker decided to smoke Smith out and went to the executive office to ask whether he intended to sign the boxing bill.

Smith puffed on his cigar for a moment, then said, "Jim, you're not going to put this bill over on me or the public."

"The public wants it," Walker insisted.

"What public?" Smith snorted. "You know as well as I do that the boxing game is nothing but a refuge for crooks, thieves and cheats. It's a rotten business."

Walker accused him of "pampering a few reformers at the expense of thousands of sports lovers," and for a few moments it seemed as though Governor Smith and Senator Walker might stage a highly illegal, gloveless match of their own on the floor of the governor's office.

Smith cooled down finally and thought up a compromise. "I'll tell you what, Jim. This is Friday afternoon. I'll keep the bill on my desk till Monday morning. If, between now and nine o'clock Monday morning, you can get one hundred representative clergymen to sign their names to letters or telegrams —legitimate and bonafide communications—and they approve this bill, then, and then only, will I sign it."

Rubbing his hands in glee, Walker started for the door.

"Just a minute," Smith called him back. "I said one hundred signatures. *And all of them must be Protestants!"*

"Protestants?" The qualifying clause worried Senator Walker.

"You heard me," Smith snapped. "If I didn't make this stipulation you'd get fifty Catholic priests who like boxing and coax fifty rabbis who are nuts about Benny Leonard [a current champion, who was Jewish]. I want one hundred Protestant ministers of the gospel to say to me personally and in writing that they are in favor of the boxing bill."

Walker hurried over to his own office to put in a call to Major Biddle in Philadelphia. "We're sunk," he told Biddle. "How in the world, especially over the weekend, can we get one hundred Protestant ministers to send letters to the Governor?"

Major Biddle told him not to worry; he'd handle everything.

On Monday morning Walker, a late riser, was awakened by a phone call from the governor's office asking him to present himself immediately. He dressed in his usual meticulous and leisurely fashion and strolled into Smith's office not much before noon.

"What goes on, Algie?" he asked.

"Don't try to be cute with me," Smith roared, pounding his desk, which was covered with telegrams and letters. "I don't know how you did it."

Neither did Walker. He gathered that the litter on the governor's desk represented Major Biddle's efforts over the weekend, but until he walked into Smith's office he had no idea they had succeeded so well.

"It's very simple," said Walker blandly. "Protestants also like boxing."

"Baloney," Smith said. "There are over 600 telegrams and letters on my desk. I'll never know how you did it."

"Did you call me over," Walker asked with a grin, "to watch you sign the bill?"

"Get out!" Smith shouted.

A few minutes later Walker was calling Philadelphia and learning how Major Biddle had put over the telegram and letter-writing campaign. "I recently gave another half-million dollars to my Bible society," Biddle explained. "I merely requested our New York office to notify the state membership about the worthiness of the boxing bill. We are a congenial organization."

Smith may have felt he had been tricked somehow into signing the Walker bill legalizing prizefights, but he remained Walker's best political friend and severest critic and proved his friendship several years later at a turning point in Walker's career. Walker's attitude toward himself and his career—his wisecracking and general frivolity—worried Smith, to whom politics was a deadly serious business. That explained why he was alternately harsh and indulgent toward the eternal spring lamb of the Democratic Party in New York. In politics, as in religion, wit and humor are dangerous qualities; even more so to flaunt any tendencies toward profligacy, and one of Jimmy Walker's greatest vices as a politician was his refusal to play the hypocrite. Despite his intuitions, Smith would be not the least of the victims of the Walker charm.

9

Downtown Boy Moves Uptown

THE possibility that Alfred E. Smith might carry the Presidential standard for the Democratic Party was first mentioned early in 1920, just after he began serving his second year as governor. A sort of boomlet had developed to send the state delegation to the San Francisco convention that summer with Smith as a favorite-son candidate. By spring political writers had advanced him to the status of a dark horse candidate, and the Democratic boss of Illinois, George Brennan, had let it be known he was favorable to Smith's candidacy. The anti-Prohibition segment of the party, a sizable element, liked Smith for his outspoken opposition to the Volstead Act.

Smith knew the danger of succumbing prematurely to Presidential fever and refused to let his hopes run away with him. He realized that he wasn't well known nationally and also that President Wilson, though disabled by a stroke, was cherishing hopes for a third term.

Presidential yearnings were especially dangerous for a governor of New York, he believed. "Say," he said during a bull session in his office on the subject, "you know what happened to every Governor who went to Albany and instead of tending strictly to business sat up in the dome of the Capitol with his eyes glued to a pair of field glasses trained on the White House."

Smith, his wife, his son Alfred and daughter Emily were

aboard the private car, shared with Boss Murphy and other bigwigs, of the special train engaged by Tammany to take its delegation to the national convention in style. Cases of liquor were
hoisted aboard; the country was legally dry, but most of its
politicians were wet. The train departed for San Francisco on
June 17, and all along the way toasts were drunk to Al Smith's
candidacy and the retirement of Woodrow Wilson, with whom
machine politicians were never comfortable.

Mr. and Mrs. Smith checked into the St. Francis Hotel. It
wasn't much of a convention from the spectator-sport viewpoint. It opened with a bang, though, when the party's national
chairman, Homer S. Cummings, delivered a stem-winder of an
oration in defense of Woodrow Wilson and the League of Nations. That was the signal for a demonstration. A huge oil paint-
ing of Wilson was unveiled on the platform; delegation after
delegation poured into the aisles to march and shout for Wilson's renomination. In the New York delegation there was an
undignified scuffle between pro-Wilson men and Tammany
braves. Franklin D. Roosevelt, then Assistant Secretary of
the Navy, managed to seize the standard of the New York delegation and bear it aloft in the demonstration. Maybe there was
something symbolic about FDR's moment of triumph, which
was to be immeasurably magnified a dozen years later.

The New York delegation as a whole reserved its enthusiasm for the moment when W. Bourke Cochran would rise
and present the name of Alfred E. Smith, favorite son, to the
convention. Cochran—whose name was always coupled in the
same breath with the term "silver-tongued"—had retired
from politics during the last years of Croker's management of
Tammany Hall but had become reconciled with Tammany
when Murphy took over and was now a Congressman. He had
been the oratorical idol of Smith's youth. Smith, who had filled
a scrapbook with newspaper clippings of Cochran's blarneying
speeches, was thrilled that the older man was going to propose
him for the Presidency.

The night before he made his nomination speech, the old

war-horse went up to Smith in a corridor of the St. Francis and told him, "I am about to achieve the joy of my life. For as long as I can remember at national conventions I have been fanning the wind either against somebody or against something. At last I have an opportunity to be *for* somebody."

The next day Cochran got up and placed Smith's name in nomination, ending with this organ-toned injunction: "We offer him to you as President of the United States. We will accept no compromise in the convention. If you take him we will give you the state of New York and if you reject him, we will take him back and run him for Governor!"

A mini-demonstration followed, in which the pennants of Illinois and New York fluttered and a Tammany band played "The Sidewalks of New York." Otherwise, there wasn't much enthusiasm. The convention than labored through forty ballots and eventually nominated James M. Cox, the reformist governor of Ohio, and Franklin D. Roosevelt to head the national ticket.

As promised, the New York delegation took him back and ran Smith for governor again. The state party leaders met in Saratoga with the resort hotels' meeting rooms filled with what one jaundiced journalistic observer called the types who participated in such proceedings: the city bosses (hard-eyed men wearing derbies and fat cigars); the reformers ("serious gentlemen with vague blue eyes who are elbowed and pushed and shoved aside by the regulars"); the county leaders trailing jobholders in their retinue; those new discomfiting phenomena, the female politicians ("determined middle-aged ladies who are thrilled at their proximity to what is going on, but carefully excluded from the inner councils"); and various small fry from the backwoods ("less important than the Japanese vote in California").

His opponent in the November election would be Judge Nathan L. Miller, and it would be a tough fight. Every fairly sensitive politician knew a Republican landslide was building up, and that it would carry statehouses as well as the White

House. As the progressive Senator Hiram Johnson of California gloomily told a newspaperman, "The war has set back the people for a generation. They have bowed to a hundred repressive acts. They have become slaves to the government. They are frightened at the excesses in Russia. They are docile; and they will not recover from being so for many years. The interests which control the Republican party will make the most of their docility."

Those foreboding words did, indeed, usher in a long period of docility, or indifference, in a country increasingly obsessed with maintaining prosperity at home and ignoring the rest of the world. No more adventurism. Thousands of Americans had been killed overseas, and Europe was in a worse mess than ever before, and Winston Churchill was saying it would have been better if the AEF had never sailed and the warring powers had been forced to arrive at a negotiated peace.

The Republicans made the most of the country's mood. They had always scorned the Democrats as a polyglot collection of imperfectly Americanized minorities. Now they played the minority game for all it was worth. Their propagandists persuaded voters of German descent, even the Catholics who traditionally voted Democratic, that a Republican President would manage to ease the harsher terms of the Versailles Treaty. The Irish were told that Wilson had neglected to work for a free Ireland even while he was superintending the birth of republics in Poland, Yugoslavia, and Czechoslovakia. The Italian voters were promised that a Republican administration would see that Italy acquired Fiume.

Liberalism was dead, and Warren G. Harding and Calvin Coolidge, along with the men who would engineer the Teapot Dome stealage, were its pallbearers. Back to normalcy. Smith could only try to buck the tide by denouncing Judge Miller as a "tool of the interests," because as a corporation lawyer he had represented the New York City traction companies, and make vague promises about Cox and Roosevelt recognizing the Irish Republic if given the chance. Miller meanwhile was accusing

Smith of having been extravagant, although the latter had actually trimmed several million out of the budget proposed by the Republican-controlled legislature.

The election constituted a Democratic disaster, but a sort of moral victory for Smith. He lost to Miller by about 75,000 votes, but ran 1,090,929 votes ahead of the national ticket of Cox and Roosevelt. Harding carried sixty-one of the sixty-two Assembly Districts in New York City, the lone exception being Smith's home district. An old opponent, William Church Osborn, sent him a telegram: "EVEN IN DEFEAT YOU CAME NEARER TO SWIMMING UP NIAGARA FALLS THAN ANY MAN I HAVE EVER SEEN."

Even so, his first loss in an election so dismayed him that he announced that he was "through with politics for good." The groan that went up from his admirers and supporters evidently produced a quick change of mind. This was evidenced by his choice of the jobs offered him in "civilian" life, during the two-year interim before he could run for governor again. While he was still finishing out his term up in Albany, he was being sought for a number of financial and corporate posts. He knew he couldn't ally himself even temporarily with a bank or traction company or any corporation that did a considerable business with the state. One of his charges against Governor-Elect Miller, after all, had been that he was legal counsel for the traction companies.

His choice of a nonpolitical job was also dictated by sentiment. It was offered by James J. Riordan, president of the United States Trucking Company, and George F. Getz, whom Smith and other friends called Uncle George. Getz owned a large share of the stock in the trucking company. After his term in Albany expired, Smith adjourned to the then-fashionable winter spa at French Lick Springs, Indiana, where he met with Riordan and Getz. With the latter he shared a great love of animals. Getz kept a private zoo, while Smith turned the rear of the grounds of the Executive Mansion into a menagerie with various dogs—six, including Caesar and another Great Dane named Thomas Jefferson—an eagle, a fox, a tiger cub, several bear cubs, and goats. With Riordan he shared something of the same downtown background; Riordan had driven a truck before rising in the world. Smith was offered the post of chairman of the board of United States Trucking at $50,000 a year, and he accepted it. In a way, it was a return to the old family business. His father had earned about $10 a week driving horse-drawn truck wagons, and Al would earn about 100 times that for sitting in an office in the Cunard Building at 25 Broadway.

The Smiths returned to the old house on Oliver Street, which they had refurnished, but from then on the neighborhood in which he had been raised would see less and less of him. The downtown boy, who once boasted that he never went north of Canal Street unless it was to go to the theater, had moved uptown. He kept a suite at the Hotel Biltmore, where his headquarters for the gubernatorial campaign had been, and his family spent much time at various summer and winter resorts. There were even reports that he had been sighted riding in a limousine, with a chauffeur driving.

As chairman of the board of the trucking company he could have contented himself with serving as window dressing while plotting his political comeback, but he insisted on getting out and hustling business. The company had a fleet of several thousand trucks that had to be kept busy, and besides, Smith had a sense of honor about money and felt that he was required to earn his thousand a week.

Probably his greatest coup in the trucking business involved one of the least-loved men in the city, Frank A. Munsey, the cannibal king of Park Row. A tightfisted Yankee who had made millions in the grocery business, Munsey had bought up a number of New York newspapers, then junked or combined them in a capricious way that made him intensely hated and feared in the newspaper business. His meanness as an employer had become a legend, and socially he was on a par with Uriah

Heep. Nominally he was a Republican because, as he said, that party "fits my point of view least badly."

At the moment Munsey owned the *Sun,* the *Herald,* and the *Telegram.* The contract for trucking the newsprint for the three newspapers was a juicy one, and Smith, despite the discouragement of his associates, was determined to obtain it.

He went to Munsey's office in the *Sun* building prepared for a cold or hostile reception, but he found that Munsey—contrary to the experiences of other people—was a rather lonely, wistful old man.

He began spouting cost estimates and other details of a proposed contract, but Munsey raised his hand and said, "Let's talk politics."

Smith was always ready to do that, without stint, and for two hours he discussed the problems of being governor and described his hopes for a reorganization of the state government, the plans for which were still kicking around legislative committees. He also told Munsey how the state hospital system had fallen into a tragic state of disrepair and how he hoped it could be rehabilitated. Munsey listened attentively. Finally, Smith rose to leave his office without bringing up the matter of the trucking contract. Munsey called him back, then summoned a secretary and, without looking over the estimates Smith had brought with him, ordered that the contract be given Smith's company.

During the several years before Munsey's death, his newspapers supported many of Smith's programs despite the opposition of his fellow Republicans, and he and Smith kept up a frequent correspondence. Smith wrote the *Sun* when Munsey died and revealed that he had frequently dined with the publisher and discussed various projects. ". . . It never failed to come to this point in his mind, 'Is that the best thing to do and the right thing to do?' . . . I say truthfully that I have felt rewarded richly for my hardest work as Governor by the warm, honest, confidential friendship of Frank Munsey." It was the warmest tribute that closed-in man received on his death. It was also a tribute to some of Smith's best personal qualities, his willingness to judge a person on his merits and not what someone else said about him, his ability to thaw out the most chilling personalities.

Smith enjoyed his nonpolitical period of success and affluence, but the instincts of the political animal undoubtedly were awakened early in 1922 by reports that Hearstian ambition was afoot again in the state. Smith was in no mood to forgive Hearst's charges of involvement with the milk trust, nor did he think it tactful for Hearst to make his ambitions to run for governor known before Smith had announced whether he would attempt to regain the Executive Mansion.

A little later Smith learned that Hearst's supporters were active in the towns and cities upstate, trying to start a boom. Now the word was that he would be satisfied with the nomination for U.S. Senator if the gubernatorial nomination were preempted. As the New York *World* reported, Hearst was determined to make the run for governor or Senator at all costs, and he was gathering considerable support. The *World* explained:

> With a few notable exceptions, Tammany district leaders in New York are holding well-paying jobs under the Hylan administration or enjoying remunerative returns from private business promoted to a large extent by their political connections. Upon all of these individuals, loyal though they are to the 14th Street Wigwam, pressure can be brought to bear through the Hylan administration.
>
> If Hearst determines to make himself the candidate for Senator, is there any likelihood of ex-Governor Smith aspiring to or even accepting the nomination for Governor? This is a question much discussed. Some Democrats of consequence, inclined to accept Hearst as a Senatorial candidate, foresee a contingency where these two bitter political and personal enemies might run on the same ticket and brave the Republican threat to placard the State with the opinion

Smith has publicly expressed of Hearst and the estimate of
Smith's fitness for office Hearst has time and again published
in his newspapers.

From then on, the pressure on Smith grew, with Hearst
haters urging him to put an end to the publisher's political aspirations once and for all and Hearst backers pleading with him
to make peace with the Chief for the "sake of the party." For
several months Smith refused to commit himself, except to let
it be known that he was happy as chairman of the board of
United States Trucking. Translated into plain language, this
was a suggestion that he would have to be coaxed back into the
arena by evidence of an overwhelming desire on the part of
the Democratic leaders and the electorate. It was apparent to
him that he could have the nomination for the governorship
merely by nodding his head. The question was whether he
would have to accept Hearst as running mate along with the
nomination.

What particularly worried Smith was that Tammany was
shaky in its attitude. Emissaries came down to the Cunard
Building from Fourteenth Street to present the views of a minority group in Tammany that Smith should speak out against
Hearst, that upstate Democrats were particularly offended by
his more or less underground candidacy. But other delegations from the Wigwam whispered that Boss Murphy was in
favor of the idea of a Smith-Hearst ticket, that many of the district leaders were also so inclined, that many Tammanyites
were fearful of losing their jobs or city contracts if they didn't
fall in line (Mayor Hylan being Hearst's man all the way), and
that the party could use the sizable campaign contributions
Hearst would make if he were suitably rewarded. Murphy,
it appeared, was afraid to thwart Hearst for fear of losing the
city patronage. In the sacred name of party regularity, Smith
was urged to forget that Hearst had called him, in effect, a
baby-killer or that he had labeled Hearst a walking pestilence.
Smith stayed silent.

The more people tried to pry an opinion out of him, the more noncommittal and disinterested he affected to be. One man who observed his study in incommunicado shrewdly noted that Smith, "conceived in the popular imagination to be an affable man, a glad-hander, one who never hesitates to express himself and whose position on all subjects is known at all times, is actually a politician keenly aware of the virtue of silence. He finds it possible to say nothing for many weeks, even when excited demands for a statement come from all sides."

By midsummer, with the state convention only four weeks in the offing, Smith still had not opened his mouth.

The undeclared war of nerves was particularly hard on William Randolph Hearst, who was burning to know whether he would be Smith's running mate that fall or his unforgiven enemy. By way of trying to budge Smith out of his rocklike immobility, he had his puppet, Mayor Hylan, dismiss George A. Colgan, the city's commissioner of markets. Colgan was notoriously an Al Smith man. When he was fired, Colgan charged that it was because, as an Exalted Ruler, he had refused to tour all the Elk lodges in the state and urge the nomination of Hearst for the U.S. Senate.

It wasn't until mid-August, with the convention only two weeks away, that Smith gave a hint of his intentions. His choice of medium, at that, was curious: an exchange of letters between himself and Franklin D. Roosevelt. He and Roosevelt had become acquainted when the latter served in the State Senate; then Roosevelt went to Washington as Wilson's Assistant Secretary of the Navy. Since then, Roosevelt had been stricken by polio. They addressed each other as "Dear Frank" and "Dear Al," but they were more acquaintances than friends. To Smith, Roosevelt seemed a genial dilettante, a gentleman farmer who dabbled in politics, and therefore not to be taken too seriously.

Roosevelt on August 13 wrote Smith an open letter relating that he had attended a Democratic conference in Syracuse recently at which it had been urged that "this state must put its best foot foremost in the selection of candidates this year . . . there is no question that the rank and file of Democrats want you to run. . . . Many candidates for office are strong by virtue of promises of what they will some day do. You are strong by virtue of what you have done. . . . Already unauthorized agents are saying that you will not accept, and many are being deceived and beginning to lose interest as a result. It would surprise you to know what enthusiasm would spring up overnight if we knew you would accept the nomination. . . . I am asking you personally and publicly to accede to the wishes of so many of your fellow citizens."

To "Dear Frank," Smith replied that "considering the facts as I know them, and answering your letter, I feel myself that I would be ungrateful if I were to say that I would be unwilling to assume the leadership." He would accept the nomination because "during the past twenty years I have been so honored by my party that even the members of my family would be dissatisfied if I did not answer the call."

But it was a two-part question the State's Democrats were asking, and Smith had answered only the first part. In any other profession but the political, in which unanswered questions build tension and contribute to the desired result, as in an old-fashioned melodrama, his attitude might have been called coyness. But he still refused to say whether he would accept Hearst on the ticket.

The situation was unchanged when the delegates to the state convention gathered at the Hotel Onondaga in Syracuse. In the ornate lobby, the tension was palpable. Hearst himself did not appear but was well represented by Mayor Hylan and Boss McCooey of Brooklyn and a battalion of Hearst hirelings, headed by his personal attorney, William A. De Ford.

Smith, too, was invisible to most of the delegates. An attack of neuritis confined him to an armchair in his suite on the eighth floor. The racking pain only increased his irritability as delegation after delegation, particularly the iron-hat boys from the sidewalks of New York with their city jobs at stake, came up to plead with him to be "reasonable."

Meanwhile, his headquarters downstairs was being supervised by an astute young man named James A. Farley, the Rockland County leader who had been among the first to mount the Smith bandwagon. Farley, whose abilities as an organizer have never been equaled in American politics, was just now venturing into the big time; he had decided to devote himself to managing other men's campaigns after recently being defeated as a candidate for county superintendent of the poor. As Smith's manager, he was making use of the opportunity to "try out my own notions of how to conduct a campaign of that kind." The fact that Smith was immobilized upstairs gave him considerable freedom, which Farley employed by sending out squads of workers to buttonhole each of the thousand delegates eligible to vote in the convention. Within hours Farley was able to take a list upstairs to Smith showing that "he could be nominated over Hearst, no matter what strength the publisher thought he had."

That informal poll undoubtedly gave Smith the sticking power he needed in the hours ahead; the self-assurance with which he held out for what he wanted also persuaded Mr. Murphy not to lean on Smith or go all out for Hearst.

"I happened to be present at one very interesting conference between Smith and W. H. Fitzpatrick, the leader from Buffalo," Farley has recalled. "The blunt old fellow told Smith that he thought a great deal more of Murphy than he did of him. But he added that Murphy was making a mistake in supporting Hearst, due to wrong advice given him by people in New York City, and that he was going to support Smith merely to save his friend Murphy from the folly of his own judgment. He repeated again that he would rather have Murphy's 'little finger' than Smith's whole body and he wanted the latter to know that fact. Then he walked out. . . ."

Farley was also present when McCooey of Brooklyn came

up to present a plea for party harmony. "Flushed with anger, Smith lashed out at McCooey in a blistering reply. . . . Mc-Cooey went out flustered and upset. . . ." Even Bourke Cochran, who had nominated Smith for the Presidency, failed to move him. He orated at length, Farley said, while Smith sat "arms folded, a black scowl on his face." He heard Cochran out, then "fairly exploded in a scorching denunciation of the attacks made on him in the Hearst newspapers. . . . His short, harsh sentences were unlike the polished utterances of Cochran's but it was a magnificent performance." When Cochran stood up to leave, as Farley recalls, he gave Smith to understand that he had entered his plea for Hearst only at the urging of Mr. Murphy, saying, "Al, I wish you to understand distinctly that I did not come here of my own volition."

Apparently Smith's temper grew more volcanic as the day wore on, and the lava spilled over those whom he owed debts of personal and political gratitude. Norman E. Mack of Buffalo, long one of the most loyal supporters, came up to the eighth floor to plead for a compromise: Let Hearst have the governorship while Smith took the Senatorial nomination.

"The answer is no," Smith roared. "No, no, no! I won't do it for you, Murphy, McCooey, or all of you together."

With all the scheming, seething passions and bargaining turning the Hotel Onondaga into a pressure cooker, only Mr. Murphy seemed to keep his cool, by the account of Ed Flynn, the Democratic leader of Bronx County. "As I sat with Mr. Murphy that day, delegation after delegation arrived and announced support for Hearst. Mr. Murphy would listen until they had concluded their arguments, and then he would simply tell them to call on Smith and repeat to him what they had said. When a delegation arrived and announced support for Smith, Mr. Murphy would say nothing."

Obviously Murphy hoped that Smith would decide to take Hearst, but he would not go up to his suite and plead with him. That would be unsachemlike behavior. Probably he also feared that Smith would reject his argument on behalf of Hearst, and that might result in a break in a relationship which had endured a lot longer than his temporary concern for Hearst and his ambitions.

He sat tight, Smith sat tight, and all day and most of the night the wrangling went on in the rooms and corridors of the Hotel Onondaga.

The impasse was broken early the next morning when a telegram arrived from New York. Hearst told his supporters they should abandon his candidacy and asked that Dr. Royal S. Copeland, then commissioner of health for New York City, be nominated for the Senate. Within a few hours Mayor Hylan and all the other Hearstlings had decamped on trains for New York, fleeing like a defeated army from the battlefield. "By 4 o'clock this afternoon," wrote Charles S. Hand of the New York *World*, "three hours before the first nominating speeches, there was not a Hearst boomer left in Syracuse. The Hearst bubble burst like a child's balloon that had been touched by a lighted cigarette. . . . Hearst quit cold. . . . Smith made his fight on a principle from which he never swerved. . . ."

That was the end of Hearst's political aspirations, but not, unfortunately for Smith, the end of his political influence, and a thwarted political aspirant is never more dangerous than when he is able to use the residue of his power like the sting of a dying scorpion.

10

The First Hurrah

ALFRED E. SMITH served three more terms as governor of New York, six years in which progressive legislation was enacted against the prevailing complacence with Harding normalcy and Coolidge prosperity. The whole structure of the state was rebuilt; the direction of state government was reoriented toward providing social and economic protection for the classes which had been ignored since the founding of the Republic. Smith's administration was a detailed preview of the New Deal. It combined the humanitarian with the political. It was the first hurrah, in effect, of the new politics. And Smith himself was the indispensable forerunner of Franklin D. Roosevelt, Harry S. Truman, John F. Kennedy, Lyndon B. Johnson.

"Men of many shades of political opinion saw in him the embodiment of a new liberalism, practical, rooted in the cities, and willing to confront the problems of an industrial society," Oscar Handlin has written. "He was far from being what all these anxious people thought he was. But there was enough in the program for which he spoke to lend substance to their dreams." It was Smith, perhaps instinctively, who grasped the possibility of the future coalition of forces—racial, social, and economic—which in the coming decades would keep the Democrats in power year after year, administration after administration. "In the 1920's, the children and grandchildren of the immigrants were reaching political maturity," Handlin believes. "As they acquired education and skill, moved upward on the educational ladder and outward away from the slums, they became concerned about their place in American society. For more than two decades, they had been under attack, in the long debate over immigration restriction—stigmatized as members of inferior races, barred from desirable trades, and challenged as to their capacity for citizenship. Now their numbers had grown and with it a potential of political power, still unrecognized by the old-line politicians. Smith was one of them, up from the city streets, and his career was a living demonstration of the falsity of the accusations against them."

Smith also profited from the blindness of the Republican old guard which failed to understand the political significance of the growing power of the Italians, the Poles, the Jews, the French-Canadians. The GOP leadership refused to listen when Louis Marshall warned that the first generation of immigrant parents "resent the idea that they are to be treated as inferiors" and asked that they be treated with understanding, with due regard for any lingering feelings of inferiority.

Smith was able to capture the sympathy and loyalty of such groups because he could speak to them without condescension. When he said—as he said so often—"Let us look at the record," his audience could expect something more than a jumble of facts and figures. He had the ability to simplify, to popularize, without cheapening and without cheating on the truth. In 1921, when he was out of office but a member of the New York Port Authority, he was invited to address the legislature on the problems of that body. The legislators were amazed when a crowd of cleaning women packed the chamber to listen to his analysis for two hours with undivided attention. Like Horatio Seymour, he could "make tangled figures concerning the cubic yards in the Erie Canal sound like a romance."

The beautiful part of his administrations, from the viewpoint of the more conservative section of the electorate, was that he accomplished much without great fiscal expenditures.

In that sense he was conservative. He was able to practice fiscal conservatism largely because of his administrative ability and his knowledge, gained while a member of the Appropriations Committee of the Assembly, of where the "fat" was, which measures were pure pork and could be eliminated without social harm. During his second term, in 1924, he was able to trim $17,000,000 out of the state budget—an exercise in witchcraft which caused a great shuddering among Republicans, who claimed to be the party of fiscal responsibility. Smith's concern for the taxpayer naturally brought into his fold many who would have otherwise been repelled by his social reforms.

This concern was stated in his January message to the legislature in 1924, heralding that expert use of the scalpel: "I believe that it is a very great mistake to take from the taxpayers in any one year more than is needed for the actual conduct of the government, always leaving a safe reserve in the bank in case of trouble. I am satisfied after a comparison of the State's resources, plus the clear surplus over and above commitments, taking account of fixed charges and making allowances for progressing other public work of a special nature, that there can be a substantial reduction in the State income tax, to every person paying it, for at least this year." He succeeded in persuading the legislature to approve a 25 percent reduction in the state income tax.

It should be added, of course, that Smith was able to economize, to cut the budget even while carrying out a program of social reform, long before the state was swamped by the urban problems and afflicted by the racial tensions which now make such austerity impossible.

He returned to Albany for his second term on January 1, 1923, on a flood tide of public approval, receiving a plurality of 387,000 votes over his opponent, Governor Miller. Of the big metropolitan dailies, only Hearst's papers and Pulitzer's New York *World* opposed him. He also carried the whole state ticket with him. One of his first nonpolitical measures on returning to the Executive Mansion was to convert it into a zoo, mostly composed of animals native to the state and including a goat named Heliotrope—Smith had a special affinity for goats and Great Danes—a raccoon, elk, bears, barn owls, rabbits, deer, pheasants. An elk presented to the governor by Boy Scouts who captured him in Bear Mountain Park was so tame that his sons could play with him as with a pony. A fawn caught in the Adirondacks wandered in and out of the Executive Mansion at her pleasure. A small black bear was so tame that when it climbed a telephone pole and escaped over the bank fence, it was recaptured by the children of a nearby orphan asylum. For the next six years the Albany Police Department was continually bemused by the necessity of rounding up dogs and other animals which strayed into the city streets from Governor Smith's private zoo.

Occasionally the animal lover and the political animal in Smith would come into conflict. Once he was lecturing Assemblyman Clarence Jenks of the Judiciary Committee and others in a conference on the executive budget and became irked because Jenks' attention seemed to be riveted on a couple of the Smith dogs frolicking on the lawn outside the office windows. Smith gave him a schoolmasterly dressing down for his inattention, to which Jenks replied: "The Governor is right. I was interested in the antics of the dogs because the dogs are what God Almighty intended them to be: just dogs. But the Governor wants to be a King."

Witty enough, but not quite accurate. What Smith had in mind even during the early days of his triumphant return to Albany was not a crown but the Presidency. He had begun shaping himself for a try at the nomination in the 1924 national convention.

This became evident in his attitude toward the state Prohibition law. Personally Smith was "wet"; the fact that drinking had been "prohibited" did not prevent him from taking a glass of beer, a highball, or a cocktail whenever the spirit moved him, which was at least several times a day. The state—particularly New York City with its thousands of speakeasies—was also wet. But there were vast parched sections of the country, the Bible Belt and elsewhere, where Prohibition was a holy cause. A wet candidate might have a difficult time obtaining the nomination. If he chose to make a try at it, his chief opponent, it appeared, would be William Gibbs McAdoo, who proclaimed himself to be as dry as the Sahara.

A vexing situation arose almost immediately after he took office. The national Volstead Act was complemented in New York State by the Mullan-Gage Act. The 1922 Democratic state convention, however, had inserted in its platform a plank favoring modification of the Mullan-Gage Act. The state legislature, aware of widespread discontent with Prohibition, particularly the ban on wine and beer, moved to repeal it. Jimmy Walker, now majority leader of the Senate, managed to push through the repealer by a one-vote margin.

That placed the ball in the governor's court. "Literally thousands of letters poured into the executive chamber on both sides of the question," he later recalled. "Friendly warnings and threats were made as to the effect upon my political future if I signed the repeal act. . . . It was quite apparent that here was a sharp division of opinion. . . . I definitely determined in my mind that I would have to resolve the question according to my own conscience."

The question was also complicated by constitutional issues. "I am dealing with three classes of people, the radical drys, the radical wets, and those who hold moderate views on this subject. The drys seem to see a moral duty on the part of the State to maintain an enforcement act. They are undoubtedly led to this conclusion by their own frame of mind because they do not suggest that the State maintain an act merely enforcing the Eighteenth Amendment in accordance with the wishes of the majority of the people of the State, but they insist that there be a State enforcement act exactly paralleling the Volstead Act. . . . The mere omission to maintain a State statute in no way abrogates a Federal statute. It seems to me that this effectually disposes of the loose talk about the nullification of the Constitution by refusal on the part of any of the States to enact separate statutes. . . ."

Moral and constitutional issues, however, were only in the background of Smith's considerations. The repealer put him on the spot. To veto or not to veto was the question. If he vetoed it, he would improve his position as a candidate for the Presidency; if he signed the bill, he would prove himself loyal to Tammany—most of whose district and ward bosses had never stopped lamenting the closing of their saloons—and perhaps to a majority of his constituency. Edward J. Flynn, the Bronx leader, stated flatly that Smith was nursing his Presidential ambitions as he returned to Albany and that they were assuming priority over any other considerations. "The most important effect of this ambition," Flynn wrote, "was to place in a new perspective the decisions that had to be made about many public questions. This was particularly true of prohibition." The Southern wing of the Democratic Party was overwhelmingly dry, as were many of the Middle Western states, and Smith, said Flynn, "realized all too well that there would be serious opposition to a downright 'wet' from an Eastern state. Should he, therefore, rely confidently on the support of the 'Wet' element, and at the same time make a gesture toward the 'drys' by vetoing the repealer?"

As a successful politician, Smith was no stranger to the polar attractions of expediency. In his reach for the big prize, it seemed necessary to disappoint his home state in widening his appeal to the South and West. He had just successfully defied majority opinion in Tammany by turning thumbs down on Hearst as a running mate. The big, the implacable, obstacle was Mr. Charles Murphy. Their long relationship now reached a critical point. Mr. Murphy was determined that Smith should sign the repealer and take his chances on winning the Presidential nomination; parochial interests must come first. He had given Smith his head over the Hearst Senatorial nomination, but now he was determined to assert his authority.

Would Smith ever have left the Fourth Ward without the benevolent interest of Murphy and the other Tammany saloon-keepers? It was time for Al Smith to remember where he came from and how he got to Albany—time to remember that he was one of Murphy's "boys."

Murphy summoned the governor to a showdown conference at Good Ground, his Long Island estate, somewhat in the manner of the Pope beckoning to Frederick Barbarossa. The showdown was brief, and probably humiliating to Smith, since there was a third party present. The witness, as Murphy probably arranged with a Celtic sense of the fitness of things, was his new favorite "boy," Ed Flynn of the Bronx.

"When the Governor entered," Flynn recalled, "I was with Mr. Murphy and got up to leave. Mr. Murphy motioned me to stay, then turned to Smith and said, 'Al, you must sign this bill.' Governor Smith then announced that he would not sign the bill. It would be very injurious for him to do so, he said. It would kill whatever aspirations he had for the Presidency.

"Mr. Murphy seldom lost his temper. His speech was normally economical of words, and he avoided vocal emphasis. But on this occasion he was deeply moved. Quietly but firmly he told Smith, 'Al, you will either sign this bill or I will never support you again, either for the Presidency or for the Governorship.' Whereupon he got up and left the room. Governor Smith sat for some time in silence and then he, too, left the room."

He returned to Albany and signed the repealer. The effect of that signature on the 1924 national convention was calculable. By it he learned that sad old lesson of organized politics. The machine giveth, and the machine taketh away. . . .

From the beginning of his six-year period as governor, Smith gathered around him a sort of intellectual harem. The growing importance of the social worker (usually female) and the entry of women into politics had occurred almost simultaneously, but no governor made so much use of that new motive force as Smith. He was a man's man, a politician's politician, who would not be expected to be very comfortable in close and continuing association with lady reformers, idealists, and crusaders. Yet his administration was marked by the number of vital young women with which he surrounded himself.

They were the Albany extension of the settlement house workers, trade unionists, social workers, and others characterized by professional politicians as do-gooders whose numbers and influence had been rising since before the World War. A whole generation educated in social responsibility would graduate, partly to Albany, partly to FDR's Washington during the New Deal, some to both. Senator Wagner, as sensitive as Smith to their influence, remarked: "One could not overestimate the central part played by social workers in bringing before their representatives in Congress and state legislatures the present and insistent problems of modern-day life." The members of that socially conscious generation included Henry Morgenthau, Jr., Adolf A. Berle, Jr., and Herbert Lehman, who worked at the Henry Street House; Frances Perkins, Charles A. Beard, and Gerard Swope, at Hull House; Sidney Hillman at both Henry and Hull Houses: Harry Hopkins at Christador House on the Lower East Side.

It was a middle-class mission to the poor, as Arthur Schlesinger, Jr., has noted, which "coincided with the release of energy which came from the new emancipation of women" and which "produced an extraordinary group of women whose vitality and compassion reshaped American liberalism."

Foremost of these recruits to state government was Frances Perkins, whom Smith named as a member and later as chairman of the Industrial Commission and whom he retained despite complaints from party regulars that her ideas were dangerously radical. Among his closest advisers were Joseph M. Proskauer, an Alabama-born graduate of Columbia and a leading member of the Citizens' Union, who often served as Smith's ghostwriter on the occasions when Smith couldn't ad-lib; Robert Moses, who became his secretary of state eventually; and, above all, Belle Moskowitz.

If there were any gray eminences in his administration, the energetic and intense Mrs. Moskowitz would have to be chosen for the role. Some people called her the "Colonel House of the Smith administration." Tammanyites were certain it was she who persuaded him to hold out against Hearst's being placed on the 1922 ticket. A graduate of Teachers College at Columbia, she had worked with the Educational Alliance on East Broadway, had managed the labor department of the Dress and Waist Manufacturers' Association, and had been one of Smith's chief campaign workers. Her post as the governor's adviser was unofficial and unpaid; officially she was publicity director for the Democratic State Committee at $4,000 a year. Unofficially, to some extent, she managed Smith, becoming one of a matriarchal trio along with his wife and mother. She treated him with a combination of the maternal and the hard-nosed friend.

Mrs. Moskowitz, as Frances Perkins observed, was of "inestimable help" to Smith, the developer of many of the ideas which he clothed in legislative action. It was advisable, as people learned, to go through her in proposing anything to the governor. To those who failed, she would say, "Why didn't you ring me up? It's too late now. You should have seen me." In time, she became somewhat domineering, Miss Perkins noted. "She had become accustomed to power, to having the yes and no, to 'fixing things.' She knew how to manage men, programs, and politics with extraordinary success."

Doubtless at her urging, Smith pushed hard for certain social legislation which had been hanging fire during Governor Miller's administration. One bill was the forty-eight-hour workweek for women and children. It was favored by a delegation of amateur lobbyists, including Mrs. Franklin D. Roosevelt, Mary Dreier, Rose Schneiderman, Mrs. Howard Bens, who came to Albany as members of the Joint Legislative Conference representing the League of Women Voters, the YWCA, the Women's City Club, and similar organizations. It was bitterly opposed by a manufacturers' lobby titled Associated Industries, Inc.

Smith himself led the fight for the shorter week for women and children. When he failed to maneuver it through the 1923 session, he kept up the pressure for several more years until it was finally passed.

He also initiated a program of low-cost housing which would replace tenement blocks and create a Bureau of Housing, in the state architect's office, to plan the program. While formulating a series of measures designed to encourage the participation of private industry in limited-dividend corporations which would put up minimum rental buildings, he recalled that one section in his old neighborhood was called the Lung Block because of the number of tuberculosis deaths in its tenement houses. That was enough to stiffen him against charges of Socialistic planning that came from the Republican minorities in the Assembly and Senate. He got most of his program through the legislature, though he was forced to sacrifice a provision for the establishment of a state housing bank which would finance the program. The whole scheme, in fact, could serve as the working model for present-day proposals for urban renewal through cooperation between government agencies and private industry.

Nineteen twenty-four was not one of Smith's best years in either his private or his public life. Charles Murphy died suddenly, leaving the leadership of Tammany Hall in doubt for many months. A second death struck him much harder: His mother died after a third attack of pneumonia—"the first real sorrow I had ever suffered."

The two deaths distracted him at a time when he was mobilizing his forces for a try at the Presidential nomination. Franklin D. Roosevelt had been named as his campaign manager, largely because his social credentials might offset his candidate's Tammany background. The real managers were Brennan of Illinois and Mack, the Buffalo leader, who had long been Smith's most fervent admirers.

The Smith forces congratulated themselves on an initial tri-

umph when the national committee decided that the convention would be held in New York, in the old Madison Square
Garden, scene of circuses, horse shows, and the murder of Stan-
ford White. A New York convention would provide an enthusiastic crowd in the galleries cheering for Al Smith and singing a rather unfortunate campaign song titled "Al, My Pal," the
chorus of which was:

> Al, my pal, a nation's falling
> In the war 'tween might and right,
> Al, my pal, your country's calling,
>   Lead us onward in the fight!
> Al, my pal, to you we're turning,
> Through dark clouds will shine the sun.
>   Al, my pal, for you we're yearning,
> Lead us on to Washington!

The vision of palship summoned up by the song and of
Smith leading the city proletariat toward the spoils of Washington did not in fact inspire a great number of delegates to the
national convention. Smith represented much of what they
feared in modern American life: the dilution of Anglo-Saxon
stock; the suspected conspiracy of Catholics and Jews to over-
whelm the old-time religion; the loosening of morals through
short skirts, wild dances, speakeasies, country clubs, and auto-
mobiles parked in country lanes. The booboisie, the yahoos,
and red-necks, as H. L. Mencken kept reminding the readers of
the arsenic-covered *American Mercury*, were riding high. To
them, Al Smith was becoming a Satanic figure, what with his
tilted derby, his snappy checkered suits, his wisecracks issuing
from the side of his mouth, his American-Cockney style. Sure,
he and his wife, Katie, cut rather homely figures, but it was the
dark-faced city mob in the background, with their mongrel
morals and cosmopolitan grabbiness, that you had to worry
about. There was something symbolic about the fact that delegates to the convention could go up to the roof theater of the
Madison Square Garden and see the very spot where Stan-

ford White was shot and killed by the maniac millionaire Harry K. Thaw for tampering with the morals of his child bride—a New York type of murder if ever there was one.

The millions in America who wanted to shut out the world and its evils, who wanted to turn away from anything that spelled modernization, who dreaded change and the challenge of the future, were organizing to resist such pressures. Four million were said to have joined the Ku Klux Klan, the old Southern resistance which had been reborn and spread to the North and West. The KKK was now almost as strong in some states north of the Mason-Dixon Line as it was in Georgia and Mississippi. Anyone brought up in the Middle West during the twenties will recall the silent, menacing parade of mounted Klansmen parading through the streets after dark, followed at times by the burning of crosses on nearby hillsides. The Klan's millions and the millions of others who sympathized with its proclaimed objectives (before the sordid story of its leaders self-enrichment was revealed) were determined to restore fundamentalism to religion, discipline to the family, restraint in personal behavior. They were willing to overlook the fact that their former idol, Harding, had died just before the putrefaction of his administration was exposed and to place his dour Vice President, Calvin Coolidge, in the White House . . . or a Democratic candidate whose rigid morality could not be questioned.

The Democrat who proposed to ride this resurgence of nativism was William Gibbs McAdoo, with his tall, stooped figure, his deep-set, melancholy eyes, and somber manner. He appealed to Southern delegates because he had been born in Georgia, to Wilsonian liberals because he was Wilson's son-in-law. A corporation lawyer and a Wall Street operator, he still managed to affect an air of enlightenment. He had built the first tunnel under the Hudson, had served as Secretary of the Treasury and as attorney for the Doheny oil interests, which had been heavily involved in the Teapot Dome scandal. Recently he had been performing plastic surgery on himself and remaking himself in the image of Willam Jennings Bryan, so long the Populist idol of rural America. Like Bryan, he was a strong Prohibitionist and paid homage to the astringent religious passions of the Bible Belt. As the standard-bearer for the Southern and Western wings of the Democratic Party, he delighted his followers by denouncing on his arrival from California the "sinister, unscrupulous, invisible government which has its seat in the citadel of privilege and finance in New York City." Few of them questioned the sincerity of that statement coming from a man who had been a New Yorker himself for many years and one of the lords of "privilege and finance" he was denouncing.

On a hot humid June 24 the convention was called to order, with McAdoo claiming a majority of the delegates but Smith asserting that the "rank and file" hoped for his nomination. It was already apparent that rancor and recrimination would dominate the atmosphere on the convention floor and in the galleries. At issue from the outset was whether the Klan should be condemned, as delegations from the Northeastern states proposed.

Smith, of course, made his position on the Klan unequivocally known from his headquarters on the top floor of the Manhattan Club across the street from Madison Square Garden. He did not believe that the Klan was a serious threat, merely a symptom of the current "spirit of unrest." But it had to be taken seriously, he added, because it was "so abhorrent to intelligent thinking Americans of all denominations," though "in time it must fall to the ground of its own weight. The Catholics of the country can stand it. The Jews can stand it. But the United States of America cannot stand it."

McAdoo, in his headquarters at the Vanderbilt Hotel uptown, refused to make a similar denunciation.

Two days before the convention opened, the Committee on Resolutions had split down the middle on the question. It finally produced two planks in the platform for presentation to the convention: one vaguely approving of the KKK, the other forthrightly denouncing it.

The issue was brought to the convention floor on the night of June 29 in an atmosphere thunderous with tribal passions and sectional hatreds. It almost seemed to at least one observer that the "ape behind the mask," which has haunted American history from the heyday of the Know-Nothings, was abroad in Madison Square Garden that sweltering night. "So thin was the veneer of civilization, so black the thoughts in the minds of the delegates that it was a terrifying thing for onlookers to behold. The city police were on hand in added numbers. It was, in fact, only the presence of husky Irish patrolmen, who would as cheerfully have knocked in the head of a pugnacious Catholic as of a Protestant Klansman, that prevented rioting."

The galleries were packed with Tammany roughnecks, and they continually interrupted the proceedings with a roar of disapproval, of booing and foot stamping and zoolike howling, that was stilled only when William Jennings Bryan, with his elephantine dignity and the *vox humana* tone of his voice, reminded them that "it takes more courage to fight the Republican party than it does to fight the Ku Klux Klan."

When the vote was finally taken, including the fractional votes allowed some of the delegates, the mildly pro-Klan resolution was adopted by a narrow margin, 546.15 to 542.85, which left everyone resentful. But it was a McAdoo victory, of sorts, and tended to confirm his claim that he had the support of most of the delegates. The question was whether he could obtain a two-thirds majority—732 votes out of 1,098.

Much of the rest of the convention was given over the futile struggle between Smith and McAdoo to clutch at a majority, but their partisans were too bitterly committed to switch sides.

The only uplifting moment came when the gallantly smiling Franklin D. Roosevelt, still crippled from his polio attack and conveyed to the platform in a wheelchair, stood as erect as possible on his crutches at the speaker's desk and affixed the label on Smith he would wear, with increasing irony, to the end of his days. Placing Smith's name in nomination, as the Tammany-packed galleries roared in ecstasy, he hailed him as "the Happy Warrior of the political battlefield."

Then the grim deadlock set in, with Smith following the proceedings from his vantage point across the street with slowly evaporating hopes.

Day after day, through more than 100 ballots, the delegates assembled in the steaming heat, answered roll calls, dispersed in caucuses, wrangled, and refused to budge. The division in American life they represented would not permit a compromise; the psychological chasm between them, between the America of the farms and small towns and the America of the growing cities, could not possibly be bridged.

On the first ballot, Smith received 241 votes and McAdoo 431½. From time to time the balance tilted slightly, often in Smith's favor. On the fifty-eighth ballot—a record for a Democratic convention—it was Smith 331½, McAdoo 495. Smith reached his high-water mark on the seventy-sixth ballot with 368. The most McAdoo received was 530. History-minded observers were reminded of the 1860 convention at Charleston, South Carolina, when the party was divided on the slavery issue. After fifty-seven ballots that convention gave up, one wing nominating Stephen A. Douglas, the other John C. Breckinridge—and how long had it taken the party to recover from that schism?

One desperate effort to break the deadlock before the party could disintegrate out of sheer exasperation was launched by Western Catholics who had been supporting McAdoo. They suggested that Smith throw his support to Senator Thomas J. Walsh of Montana, who had won fame as the inquisitor of the Teapot Dome case, who was an Irish Catholic like Smith, but was more acceptably a Prohibitionist. In return, they promised that Smith would be supported for the 1928 nomination. But Smith refused to make any deals.

The convention staggered on to the hundredth ballot before

intermediaries, pleading that the salvation of the party was at stake, arranged a meeting between Smith and McAdoo on the night of July 8, when the convention had been in session for ten days. They met on neutral ground, with Herbert Bayard Swope, the eupeptic editor of the New York *World*, Stuart Gibboney, and Thomas L. Chadbourne, a liberal Democratic lawyer, among those acting as seconds and referees. In the swank apartment of a former ambassador at the Ritz Carlton, Smith recorded, "I admitted that I did not believe that I could be nominated. . . . In the interest of party harmony, I suggested that we both withdraw our names from consideration, throw the convention into the hands of the delegates themselves, and let them make the choice." McAdoo rather tentatively suggested that they both might throw their support to a compromise candidate, Edwin T. Meredith of Iowa, the Secretary of Agriculture in the Wilson administration, but "I told him frankly that I did not have the control of the delegates who were for me. . . . Whereupon we parted and shook hands like two old-time friends."

McAdoo subsequently yielded to pressure for his withdrawal, and the backstage managers presented John W. Davis, an intelligent, progressive lawyer, who had been Solicitor General under Wilson and later Ambassador to Great Britain, to the convention. It was a decent choice. He promised a resumption of Wilsonian liberalism but without any venturesome tendencies aboard. On the other hand, he lacked political appeal; worse yet, he had been J. P. Morgan's lawyer and was not the type calculated to appeal to either the big-city voters or the rural masses. But the convention, on the hundred and third ballot, handed him the nomination.

As a sop to his frustrated hopes, Smith was invited to address the convention and probably hoped to use it as the springboard for aspirations now deferred until 1928. He started out nicely enough by mentioning the enthusiasm of the galleries for his nomination. "If you have been annoyed in any way, by the various people with whom you have come into contact, in their zeal to explain to you why I am the greatest man in the world, overlook it." There was a ripple of laughter, and the delegates began to hope for one speech at the long dreary affair they could remember with some affection. Even delegates from the general-store-and-filling-station crossroads who wore KKK spook sheets on their night out could appreciate Irish humor. Instead of providing a little comic relief, however, Smith launched into a long dull recital of the achievements of his administration in Albany; it sounded like a chapter from *The Collected Works of Mayor John F. Hylan,* and the delegates from the hinterland went home convinced that Smith was just another boastful New York wise guy.

That fall the voters decided to keep cool with Coolidge, given the choice of Davis and his running mate, Charles W. Bryan, the Great Commoner's brother, or Senator Robert M. La Follette of Wisconsin, who ran on a third-party ticket as a Progressive Republican. Only half the eligible voters went to the polls.

11

Up at the Tiger Room

FROM 1924 on, his friends in the old neighborhood claimed, they never saw Al Smith any more until an election was coming up. "He's hanging out with a crowd of rich Catholics and rich Jews," they said; he'd gone high-hat, uptown, was even seen on golf courses wearing knickers, and the next thing you knew he'd be going to Southampton instead of Coney Island for the summer. There was some truth to the rumors. The Smiths moved out of 25 Oliver Street and put up the house for sale. They were also climbing fast socially and no longer regarded sitting on a front porch (or stoop) and drinking a glass of home brew with friends and neighbors as the way to spend a summer evening.

Smith had become the centerpiece of what might have called itself the Society for the Perpetual Adoration of Alfred E. Smith. Many of its members were indeed wealthy and Jewish or newly rich and Irish Catholic, many of the latter having gained affluence since the World War. Many were interested in politics as an outlet for reformist urges; some liked the proximity of power or the excitement of the game (the Tiger Room being a Tammany clubhouse, in effect, for the upper class). A few, undoubtedly, were keenly aware of how political connections could increase their fortunes. The founder of the group, it must be said for that essentially modest man, was not Smith himself.

154

The headquarters of Smith's circle, also known as his golfing cabinet, were on top of the building at 44 East Twenty-Third street owned by William F. Kenny, who had established a private club which he called the Tiger Room in the penthouse. It was lavishly outfitted with a banquet room, a fully equipped kitchen, bar, and cardroom, where Kenny and his friends played poker at stakes some of them could not quite afford. Most of the Democratic bigwigs in the state attended dinners there at one time or another. It soon became known among insiders, as Ed Flynn of the Bronx observed, as "A clearing house for state business and politics," the New York City branch of the governor's office. Kenny was one of the largest contributors to Democratic campaign funds and thus possessed a magnetic attraction.

It was probably the most exclusive club in New York City during its brief history between the Coolidge inaugural and the stock market crash. To be admitted you had to be well heeled, golf-happy, and political-minded; you had to agree to the proposition that Al Smith was the greatest statesman since George Washington; it helped if you were Catholic or Jewish, and it didn't hurt a bit if you were born on the Lower East Side or in the gashouse district *and* had made a success of yourself. It was a high-rolling crowd, and according to one survivor of the group, some of its members were all but wiped out long before the '29 catastrophe trying to keep up with the pace set by Kenny and the richer members. Kenny himself "more than made expenses" by winning consistently at his poker games.

The founder of the Smith protective society—and its chief enthusiast—was the hard-nosed and hard-driving Kenny. He and Smith had known each other slightly as boys. Since then Kenny had risen from driver of an ash cart to the prime contractor for practically everything New York Edison had built. He had also made millions by getting in on the ground floor of automobile and radio stocks, which had shot up like IBM or Polaroid during a later Wall Street boom.

If there was any idealism left in Kenny's system after a lifetime devoted to battling his way up, it was his conviction that Al Smith would make a great President.

Smith, in turn, admired Kenny as a self-made multimillionaire as once he had admired Kenny's father, who was foreman of Fire Engine Company 7 at City Hall Park and had drilled his horse teams to such a pitch of perfection that they won the engine company competition at a Madison Square Garden horse show. Undoubtedly, however, there was more to Kenny's ardent friendship than the rather naïve tribute Smith paid to it in his autobiography: "The old neighborhood produced men strong in their friendships and loyal to the last degree in their devotion to one another. . . . Editorial writers and newspapermen spoke of the devotion of my army of friends, and all made special mention of W. F. Kenny's great desire to promote my welfare. To those who know us both, and who come from the old neighborhood, it is easily understandable. He began, like myself, at the bottom of the ladder . . . by hard work and the devotion of his friends he attained his present position in the financial and business circles of our city." The folks from the old neighborhood would, however, have had great difficulty in obtaining admittance to the Tiger Room in the penthouse of the building at Twenty-Third Street and Fourth Avenue if their home address were all they had to offer.

Others who belonged to the charmed circle included Eddie Dowling, the Broadway actor-producer, who had become friendly with Smith after the latter went backstage during the run of Dowling's hit *Sally, Irene and Mary* in 1922 and whose recollections of high times at the Tiger Room, recorded for the Oral History Project of the Columbia University Library, provide a frank and uninhibited insight into the men who surrounded Smith during the several years when his hopes for the Presidency were rising.

The group also included Herbert H. Lehman, himself a future governor of New York and the member of a prominent banking family; John F. Gilchrist, one of Smith's chief political advisers; Tim Mara, the ex-bookmaker who had become a stockbroker and owner of the New York Football Giants; George Getz and Jim Riordan, who had found the $50,000-a-year job for Smith during his period of political unemployment; Herbert Bayard Swope, the Moskowitzes, Henry Morgenthau, Jr., and others of the rich-Democratic-liberal set; and James J. Hoey, an insurance man interested in politics.

When Smith came down from Albany now, he stayed in the suite at the Biltmore he kept the year around and spent much of his time up at the Tiger Room or out on the golf course with Kenny and other members of the group. The Tammany clubhouses saw him no more, and Tom Foley's saloon and all the other watering places where he had renewed his contact with the people were either closed or turned into speakeasies.

One night shocking news reached the Tiger Room by telephone. Kenny's oldest son, William, Jr., had been shot and killed by a taxicab driver while taking his girl home in Brooklyn. In the aftermath of that tragedy, Smith naturally acted as Kenny's personal counselor. Kenny, according to Eddie Dowling's recollection, wanted to see his son's murderer sentenced to the electric chair. Smith, as unofficial intermediary between Kenny and the law, advised him to damp down his desire for vengeance. Smith, Dowling said, had learned that the cabdriver, if he were charged with first-degree murder, would testify that the fatal fight broke out after he saw Kenny, Jr., misconducting himself with his girlfriend. Smith declared they could "throw him out the window" for all he cared about the cabby, but it would be advisable to let the man plead guilty to a manslaughter charge rather than have the Kenny name smeared in the newspaper accounts of the trial. Kenny finally accepted Smith's advice.*

After losing his attempt to obtain the Presidential nomination at the 1924 national convention, Smith was renominated

---

* It might be noted that Smith would have been placed in a most uncomfortable position if the cabdriver had been convicted of first-degree murder and sentenced to death. As governor, he would have had to sit in judgment on the man's appeal for executive clemency.

for governor and ran against Theodore Roosevelt, Jr., who had inherited his father's military, but not, apparently, his political, aptitudes. In the fall election Coolidge carried the state with a 850,000 plurality, but Smith defeated Roosevelt by 108,561 votes. He was the first governor in exactly 100 years to serve a third term. When he took the oath of office on January 1, 1925, in the Assembly chamber, he affirmed his "deep and abiding affection" for that place. "It has been my high school and college . . . the very foundation of everything that I have attained. . . ."

His position in the state Democratic Party was now unassailable. He had also assumed virtual dictation over the affairs of Tammany Hall, at least insofar as they affected him. Without any great deal of consultation with the district leaders, he maneuvered George W. Olvany into the office of Grand Sachem as successor to Charles Murphy. Olvany had served under Smith in the sheriff's office, and "beholden to" is one of the most potent phrases in practical politics.

Under the circumstances, Smith believed that he should have a loud, firm say in who Tammany would place in the office of mayor of New York. The death of Boss Murphy, who was always conciliatory toward William Randolph Hearst, who in turn was the incumbent Mayor Hylan's chief protector, made it possible to dump Hylan with little or no ceremony.

On the question of who would succeed Hylan, Smith at first was undecided. Most of his friends were booming Jimmy Walker, still majority leader in the State Senate, to run against Hylan in the primary; the big names on Broadway, including George M. Cohan, Irving Berlin, Gene Buck, and also John J. McGraw, the manager of the New York Giants, all Smith's friends as well as Walker's, had started beating the drums for Beau James. Smith, however, was fearful that Walker would be handicapped by his well-deserved reputation as a rounder and, in the currently popular term, a "skirt chaser." At the moment Walker was estranged from his wife and attached to a show girl.

Smith and a number of Tammany chiefs met on a golf course outside Atlantic City during the summer of 1925. In the locker room after a game, several of Walker's backers approached Smith and wanted to know what his attitude would be toward Walker's running for mayor.

Smith frowned and replied, "If Walker could keep out of the Broadway limelight—which he can't—and if he would rid himself of that certain party he has been going around with—which he won't—and go back to Mrs. Walker, then things might be different."

In the following weeks, Governor Smith began to receive heartening reports on Jimmy Walker. A changed man, by all accounts. He was no longer seen in the Broadway nightclubs. He was photographed in various places with Mrs. Walker on his arm. It was even said that Walker had taken the pledge.

Late in July Smith was vacationing at the Half Moon Hotel on Coney Island—the rumors in the old neighborhood that he had given up that homely resort in favor of Long Island were proved false—with his three sons. He decided to have a conference with Walker and determine whether a reformation had really taken place. When he called the Walker home on St. Luke's Place, Mrs. Walker loyally told the governor that Jimmy had just stepped out for a moment, but she'd see to it that he received the message. Actually Walker was holed up in a penthouse apartment nearby with a plentiful supply of booze. When word reached him that Smith wanted to see him immediately, he had to be shaken out of a sound, brandied sleep and hastily revived with cold showers, massage, and black coffee.

A little shaky, but sober and clear-eyed, Walker was driven in a Rolls-Royce limousine out to Coney Island, where he was received immediately by Governor Smith in his suite at the Half Moon Hotel.

Smith gave him the ups and downs, as they used to say in the old neighborhood, and decided Walker looked as good as he was reported to be. He moved over to the sideboard and started pouring himself a drink, remarking, "I gather you won't join me."

"In a drink?" Walker asked with a blue-eyed innocence. "Oh, no, thanks."

"How'd you ever do it?" Smith inquired.

"Do what?"

"Straighten up—go home where you belong—keep away from the speakeasies."

"We all grow up sometime," Walker solemnly replied.

Smith went over and placed his arm around the rescued lamb and in his warmest good-shepherd voice told him, "You've proved that you can rise to the occasion. I've checked up on you, Jim, and I've decided to approve of your candidacy. You're the man to beat Red Mike Hylan. Sure you won't join me in a drink?"

"Just," said Walker virtuously, "a glass of soda water."

He left Smith's presence without once irking him by calling him Algie, hurried back to the limousine, and opened a magnum of champagne before the chauffeur was half a block away from the Half Moon Hotel.

The next day Grand Sachem Olvany announced that Walker would run for mayor with Tammany's blessing.

It was far from the usual thing for the governor to interfere in New York City election campaigns, but his fondness for Walker and his detestation of Red Mike Hylan were so strong that he decided to make his influence felt. His animus for Mayor Hylan had been increased as a result of their clash over the $300,000,000 bond issue Smith had proposed to finance a program to eliminate grade crossings where highways and railroad lines intersected. There had recently been a number of fatal accidents in which cars had been struck by trains. Grade-crossing elimination required the railroad to pay half the cost, the state one-fourth, and the local community one-fourth. Smith persuaded the legislature to approve of placing the $300,000,000 bond issue to pay the state's share on the fall referendum ballot.

Upper left: Alfred E. Smith at the age of four at Coney Island, 1877.

Upper right: The young Al Smith with friends.

Right: Smith, costumed as Annie Oakley, with a friend as Buffalo Bill, 1908.

Al Smith with his family, 1917.

Posing with a symbol of the Democratic Party, about 1926.

Governor Al Smith as an honorary member of the pressmen's union, 1928.

Smith's acceptance speech as Presidential nominee, 1928.

Smith with reporters at a daily press conference during the 1928 Presidential campaign trip.

Laying of the cornerstone of the new building of the Society of the
Tammany at Seventeenth Street and Union Square East, January 8,
1929. In front row, left to right: Willis Holly, secretary of the society;
James J. Walker, mayor of New York at the time; John R. Voorhis
(in his hundredth year), Grand Sachem of the society; and Alfred E.
Smith, a sachem of the society.

With Franklin D. Roosevelt on the Empire State Building Observatory, May 1, 1931.

Al Smith at a dinner with Governor Lehman, Archbishop Spellman, Monsignor Lavelle, and Mayor LaGuardia.

Al Smith at his desk in the Empire State Building, 1939.

Al Smith, his wife, and their grandchildren, about 1940.

Al Smith with Herbert Hoover at an automobile show.

Mr. and Mrs. Al Smith leaving St. Patrick's Cathedral on Easter Sunday, April 13, 1941.

Mayor Hylan then outraged him by making a speech against the bond issue, asserting that the railroads should be forced to pay the entire cost of eliminating the grade crossings. It was an easy thing for a mayoralty candidate to say, but it made Governor Smith and the Democratic majority in the legislature look bad.

Thus Smith took the stump for Hylan's opponent and also took on Hylan's chief sponsor, Hearst. On September 2, 1925, with the primaries only thirteen days away, he sent an open letter to Hearst, which Hearst's *American* obligingly published on page one, denouncing the publisher as a "liar" and a "debaser of journalism" who "had the nerve of a Bengal tiger to be loafing in the splendor and grandeur of his palatial estate on the Pacific Coast, and attempting to dictate the politics of the greatest city in the world."

Smith was greatly pleased by Jimmy Walker's victory at the primary over Hylan and his subsequent election as mayor. There were less pleasant sequels to come.

During those several years when Smith was preparing to make his all-out try for the Presidential summit, compiling the record which many historians have acclaimed the finest of any governor of New York and at the same time trying to create an image of himself in the nation as the kind of man who would bring dignity, as well as social justice, to the White House, he was occasionally distracted by domestic affairs. The social demands on him and on Katie probably prevented them from keeping as close a control over the lives of their children as they would have exercised if they had stayed in the closely knit fabric of the old neighborhood.

Thus the elder Smiths were surprised, shocked, and dismayed when two of their sons, Alfred, Jr., and Arthur, both eloped and married hastily and unwisely.

They had better luck with their two daughters, Emily, who was her father's favorite and who probably resembled him in character and spirit more than any of the other children, and her younger sister, Catherine.

Emily was married to Major John A. Warner, the superintendent of the state police. Aside from whatever Freudian complications may have beset him, Smith at first was inclined to view Major Warner with disfavor. He was a Harvard man, which was forgivable, but he was also a Republican, which was harder to swallow.

Smith yielded gracefully, however, and the wedding he gave Emily has been compared as a politicoromantic spectacular event with that of Alice Roosevelt and Nicholas Longworth. It took place on June 5, 1926, at the Cathedral of the Immaculate Conception with Patrick Cardinal Hayes officiating. Fifteen hundred guests were invited to the reception. Among them were Owen D. Young, chairman of General Electric; Louis Fook, the "mayor of Chinatown"; and the boys from Tammany, red-faced and ill at ease in their cutaways, silk hats, and party manners. A truckload of gifts including everything from gold candlesticks to Boswell's *Life of Johnson* was on display, and there was a railroad car full of other gifts waiting to be hauled up to the Executive Mansion.

Smith surveyed the tables laden with gifts and with a forced smile commented, "I guess I'll have to run again in the fall. Emily's going to live in a four-room house. She'll need the basement of the Executive Mansion to store all this junk in."

He did run for governor again in the fall, not so much to use the mansion as a storehouse for his daughter's wedding gifts as to keep himself in the forefront of possible candidates for the Democratic nomination for the Presidency in 1928. His Republican opponent was Ogden L. Mills, a wealthy and socially prominent man currently a member of the House of Representatives, future Secretary of the Treasury, intimate of President Coolidge, and determined to make a strong attempt to dislodge Smith from Albany and, more important perhaps, to eliminate him from the Presidential race. The unofficial slogan of the Republican strategists in the 1926 campaign was "Beat Smith now and you won't have to beat him in 1928."

In that determination, Mills accepted as his chief campaign issue the old charge that Smith was somehow responsible for the milk drunk by New Yorkers. This time it was not how much the milk cost, but the allegation that it was contaminated. POISONED MILK, screamed the Hearst papers' headlines. MAYOR'S ACCUSERS SAY AL SMITH IS IN LEAGUE WITH WATERED MILK SELLERS, blared a headline in the New York *Sun*.

Up and down the state Mills dragged the milk issue, charging that the milk sold in New York City was deficient in butterfat, that it was watered, that it was contaminated, and it was all Governor Smith's fault for not regulating the distribution of fresh milk. That issue evaporated, however, when the scientists on whose report the Republican charges were based admitted that New York's milk supply tested as rich in butterfat as that of the rest of the state.

One result of the hullabaloo over milk was the first meeting between Smith and John J. Raskob, the industrialist who was to make himself Smith's staunchest political supporter and generous personal friend or, depending on the viewpoint, his evil genius and Mephistophelian guide toward a more conservative outlook. Eddie Dowling, the actor-producer, made the introduction, as he recalls, after Raskob, a stagestruck amateur magician, as well as the big wheel at General Motors, expressed the desire to meet Smith. At that first meeting, Dowling says, Raskob declared that he was outraged by the Republican attempt to whip up a milk scandal, and therefore, he was giving the Democratic State Committee $25,000 to be applied toward Smith's campaign expenses. From then on Raskob played a very important role in Smith's calculations about the White House.

He brought his campaign against Mills to a climax with a speech at the Metropolitan Opera House which found him at the top of his form as a political orator, as a popularizer of abstruse issues. For the benefit of his audience, gesturing, tiptoeing, raising and lowering his voice melodramatically, he pictured an imaginary conference of the leaders of the Republican Party searching for a way to beat Smith. The title of this tableau of political desperation, he announced, was: "The Republican Dilemma, or Looking for an Issue." Today, under the magnifying lens of the television camera, such a performance would show up, doubtless, as unbearably hokey and overdone; but Smith's medium was the platform, living theater in the era of the Barrymores, and the farther he stayed from the magnification of modern communications (even radio), the better for him. Smith had to be seen and heard in the flesh.

So, acting his heart out, sublimating a talent for the theater which fate had not permitted him to use professionally, he pranced through a triumphant performance on the stage of the Metropolitan Opera.

"One of the leaders said, 'Now, wait. Don't go too strong on tax reduction; don't stress that because we made an awful mistake in 1925. We stood up in Albany and we bitterly opposed tax reduction. We fought the governor. We made wild and foolish statements to the effect that the Governor's policy would impair the State's surplus.'

"Another one said: 'Wait a minute. You ain't said the half of it. Tell the conference about that night we sat up until four o'clock in the morning trying to find things to spend money on, and tell about the list of appropriations we suggested, amounting in total to over $13,000,000, which, if adopted by the legislature and signed by the Governor, would have made tax reduction impossible. And listen, while you're at it tell the whole truth.

" 'Tell the conference what Smith said about the $13,000,000. You remember how stupid we were about it. We put $2,500,000 in it anticipating a verdict in a damage suit that hadn't been decided yet. And above all things, don't overlook that night Smith had the General Electric Company rig up a radio [broadcasting studio] in the Executive Chamber and sat talking into it up to 12 o'clock. Don't forget the advice that he gave to the people of the state to write to their Senators and Assemblymen and let them know what they thought about it. And don't forget the wagonload of mail that came up Capitol Hill the next day and saturated the post office. . . .' "

For two hours Smith held his audience enthralled while he mimicked the imaginary conference of opposition leaders trying to find a chink in his armor.

Then, with a nice sense of theater, he abruptly switched from the satirical and launched into a tigerish attack on William Randolph Hearst as inventor of the milk issue. He held up a newspaper cartoon showing Mills with a menacing shadow looming behind him.

"You know who that is?" he cried, pointing to the shadow. "That is Hearst. Lowbrow, sinister looking creature that lurks behind the candidacy of Ogden Livingston Mills, and he is the man that made the issue. Well, he made a regular Hearst issue. The business of the State of New York or the material financial prosperity or the betterment of the people does not mean anything to him and he invented the issue of milk.

"If I hadn't worked hard for the State, the little conference that has just suspended would not have been forced to drive the aristocratic and intelligent son of an aristocratic family out in the gutter to pick up Hearst for his issue.

"The conference could find no issue, because I have faithfully, honestly and solely given every minute of my time to the business of the State of New York. I have bettered its business side. I have bettered its human side. I have bettered every phase of it. I have never failed to tackle any problem that came up before it."

Smith's campaign was helped along almost on the eve of the election by the careless remark of a Mills sloganeer, who dropped a clinker when he said, "Al had to work or starve; Mills never had to work," as though a citizenry which made work a high virtue would find something sympathetic about that. "We don't know who the publicity man was who opened

THE FIRST HURRAH   166

up this jug of asafetida in Mills' office," the New York *Times* commented. "Whoever it was, Mills should turn him loose to work at something else or starve."

Smith, running up a plurality of 257,000 votes, carrying along Robert F. Wagner, Sr., to a seat in the U.S. Senate, was returned to Albany for his fourth term.

"The man you run against," Will Rogers wrote him, "ain't a candidate. He is just a victim."

Now the man in the Executive Mansion at Albany was floodlighted by the converging beams of publicity, national interest, and political scrutiny. He was the front-runner for the 1928 Democratic nomination; William G. McAdoo announced that he would not be a candidate, and there was no other serious rival on the horizon. A misstep would be magnified into a sprawling pratfall. Everything he said would be dissected for meaning or twisted out of shape by the opposition. His private life, past and present, would be torn apart. If the Democratic National Committee's publicity apparatus pictured him as the hero of a real-life Horatio Alger tale, the Republicans would turn the fable inside out and present him as a loudmouthed vulgarian who'd fought his way out of the dockside stews. Even his wife—and Smith was touchy about that—would be scrutinized mercilessly to see whether she could live up to the demands of being the First Lady of the Land. Long before the campaign really started, the story was circulated that Katie Smith, on being complimented by an ambassador's wife on the smartness of her gown, would undoubtedly reply, "You said a mouthful!"

He was also intensely aware that the religious issue would be raised against him, that only the tip of the problem had presented itself in the vituperative course of the 1924 convention. If he actually became the nominee of the Democratic Party, his faith and the unconcealed ardor with which he practiced it would be attacked without, as later became the case, any shame or stigma attaching itself to the attacker. He also knew that some Catholics of a more conservative bent feared that his candidacy would harm the church by arousing such unruly passions.

Joseph Tumulty, who had been one of President Wilson's chief aides, warned him in 1927: "You must flatly, once and for all, dispose of the notion that the Pope will be the Colonel House of your administration."

Louis Howe, as Franklin D. Roosevelt's agent at large and the man who was devoting his career to placing FDR in the White House eventually, which made him a trifle bitchy about all other aspirants, reported in full on the trip Katie Smith made to Europe, particularly her audience with the Pope:

"Mrs. Smith is back from Europe and complains to your 'Missus' that there were too many ruins in Rome. She is talking too much for Al's good, describing with much gusto and detail their special audience with the Pope and how he referred to Al as his son and the great knowledge he showed in the political campaign. One of her stories is particularly delicious. She says that the Pope turned to McCooey [the Tammany boss in Brooklyn], who was with them, and said, 'I know how hard you have worked for my beloved son, Governor Smith, but next time you must work even harder.' She also is announcing that she brought back a photograph of the Pope personally inscribed 'To my beloved son, Alfred E. Smith.' "

The Republicans could be depended on to pluck several instances on the Smith record in which he might be accused of having espoused Catholic causes. At the Constitutional Convention of 1915 he had offered a controversial amendment proposing to strike out of the constitution a clause preventing the state from making direct contributions to parochial schools, an issue still alive in New York state politics. Smith later explained that he had offered the amendment to counter a proposal that church property be taxed. His opponents could and would point out that New York City, with the governor's approval, had paid as much as $4,000,000 in one year to parochial schools. On the other hand, Smith had also acted contrary to the church's dogma by approving a bill providing for the extension of the grounds for divorce in the state, and he had vigorously opposed most forms of public censorship, despite the fact that they were strongly favored by the church.

In a time when prosperity and its continuance were all-important to the voters, he was also vulnerable to charges that he was dangerously liberal. If he was noted for one thing throughout the nation, it was for legislation he had proposed or encouraged which provided workmen's compensation, shortened the workweek for men, women, and children, safeguarded working conditions, and provided for the widows and orphans of the working class. Actually he was a social liberal, an economic conservative. Both as a legislator and as governor, his career had been marked by his efforts to reduce taxes, often against the opposition of the Republicans. At most he was a Jeffersonian liberal, and his unqualified admiration for men who had made good by their own efforts testified more than adequately to his devotion to free enterprise.

He could also be scored heavily against on the still-lively subject of liquor. The country as a whole was fed up with the Noble Experiment; the saloon had merely been replaced by the speakeasy, the distillery by the bootleg gangs, and few Americans suffered from thirst, though many from inconvenience. Many Americans who drank, however, perversely liked to think of their public servants as too high-minded to touch the stuff themselves. Others who didn't drink shuddered at the thought of a tosspot managing the affairs of city, state, or nation.

It was fairly well known that Smith looked kindly on a drink, before or after sundown. Back in 1923, he and the legislative correspondents were sitting in his office, talking about the "good old days," when swinging doors instead of peepholes stood between a man and his pleasure.

"Wouldn't you like," Governor Smith nostalgically asked, "to have your foot on the rail and blow the foam off some suds?"

The remark, of course, was strictly off the record, but a reporter who had not been present at the press conference heard about it and wrote a story which was picked up by the wire services. It echoed hauntingly, even though Smith had written a letter of explanation to a well-known dry, U.S. Senator Simeon D. Fess of Ohio: "You may have noticed recently in the newspapers a statement coming from me about bar rails. I think that on my record you will join with the people who know me well and do me the credit of believing that I have enough common sense and experience of life to understand that the saloon is and ought to be a defunct institution in this country. . . . My remark was intended for gentlemen with a sense of humor, and not for use by an intolerant and prejudiced adversary, spying for a chance to misrepresent the real meaning of a casual jest. . . ."

Smith's drinking habits were a matter of continuous interest to both sympathetic and hostile observers who weighed his chances of obtaining the presidency. Louis Howe, as FDR's watchdog in Albany, reported to his master that "I took lunch today with some of the Albany boys and they told me in some ways at least Smith is much drier than he used to be. How long he has sworn off for this time, God knows. Let us trust until after the national convention."

Smith's trouble was that he refused to be a hypocrite and to unstopper the decanter only after bolting his door, pulling down the shades, and stuffing the keyhole. Ed Flynn recorded "a cocktail or highball" was "always available" to callers at the Executive Mansion. Technically, of course, Smith, like tens of millions of his fellow Americans, was breaking the law every time he brought cup to lip, but he evidently regarded as a matter of civil liberty what type of fluid he chose to refresh himself when the sun disappeared behind the Capitol dome. If the Volstead Act had been observed to the letter, instead of in the breach, it would have taken a concentration camp the size of Texas to hold all the lawbreakers. And there were plenty of other rationalizations available, as every survivor of the dry decade can testify.

But Smith's taste for alcohol, of course, had become a matter of national interest, even touching on his fitness to hold high office. A correspondent asked Oswald Garrison Villard, editor of *The Nation*, "Does Al drink and does he drink too much?" Villard published the question and his own answer: "I am reliably informed that he drinks every day, and the number of his cocktails and highballs is variously estimated at from four to eight." Later Villard, embarrassed at the wide circulation this exchange was given, stated that he was supplied the information on Smith's intake by Belle and Henry Moskowitz, who were not likely to exaggerate it.

Smith himself became a trifle defensive on the subject, as Ed Flynn, the Tammany leader in the Bronx, recalled from a visit to Albany. He had been closeted with Smith when Josephus Daniels, Wilson's Secretary of the Navy and a notorious tee-totaler arrived. "We suddenly realized that many cocktail shakers, bottles of liquor and glasses were scattered about. Governor Smith, in his usual jovial manner, told me to go down and talk to 'the old geezer' until these evidences of conviviality could be removed. I hurried down and chatted with Daniels until I felt the coast must be clear. The subsequent conference between the Governor and the former Secretary of the Navy was consequently carried on in a most conventional and 'dis-spirited' atmosphere."

To a fairly sympathetic observer like H. L. Mencken, who as a champion beerbibber liked Smith's wetness, it appeared that his boom for the Presidency might have started too soon. In July, 1927, he pointed out that Smith had more than a year in which to trip himself up. "He may say something grossly of-fensive to the Ku Kluxers who now cast sheep's eyes at him, and so send them fleeing to their klaverns. Or he may say nothing, and so lend support to the growing suspicion that, after all, he has nothing to say." There was a danger to Smith in his silence on national issues because people would begin to suspect that "he esteems delegates more than he esteems principles, and is willing to get them by false pretenses." No one knew what Smith thought about the Muscle Shoals Dam project, Secretary of State Frank B. Kellogg's foreign policy (including the small war the Marine Corps was fighting in the Nicaraguan jungles against Augusto César Sandino and his guerrilla bands, a preview of things to come), the Teapot Dome scandal, freedom for the Philippines, income-tax reduction, or other matters rippling across the national scene. Mencken was inclined to attribute Smith's silence to his parochialism. "The plain fact is that Al, as a good New Yorker, is as provincial as a Kansas farmer. He is not only not interested in the great problems that heave and lather the country: he has never heard of them."

Even though "villagers in the remotest deserts of Texas" were beginning to think kindly of him, Smith's greatest trials were in the offing, Mencken believed, when he would have to keep interest in his candidacy alive and prospering. "It is in the nature of enthusiasm to cool. It is the essence of politics that the hero of today is pursued by wolves tomorrow."

It was also apparent to Smith and his advisers that he would enter the Presidential race with handicaps that couldn't be shucked off. His principal argument, as always, would be to "look at the record." And his record was good. After years of effort, the state government had been reconstructed along the lines suggested by the commission he created in his first term; it had been streamlined for efficiency, many departments had been consolidated and brought under control of the chief executive, and the state's voters had ratified the necessary amendments by overwhelmingly favorable referendums. Many years later Robert Moses, who was his secretary of state and administrative second-in-command, concluded that Smith was the "greatest governor of our time." It should be remembered that Moses has always been noted as a man of merciless objectivity, but he wrote:

"He was a great executive because he had a warm heart, vision, shrewdness in picking men, and the generous impulse of all great administrators to build up his associates, trust and reward them. If he had any ignoble prejudices or mean qualities, I never saw signs of them. In a strange way Al Smith always reminded me of Mark Twain, not the later embittered Mark, erupting, fulminating, kicking at the savage indignities of the world, but the eager, happy, frontier boy, footloose and fancy free, who set type, messed around Mississippi boats and, like Huckleberry Finn, played hookey and thumbed his nose at the Three R's. Too much schooling cramps the style of men like Clemens and Smith."

In a sense perhaps not intended by Mr. Moses, that warm tribute raised the paramount question about Smith for voters who were not prejudiced against his Catholicism and who were tolerant of his views on Prohibition. There was no doubt about the warmth and generosity of the man, or the largeness of his spirit, or his lovableness. The question was whether anyone could visualize the Honorable Huckleberry Finn as President of the United States.

PART II

Unhappy Warrior

> *But that, alas, is always the*
> *fate of Democrats. Either they*
> *must lie with their natural*
> *enemies, or they must go without*
> *sleep at all.*
>
> —H. L. MENCKEN

12

The Remaking of an Image

It was H. L. Mencken's later theory that Smith was "ruined by associating with rich men—a thing far more dangerous to politicians than even booze or the sound of their own voices." By the time he began shaping his renewed effort to obtain the Democratic nomination for the Presidency, certainly, he was often to be found in the watering places of the rich and mighty; his companions were more likely to be millionaire industrialists or intellectuals on leave from their academic duties than Tammany leaders or old friends from the Fourth Ward. Some candid insights into Smith's mood during the months preceding the Democratic convention have been provided by Professor Lindsay Rogers, who found him unspoiled by his sojourning among the upper classes.

Rogers had taken leave from the Columbia University faculty under an appointment from Governor Smith to investigate reports of fraudulent claims being paid as workmen's compensation. There were hints of a scandal in the State Department of Labor, and Smith obviously wanted to root out any corruption or inefficiency himself rather than have them exposed by his political enemies. The industrial commissioner then was James A. Hamilton, whom Rogers characterized as "perfectly honest but afraid of his own shadow," Frances Perkins having been advanced to chairman of the Industrial Board, the ap-

pellate body for workmen's compensation cases. At any rate
Rogers found nothing "shockingly collusive," merely that Hamilton wasn't a tough enough administrator.

Smith was "an admirable man to work for," Rogers recently
recalled. "I played golf with him, sat up and held his hand at
night, and he never asked me a damn word about whether my
report was going to be embarrassing to the administration or
not. Not a single word! The first thing he knew about the report was when I sent it to Albany."

Smith and Rogers got along so well together that the professor was summoned to the fashionable mountain resort of
Asheville, North Carolina, while Smith was making preparations for the campaign. "I'd write a memo for him," Rogers remembered, "he'd read it and master it, but he would talk ex-
temporaneously." In discussing campaign strategy with the
governor, Rogers always spoke his mind, often in the bluntest
terms, to which another Smith adviser, Joseph M. Proskauer,
objected.

Once he became involved in an argument with Smith and said,
"Listen, Governor, don't make a God damned fool of yourself!"

Proskauer chided Rogers for having been "disrespectful to
the next President of the United States."

Rogers turned on Proskauer and tartly reminded him that
he wasn't there to "discuss your prophetic gifts."

"Joe," Smith interceded, "shut up. Of course he should
say anything he wants to me."

Smith and his advisers were camping out at the Biltmore
Estate, which Smith valued for its proximity to a splendid golf
course. So far as Rogers could observe, Smith was unaffected
by the splendor of his surroundings or the elegant tone of the
horsey, fox-hunting crowd at the resort. Once they made a
long trek over thick-napped carpeting through marbled corridors to the bathroom. Smith glanced at the huge marble tub
and commented to Rogers, "It ain't right for any son of a bitch
to have this much."

He was also unabashed in the presence of society women, according to Rogers. One of the local matrons demanded to know why he wasn't taking more interest in the Asheville horse show, and he replied: "Madame, the only horses I've had any dealings with were trucking horses."

Professor Rogers became the headman of a number of writers and intellectuals and teachers gathered to formulate his strategy against the Republicans: the *"New Republic* crowd," as Mencken scornfully called it. His leading advisers, however, were Belle Moskowitz, Joe Proskauer, and Robert Moses, and later John J. Raskob as his official campaign manager.

One of the first issues to be met and firmly dealt with was Smith's Catholicism, a matter raised more than a year before Smith was officially the candidate of the Democratic Party. Early in March, 1927, Ellery Sedgwick, the editor of the *Atlantic Monthly*, sent him galley proofs of an article titled "An Open Letter to the Honorable Alfred E. Smith," which was to appear in the April issue. The author was Charles C. Marshall, a New York City attorney and a leading Episcopalian layman. Marshall argued against a Catholic in the White House in the loftiest constitutional terms; no one could accuse him of being a bigot because he didn't use the language of backwoods bigotry. The Marshall letter, however, raised the question of "certain conceptions which your fellow citizens attribute to you as a loyal and conscientious Roman Catholic, which in their minds are irreconcilable with that Constitution which as President you must support and defend, and with the principles of civil and religious liberty on which American institutions are based."

In the style of a legal brief, Marshall referred to and quoted from papal bulls, encyclicals, and other church documents to support his case that neither Smith nor any other good Catholic could faithfully serve both the United States government, as chief executive, and his church. Marshall wanted to know "if you accept both teachings," that of the church and that of the Constitution, "how you will reconcile them." If there were a conflict between the civil and ecclesiastic powers, which would govern Smith," the jurisdiction of Rome or the decision of the United States Supreme Court?" He pointed out that the Supreme Court had ruled that "in matters of religious practice which in the opinion of the State are inconsistent with its peace and safety, the jurisdiction of the State shall prevail." Marshall also discussed several issues over which state and church were at odds, funding the parochial schools and the divorce laws among them.

Smith was outraged by the open letter; he thought he had more than adequately answered the questions it raised by his actions as governor of New York, and he was disposed to ignore it. Mrs. Moskowitz and Judge Proskauer were rightly convinced that he could not afford to let the letter go unchallenged. They tackled Smith on the subject at his New York City "branch office" in the suite at the Biltmore.

Proskauer, gesturing with the galleys of the Marshall article in his hand, asked when Smith was going to start work on his reply.

"I'm not going to answer the damn thing," Smith retorted, his face red with anger.

"You *have* to answer it, Al," Proskauer told him. "Here's a man who throws down the challenge to you that your religion makes it impossible for you honestly to be sworn in as President of the United States. You owe it to yourself, to your party, and to your religion to answer it."

"To tell the truth," Smith replied shamefacedly, "I don't know what the words mean. I've been a Catholic all my life— a devout Catholic, I believe—and I never heard of these encyclicals and bulls and books that he writes about. They have nothing to do with being a Catholic, and I just don't know *how* to answer such a thing."

There was a long silence; then Smith grinned and suggested, "You answer it, Joe."

"Well, that would make it perfect," Proskauer replied. "A Protestant lawyer challenges a Catholic candidate on his religion, and the challenge is answered by a Jewish judge."

Finally, it was decided that the reply, which appeared in the May issue of the *Atlantic Monthly*, was to be drawn up in collaboration between Judge Proskauer, and Father Francis P. Duffy, the legendary chaplain of the "Fighting 69th," now a parish priest in the Hell's Kitchen section of New York City. The riposte was revised over and over by Smith himself and finally submitted to Cardinal Hayes for his approval.

The article appeared under the title "Catholic and Patriot: Governor Smith Replies." It stated at the outset that Smith had sought counsel from Father Duffy because "I am neither a lawyer nor a theologian" and Father Duffy's patriotism could not be questioned since he "wears upon his breast the Distinguished Service Cross of our country, its Distinguished Service Medal, the Ribbon of the Legion of Honor, and the Croix de Guerre with Palm of the French Republic."

If there had ever been a conflict between his devotion to the church and his service to the state, the article stated, "I, of all men, could not have escaped it, because I have not been a silent man, but a battler for social and political reform. These battles would in their very nature disclose this conflict if there were any."

Many years later John F. Kennedy was to be praised for his political courage in confronting the Protestant grandees of Texas on the same issue, but certainly Smith broke the ground for him in his reply to Marshall. Smith met the Marshall charges and innuendos head on: "Instead of quarreling among ourselves over dogmatic principles, it would be infinitely better if we joined together in inculcating obedience to these Commandments in the hearts and minds of the youth of the country. . . . What we need is more religion for our young people, not less; and the way to get more religion is to stop the bickering among our sects. . . ."

That Marshall's imputations were false, he continued, could be proved by the records of two Chief Justices of the Supreme Court, Roger B. Taney and Edward D. White—who happened to have been Catholics and who had never been accused of having been swayed by "any unwarranted religious influence."

Marshall had quoted from the *Catholic Encyclopedia* to support his claim that the church taught its followers to be intolerant of other faiths. Smith refuted that by quoting from the same source: "The intolerant man is avoided as much as possible by every high-minded person. . . . The man who is tolerant in every emergency is alone lovable." And he forcefully added, "You seem to think that Catholics must be all alike in mind and in heart, as though they have been poured into and taken out of the same mould. You have no more right to ask me to defend as part of my faith every statement coming from a prelate than I should have to ask you to accept as an article of your religious faith every statement of an Episcopal bishop, or of your political faith every statement of a President of the United States."

He quoted a series of American Catholic archbishops declaring their belief in the separation of church and state and in the guarantees of religious freedom, particularly that of Archbishop John Ireland of St. Paul: "Violate religious freedom against Catholics, our swords are at once unsheathed. Violate it in favor of Catholics, against non-Catholics, no less readily do they leap from the scabbard."

In his administrations as governor, he declared, he had never shown any preference for Catholics in his appointments. "In the first month of this year there gathered in the Capitol at Albany the first Governor's cabinet that ever sat in this state. It was composed, under my appointment, of two Catholics, thirteen Protestants, and one Jew. The man closest to me in the administration of the government of the State of New York is he who bears the title of Assistant to the Governor. He had been connected with the Governor's office for thirty years, in subordinate capacities, until I promoted him to the position that makes him the sharer with me of every thought and hope and ambition in the administration of the State. He is a Protestant, a Republican, and a thirty-second-degree Mason. In my public life I have exemplified that complete separation of

Church from State which is the faith of American Catholics today."

Regarding his position on education, he wrote: "You admit that the Supreme Court guaranteed to Catholics the right to maintain their parochial schools; and you ask me whether they would have so ruled if it had been shown that children in parochial schools were taught that the State should show discriminations between religions, that Protestants should be recognized only as a matter of favor, that they should be intolerant to non-Catholics, and that the laws of the State could be flouted on the ground of the imaginary conflict. My summary answer is: I and all my children went to a parochial school. I never heard of any such stuff being taught or of anybody who claimed that it was. That any group of Catholics would teach it is unthinkable."

Smith summed up by affirming that he recognized "no power in the institutions of my Church to interfere with the operations of the Constitution of the United States or the enforcement of the law of the land."

It should have stilled any doubts on the religious issue, being as forthright a statement as any man could make. Undoubtedly it made an impression on the quality folk who read the *Atlantic Monthly* and on many others who saw excerpts quoted in the newspapers, but it did not penetrate into those regions, mainly in rural America, where it would have done the most good.

Robert Moses was one of those who believed that the Marshall challenge should have been answered by Smith in his own forthright idiom rather than the loftily intellectual riposte pieced together by his advisers. "I attended one of the editing sessions," Moses recently recalled, "which seemed like a joint meeting of the Sanhedrin and the Rota. I told Father Duffy, the great war chaplain, that it was no place for me in my thin, muslin gown and sneaked out to Keeler's Bar to blow the froth off a couple of tall ones. The result of all this editing was brilliant, scholarly, rhetorical, noble, sublimated and probably, as a matter of sheer logic, unanswerable, but it wasn't

Smith. It lacked his natural brevity, roughness, downrightness and instinct for the jugular."

By mid-1927 Smith was mentally and emotionally geared for the 1928 election. Political intelligence informed him that he could probably win the Democratic nomination without much difficulty; the struggle would come when he was confronted with Republican claims that they had invented and sustained the New Era, by which they meant prosperity unlimited and everlasting (so long as the Republicans stayed in power). Yet he would not allow even the claims of his supreme ambition to interfere with the more human rites of grandfatherhood.

All those who were close to him urged that he attend the 1927 Governors' Conference that summer on Mackinac Island, which he might use as a stage for dramatizing himself as a probable Presidential candidate.

Belle Moskowitz was especially urgent in insisting that he should attend the conference, and both Moses and Proskauer joined in the plea. At first he was evasive about his reasons for not wanting to go to Mackinac; he'd have to be gone for a week, and the state's business came before politicking, etc.

"You haven't given us a single good reason for not going," Mrs. Moskowitz bluntly told him, arguing that Secretary of State Moses could hold down the fort for a week without difficulty.

"Listen," Smith replied, "I'm not going, and this is the reason why. Emily's going to have a baby this month, and I've got to be here."

He added that becoming a grandfather for the first time was more important, at the moment, than advancing his prospects for the Presidency.

Later that day Emily Smith Warner encountered Mrs. Moskowitz in a corridor of the Capitol.

"We could kill you," Mrs. Moskowitz told the mother-to-be in pretended anger.

"Who?" asked the bewildered Mrs. Warner.

"Judge Proskauer, Bob Moses and I."

"But what have I done?"

Mrs. Moskowitz explained the situation.

"You know Father," Mrs. Warner said.

Nothing would budge Smith from Albany until Mrs. Warner gave birth to her daughter Mary on July 25, by which time the Governors' Conference was in session.

In the ensuing months Smith and his advisers addressed themselves to the problem of image making. Madison Avenue and the polltakers had not yet assumed the burdens of political campaigning, and Smith was opposed to presenting himself in anything but his true light, but it was still important that his political personality and what he stood for not be distorted by his enemies.

The campaign he conducted was remarkable for many things, but perhaps the most historically important was the fact that his candidacy staked out the arena in which today's politics are fought, the country-city cleavage, the rural-urban struggle that now lies behind not only political campaigns but the struggle between Congress and the President. It lurks in the background of the one-man, one-vote reapportionment struggle. It defines the frontier between the Old and New Politics. And the "line he drew across the map of American politics," as Samuel Lubell noted, "has never been erased." His struggle for the Presidency catalyzed the newest and most urgent forces in American politics, and serves as a marker, in more than political ways, between the American past of Main Street, farms and villages and the present of cities and their suburbs. "The startling fact," Lubell pointed out in *The Future of American Politics* (1952), "is that through the booming twenties Republican pluralities in the large industrial centers were dropping steadily. Even when the stock market tickers were clicking most gratifyingly the forces of urban revolt were gathering momentum."

The new split in the political consciousness of the country,

the width of which was just being suspected by a few, was de-
fined in the intemperate letter of George Fort Milton, a strong-
minded Tennessee publicist and politician, to William G. Mc-
Adoo. Smith, he said, would appeal to "the aliens, who feel that
the older America, the America of the Anglo-Saxon stock, is a
hatefull thing which must be overturned and humiliated; to the
northern negroes, who lust for social equality and racial dominance; to the Catholics who have been made to believe that they
are entitled to the White House, and to the Jews who likewise
are to be instilled with the feeling that this is the time for God's
chosen people to chastise America yesteryear." If it was true, as
Milton believed, that "the dominance of such groups represents
the New America, the Old America, the America of Jackson,
and of Lincoln and Wilson, should rise up in wrath and defeat
it."

Smith, of course, would attempt to ameliorate the resent-
ments of people like George Fort Milton, who were shrewd
enough to sense the changes soon to occur but too inflexible to
make their peace with them. The irony was that in some ways
Smith represented Milton's "Old America" as much as any
bald eagle of Republican, Protestant, Anglo-Saxon ancestry.
He was liberal and progressive when it came to bettering the
lives of the working class from which he rose, but bone-deep,
which is to say morally, he was a conservative, a man of the ancient verities, to whom the rouged kneecaps of the flappers and
the wild sounds of the jazz bands were premonitions of a new
Babylon.

During his terms as governor, his economic conservatism had
displayed itself in his stern budget cutting and his efforts to reduce taxes. Four years before, he had promised to halt the extension of federal government and reassert the rights of the
states, and in 1925 he wrote: "We must stop the dangerous
overcentralization of the Federal power," which placed him
slightly to the right, for the moment, of President Calvin Coolidge. That same year Walter Lippmann called Smith "the

most powerful conservative in urban America." And when he called for an "unflinching application of Jeffersonian principles to the problems of the day" in 1928, he alarmed the more liberal members of his own party, including Rexford G. Tugwell, who admonished him in the *New Republic*, "Cannot Governor Smith understand that—ridiculous as it sounds—the stronghold of Jeffersonianism has shifted from the South to the Northeast and that its latterday prophet is Coolidge?"

Libertarians would also be offended by his stance on public morality. His opposition to the blue laws, which the urban masses resented originally because they closed the saloons on Sunday in a backlash of puritanism, was more apparent than real. He signed the so-called Padlock Bill in 1927, which closed any theater for one year if it presented a play judged indecent by the courts. The governor's signature went on the bill after he had unwittingly attended a performance of a play dealing with the subject of lesbianism (and Broadway defiantly produced a musical starring Texas Guinan and titled *Padlocks of 1927*).

On the issue of Smith's urban parochialism, his hazy knowledge of American geography, and his even greater weakness in the field of world affairs, it was obvious that he and his supporters would have to hope for the best. No crash course in those subjects could have brought him up to date. Even that apparently most fervent of his supporters, Franklin D. Roosevelt, could not resist taking a few digs at Smith's ineradicable New Yorkishness, or perhaps Roosevelt had already, subconsciously, begun thinking of himself as a worthier candidate for the Presidency.

Claude Bowers, journalist, diplomat and author of the classic *The Tragic Era*, was asked to call on Roosevelt shortly after Bowers had been selected to make the principal speech at the Jackson Day banquet. Roosevelt unburdened himself of a number of doubts about the coming campaign which had arisen after a recent conference at which naming the campaign management was discussed and the New York politicians present had agreed at Roosevelt's insistence to name one Western man as "window dressing." This, Bowers gathered from Roosevelt's conversation, "was because Smith had won his victories in the cities; the Tammany men did not realize that while the cities dominated New York State, they did not then dominate the nation."

Perhaps a trifle cattily, Roosevelt laughed over his recollection of Smith being confronted by some Kansas delegates during the national convention of 1924. As Roosevelt told it, Smith appeared "entering like a breeze, in a swallowtail coat, a silk hat at a rakish angle, and with the usual cigar in his mouth. 'Hello, hello, my boy, and how's things?' he said, addressing Roosevelt. The latter introduced his callers as delegates from Kansas. 'Hello, boys,' said Smith, shaking hands. 'Glad to see you. Y'know, the other day some boys were in from Wisconsin, and I learned something. I always thought Wisconsin was on this side of the lake. It's on the other side. Glad to know it. Glad to know more about the place where the good beer comes from.' And this to delegates from a strong Prohibition state."

Among the more influential opinion makers whose doubts and questions Smith would have to confront was William Allen White, not only the editor of the widely quoted Emporia *Gazette,* but the energetic author of magazine articles and books with a nationwide reputation for sagacity and objectivity. In his editorial columns, articles, and books, White's attitude toward Smith wavered from bleak suspicion to tempered enthusiasm. Everything about White's background, of course, worked against acceptance of an Al Smith in the White House; he was a dry, a Middle Western Protestant, a country boy who had grown up at a time when Tammany Hall, to non-New Yorkers, was a Babylonian temple.

Some of his initially equivocal attitude toward Smith was visible in an article he wrote for *Collier's Weekly* in 1926. White admittedly was offended by Smith's habit of wearing a "pink-and-crimson tie." He believed that the 1924 convention battle was between "the hard, ascetic moralities of Puritanism" and the "lighter, brighter, happier philosophy of Catholicism." He was also certain that it would take ten years to educate Smith sufficiently to hold national office, but conceded that there was "no stronger brain in America than Smith's."

In a book titled *Masks in a Pageant*, written in 1927 and published in 1928, White was still essentially well disposed, granting that as a follower of Tom Foley, Smith had acquired a "capacity for teamwork, a habit of industry and the precious moral precept that it does not pay to lie." Tammany's system made "square men who, according to the morals of their day, played a fair, brave game, even when it was dirty. When the morals changed, the habits of the game did not . . . it was as square as the game that Lincoln learned. . . ."

As the 1928 campaign warmed, however, all of White's doubts and suspicions rose to the surface, particularly after he received a slanderous and misleading pamphlet from the Reverend O. R. Miller, superintendent of the New York Civic League. Actually the circular had first been published in 1918 by the Anti-Saloon League as a summary of Smith's legislative record between 1904 and 1916. The pamphlet falsely charged that Smith had favored laws favorable to prostitution, as well as opposed those designed to close the saloons. With that pamphlet, apparently, as his documentary evidence, White assailed Smith before a Kansas political gathering as the sponsor of organized vice. Four times, White charged, Smith had "voted against stopping gambling and prostitution in connection with saloons. . . ." He conceded that Smith was a man of "unusual intelligence, splendid courage and rare political wisdom," but his Tammany indoctrination made him unacceptable to the American heartland. "It is not that Governor Smith is a Catholic and a wet which makes him an offense to the villagers and town-dwellers, but because his record shows the kind of President he would make—a Tammany President. . . . Tammany is Tammany, and Smith is its prophet. . . ."

The coming election, as White saw it, was a struggle for the

American political soul, a battle between two opposing concepts. One was that of rural America, soundly conservative and dedicated to proven values. The other was represented by the growing urban masses, with their unconscious affinity for change and experiment.

Time would show that Smith essentially was as conservative as White or any of his followers, but meanwhile, it was Smith's problem to present himself to the sizable portion of the electorate represented by White as a man who had outlived his Tammany beginnings. The doubts of a William Allen White, though misconceived, could not be shrugged off.

After the legislative session of 1928 ended, Smith spent much of his time commuting between the Executive Mansion in Albany and the Hotel Biltmore suite in New York City. There was considerable debate among his supporters on how to handle the various campaign issues, and Smith considered himself the rightful arbiter of those controversies. He was highly indignant when the New York *World,* an independent Democratic organ never particularly friendly to him, tried to maneuver him into making a declaration on the Prohibition question, which still stood as a monument to American hypocrisy. ("If you think this country ain't Dry," Will Rogers observed, "you just watch 'em vote; and if you think this country ain't Wet, you just watch 'em drink. You see, when they vote, it's counted; but when they drink, it ain't. If you could register a man's breath that cast the ballots, that would be great. But the voting strength of the country is Dry.") There was also the perennial tariff question, with many Democrats urging that the high protective tariff of the Republican administrations not be opposed.

An amusing portrait of Al Smith during those preconvention months was composed by Claude Bowers, who was to make the keynote speech and whom Smith summoned to the Biltmore one day to discuss "some ideas about taxation." Bowers soon learned that Smith had something besides fiscal policy on his mind. When Bowers arrived at the Smith suite, the governor had just arrived from a party conference in Buffalo and taken a bath. "He wore a bathrobe, which was thrown back," Bowers remembered, "and oldfashioned underwear that reached to his ankles and fit like tights, giving a grotesque appearance to his thin legs.

"When, frequently, he had to go to the door to turn someone away, he went at a dogtrot, his skinny legs in tights most conspicuous as he ran. But his thin face, actor's profile and penetrating blue eyes, his fluency and clarity in explaining what he had in mind, his magnetism and dynamic force, stamped him as an outstanding individual, a real person.

"It was not taxation he had in mind. Sitting down at a table in front of one of the tall wall mirrors and motioning me to a chair beside him, he said in his husky voice, 'I'm afraid that at Houston [the site of the 1928 convention] an attack will be made on Tammany. If it is it should be answered on the spot. When Bryan made his attack in the Baltimore convention I told Charlie Murphy it should be answered right away, but he thought differently. The next day, when it was too late, he changed his mind and put up Stanchfield [John B., a prominent New York lawyer and Tammanyite], who made a botch of it. Now, if an attack is made at Houston it should be answered on the spot, and *you're the man to make the answer.* You're not a member of Tammany—I don't suppose you've ever been in a Tammany club in your life. The Democrats over the country respect you, and you're the man to make the answer.'

"He then proceeded to set forth what he thought should be said. Talking earnestly, gesticulating with clenched fist, looking in the mirror as he talked, the way an actor would, he set forth the argument. It was a good one. But it was startling to be asked to assume this responsibility in addition to that resting on the keynote speaker. It was in direct contradiction to the agreement I had heard made by the inner circle of his advisers not to reply to any attack."

As it turned out, Bowers' services as Tammany's defense attorney were not required; no attack was made.

Once that piece of business was out of the way, Smith entertained Bowers—and no doubt himself—with stories about the eccentric ex-Governor William Sulzer, his old political enemy. "It has often been said that a great actor was lost when Smith went into politics," Bowers observed, "and on this occasion he gave an exhibition of his histrionic talent." Sulzer had campaigned for governor among the people of the Lower East Side, many of them recent refugees from czarist repressions in their homeland, by falsely claiming credit for having forced on Congress an abrogation of a treaty with Russia. Smith imitated Sulzer as the latter told his audience that "All over Russia tonight the Jewish people are on their knees praying for Bill Sulzer." Sulzer had to be reminded by his more knowledgeable running mate, Martin Glynn, that Jews did not pray on their knees.

A few days later Smith met with several of the men who were drawing up a proposed platform and demonstrated his ability to winnow out advice, to yield to superior knowledge or present his own arguments most forcefully when he considered himself on firm ground. The meeting was held at the Lotus Club, in a conference room with the austere portraits of Whitelaw Reid, the aristocratic Republican and late publisher of the New York *Tribune,* and William Winter, with all the astringent dignity of an eminent theater critic and historian, frowning on the Democratic cabal. Among those present were Senators Robert F. Wagner and Key Pittman, Claude Bowers, and Judge Proskauer, who had drawn up a first-draft platform to try it out on Smith.

Senator Pittman, a Nevadan with some competence in foreign affairs, read the plank on America's role in the world. It was phrased in the language of diplomacy, and Smith's face reddened, his manner grew fretful as the ponderous sentences unreeled from the Senatorial mouth.

Smith finally reached over, took the paper out of Pittman's hands, and reread himself with mocking emphasis on its more pompous phrases.

"Now what the hell does all that mean?" he exploded. "No one knows what it means. I know a little, but it gives me a pain in the back of the neck to get it. Our people are not the professors and the fancy boys down at the Union League Club. We want a platform the man in the factory and the corn row can understand. Now let me try my hand."

Clenching his fists, gesticulating as he would have on the stump, he ad-libbed his own version of a foreign-policy plank. ". . . the cords in his neck stood out," one man present at the meeting recalled, "his face flushed, he looked at the floor, and he delivered a speech instead of a plank, but one that astonished . . . by its keen comprehension of world problems and our relations to them. His lack of familiarity with federal procedure was occasionally shown by his frequent questions as to the relative roles of the President and the Senate, but there was everything disarming in his honesty in asking, and admirable in his instant comprehension."

There was a moment of silence when he finished, broken when Judge Proskauer quietly commented: "Al, that comes very near to the League of Nations." The League, of course, was then anathema to the American electorate.

Occasionally as the rest of the platform was read, Smith would argue a point, would listen to Wagner's or Pittman's reply, then subside with a grin, saying, "I'm licked."

The Prohibition plank was a rather weasel-worded, play-it-safe pledge to enforce the Volstead Act as being part of the law of the land. Smith strongly objected on the grounds that everyone knew it couldn't be enforced and it would be dishonest to promise people that it could be.

Finally, he took a piece of paper and hastily scrawled his own concept of how the plank should read: "The Eighteenth Amendment is part of the fundamental law of the United States.

We hold it to be an economic not a political question. We promise a solution of its enforcement or its amendment as experience
may teach."

Wagner interjected that Smith must mean "social," not
"economic," but the latter replied that he was questioning how
much money people were willing to pay in support of a bureaucracy trying to enforce an unenforceable law. In the end, he
tore up his suggested Prohibition plank and threw it on the
floor. It was a pity that the whole issue could not be so easily
disposed of.

As convention time approached, it appeared that Smith was
so far out in front that the nomination could hardly escape his
grasp. There were several other candidates in the running.
Governor Albert Ritchie of Maryland offered himself as a wet,
a conservative states' rights man, but he wasn't well known outside the Eastern Seaboard. Edwin T. Meredith, proposed as a
compromise as in 1924, inherited some of the dissidents from
the Bryan-McAdoo wing of the party, but he died ten days before the convention began. Senator Thomas J. Walsh of Montana presented himself as a Catholic, a dry, and the hero of the
Teapot Dome investigation, but the inquisitorial type rarely
gains wide popular support, and he had withdrawn his candidacy after suffering a sharp defeat in the California primary.
Senator James A. Reed of Missouri was hauled out as a final
stop-Smith candidate by the Bryan-McAdoo forces, but he
also had shown up poorly in several primaries.

Alfred E. Smith's great moment, the storming of heights
whose attainment should have been all but unimaginable for a
boy from the South Street docks, was now approaching.

13

Once Again the "Happy Warrior"

ONE man who did not envy Alfred E. Smith his approaching moment of triumph was H. L. Mencken, whose acerbic observations on the national conventions during the 1920's provided the country with a much-needed antidote for what he called political buffoonery. Mencken, shortly before the Democratic convention assembled, wrote that he did not envy Smith or "any of the other gentlemen who make of our America the greatest show since Rome caved in. There is such a thing as sitting in the audience without getting stage-struck, as going to the bull-fights without wanting to be either the matador or the bull. After all, it is the spectator who has the fun, not the clown. . . ."

Mencken was a better satirist than prophet, but he was on target when he predicted that the Democrats, as the inveterate party of the opposition, which had forced all the important issues since the Civil War, would soon tip the balance between rural and urban America. He was writing in the Baltimore *Sun* on July 23, 1928, when he boldly predicted: "The essential issue in America during the next fifty years will be between city men and yokels. The yokels have ruled the Republic since its first days—often, it must be added, very wisely. But now they decay and are challenged, and in the long run they are bound to be overcome."

That first challenge came from Smith, not the wealthy, well-educated, cosmopolitan gentleman from West Branch, Iowa, whom the Republicans nominated for the Presidency. He was Secretary of Commerce Herbert Hoover, who, wary and self-contained, had sat in the Cabinet with Harding and the boodlers without being tarred by the same oil-smeared brush. Despite an adventurous career as a mining engineer in China, Australia, the Malay States, and South Africa, he looked and acted more like a small-town banker than a Richard Harding Davis hero, with his broad, pudgy face, his high-starched collars, his mouse-colored hair and cautious hazel eyes. Politically, he was unappetizing; his manner was chill and forbidding in public or private. Yet he was most famous for his humanitarian efforts as the head of American relief in wartime Belgium and post-revolutionary Russia. The contradictions of his personality—the gold miner driving his coolie workmen, the man later dedicated to feeding other coolie masses—were carried over into his public philosophy. This was expressed in his book of half a dozen years before, *American Individualism*.

What he believed in, Hoover wrote, was a "progressive individualism" uniquely capable of being nurtured on American soil. Perhaps he was thinking of the piebald aspects of his own career when he declared that the American form of individualism was superior to the reprehensible European brand because we had removed the self-centered aspects by affirming the principles of equality in opportunity and of service. Americans attained their goals by merit. Then, inspired by the "rising vision of service," they had repaid society by helping those less fortunate. It was the glory of this system, he believed, that capitalism now meant a great enterprise was owned, not by a plutocrat and his family, but by thousands of stockholders. The inequity of their holdings did not enter into his calculations. Thus he declared that America was changing from "extremely individualistic action into a period of associational activities" —a phrase which would surely have caused Al Smith a bout of nausea had he ever attempted to read his future opponent's book.

One man who was unhappy over the Republican choice was President Coolidge, who, almost a year earlier, had removed himself from consideration for reelection with the seemingly adamant statement "I do not choose to run." Coolidge did not like Hoover, did not believe the "Great Engineer" could make American society continue to run smoothly, apparently mistrusted the didactic tendency he had noted in his Secretary of Commerce. "That man," Coolidge told another Cabinet member, referring to Hoover, "has offered me unsolicited advice for six years, all of it bad!" His associates said Coolidge was deeply distressed when Hoover was nominated. A certain amount of disaffection could be noted elsewhere in the GOP, too, and only the business community seemed to be entirely taken with the aloof and reticent Mr. Hoover. Even his greatest admirers would not claim that he possessed the power to inspire.

If there was a lack of enthusiasm in the Republican camp, the Democrats were determined, for once, to rise above the brawling factionalism that usually marked their national conventions. "One big happy family" was to be the keynote. Arguments over the platform would be settled in the committee rooms. Rancorous sectionalism would be subdued. Party harmony was more important than bickering over the KKK and the Anti-Saloon League, Tammany and the League of Nations. The Democrats had been out of power for eight years now, and thousands of the faithful were urging on their leaders the need for unity, behind which lay the hopes of those thousands hungering for public office and other good things that came when the levers were in Democratic hands.

At the 1924 convention, outlanders had been enraged by Tammany's steamroller tactics, the hooligans howling from the packed galleries, the noticeably large number of Catholic priests in attendance. This time the fervor of Smith's supporters would be subdued. No cases of liquor were loaded aboard the train which took the New York delegation to Houston. The floor fight for Smith would be led by two well-mannered gentlemen from upstate, Franklin D. Roosevelt and George R. McNamee, the state Democratic chairman. Some Tammany-ites were seen carrying books of poetry. Senator Walsh observed that there was "no better dressed, more polite, less demonstrative delegation in the convention than the delegates sent by Tammany Hall." A delegation from the Holy Name Society could not have been soberer and more deferential.

Smith, having curbed the exuberance of his old comrades from the Wigwam, also assured the convention in advance there would not be a repetition of the ballot ordeal of 1924. He would withdraw his name if he was not nominated by the tenth ballot.

The delegates assembled in the torpor of a Texas summer while Smith stayed in Albany, as he believed was befitting his position as the all but unchallenged front-runner. He stayed in constant touch with the New York delegation by wire, but according to his daughter Mrs. Emily Warner, he intervened in the proceedings only when it came to the Prohibition plank in the platform.

"That isn't on the level," he snorted. He then dictated a telegram in which the party would promise a strict enforcement of the Volstead Act as long as it was the law but made it clear that a Democratic administration would work for its repeal. Anything less straightforward, any attempt to equivocate, would be hypocritical and dishonest.

"If you send that telegram," one of his advisers told him, "you may not be nominated."

"I don't care," Smith snapped. In his autobiography he later stated that he didn't want the nomination if "I had in any way to compromise with the principle involved" in the Prohibition controversy. It was not the first time he had dug his heels in and refused to compromise for the sake of his personal ambitions.

Claude Bowers, one of the few journalists who ever made a

highly effective orator, got the convention off to a rousing start with his keynote speech. (After that, as one Tammany man, brooding over conventions past, said, "it was the longest wake any Irishman ever attended.") Bowers struck hard at the fallacies and contradictions of Republican ideology, particularly the GOP's devotion to both Abraham Lincoln and Alexander Hamilton. "You cannot believe with Lincoln in a government 'of the people, by the people and for the people' and with Hamilton in a government of the wealthy, by the powerful and for the privileged. . . . There are Lincoln Republicans and Hamilton Republicans, and never the twain shall meet until you find some way to ride two horses going in opposite directions at the same time!"

The greatest enthusiasm, however, was aroused when Bowers mentioned the legitimate grievances of the farmers, who were particularly restive in the midst of affluence in other sectors of the economy. "We do demand," Bowers proclaimed, "that privilege takes its hands out of the farmer's pockets and off the farmer's throat."

Somewhat to Bowers' surprise, that touched off a demonstration in the aisles, which was started by delegations from the agricultural states but was soon joined by many other groups. Mencken was amused when the "horny-handed sons of toil" from Tammany joined with the New York delegation in demonstrating their warmth at the federal government's treatment of the farmers, whom privately they were inclined to refer to as apple knockers and turd kickers. But it was all part of the spirit of amity that had been decreed from the top, and Tammany men knew how to obey orders.

Radio, despite the static that marred many broadcasts, was then the hot medium. Millions listened to the Houston proceedings over their superheterodyne sets, among them Governor Smith.

He and his family, friends, advisers, and newspapermen gathered around a radio set in the Executive Mansion to hear the nomination speech by Franklin D. Roosevelt, ending with the now-familiar salutation: ". . . one who has the will to win—who not only deserves success but commands it. Victory is his habit—the happy warrior!"

With a crackle of static, the cheers from the Democratic multitude poured out of the loudspeaker in Albany. So far the convention, running from June 26 to 29, had operated like "clockwork," as Roosevelt said. The Smith forces were perfectly organized, supremely confident. Little attention—perhaps too little—was paid to a number of odd events occurring near the hall in which 18,000 persons were crowded for the climax to the convention. Street-corner evangelists predicted that God would intervene to prevent Smith's nomination. Nearby a Baptist church was holding a round-the-clock prayer meeting beseeching God to interpose Himself between the nation and the possibility of a Catholic President.

All to no avail. The nominating process, too, went like clockwork. State after state declared itself for Smith.

In the Executive Mansion at Albany, everyone was tense with excitement, not so much over the predictable outcome but over the completeness of the victory. To stand a chance of winning, there must be evidence of overwhelming approval by his party. Smith, however, was "quite the calmest of us all," according to his daughter Emily. "Occasionally his cigar would go out and he would light it again or replace it with another. Now and then he would reach over and turn the radio dial a little, or smile and make some passing remark, or answer a question . . . he was relaxed and surprisingly at ease."

He was easily nominated on the first ballot when Ohio announced it would change its vote in his favor. There was a flaw in the victory, however, when the convention refused to nominate him by acclamation. It then proceeded to nominate Senator Joseph T. Robinson of Arkansas as his running mate. Robinson as a Southerner and a dry, it was hoped, would lend balance to the ticket, but at least one observer thought it was like trying to carry fire and water in the same bucket.

A crowd had gathered outside the Executive Mansion and

was watching through unshaded windows. When they saw his daughter Emily jump up and embrace Smith, they knew he had been nominated, and "they swept abruptly up the steps, across the porch and into the house itself. Cheering, laughing, and shouting their congratulations, they poured into room after room." Smith beamed, puffed on his cigar, and shook hundreds of hands.

It was the high point of his life.

Almost from the moment the prize was within his grasp, Smith made it evident that he would not enter the campaign against Hoover from the left wing of the political theater or wrap himself in a Bryanesque, neo-Populist mantle. The country must be assured, he believed, that the party was not the enemy of business and most emphatically that it would not endanger prosperity by radical innovations in government.

Those Democrats who hoped the campaign would be conducted along progressive lines were immediately disappointed, in fact, by his decision to persuade business that his party was its friend, that he would not go along with the liberals' pleas for restraint of its power over national affairs. Smith was strongly in favor of social justice and public ownership of electric power, but he would not go beyond that. Even the generalized sympathy for the farmers' low incomes contained in Claude Bowers' keynote speech before the national convention caused him to back off in alarm at the possibility of losing support of the business community. "My first intimation that the speech had frightened some of his advisers," Bowers related, "came with the discovery that, contrary to custom, it was not printed and distributed by the National Committee."

The Socialist candidate, Norman Thomas, as usual, pointed out that there was little actual difference between Smith and Hoover, that Smith "accepts Hoover's general philosophy and reduces the battle between them to the comparatively insignificant question of power at Muscle Shoals and Boulder Dam."

Even in the right wing of the party there was a certain

amount of dissatisfaction with the party's choice. In the case
of the aristocratic James W. Gerard, who had been Wilson's
Ambassador to Germany from 1913 to 1917 and who was treasurer of the Democratic National Committee from 1924 to
1936, it was expressed in terms of personality. Discussing Smith
with an interviewer for the Oral History Project at Columbia
many years after the campaign, Gerard recalled that in the summer of 1928 Smith was "confident that he would win" and indicated that Smith's cockiness was only one of the reasons he,
Gerard, disliked him quite intensely. Gerard's statement is
notable in that it is one of the very few expressed by his former associates in which personal dislike, if not something
stronger, is apparent.

"He was a very conceited fellow," was the way Gerard recalled Smith, "and the most selfish man in politics that I have
ever met. He was for Al Smith, and you must be for Al Smith.
If you asked him to be for anybody else, he wasn't."

If it was all-out enthusiasm Smith most valued in a close associate, he found that quality in the man whom he had
named as chairman of the national committee—John J.
Raskob. A stranger to the national political scene, he had been
a fervent Smith man since the 1924 gubernatorial campaign.
He was also heartily disliked by many Smith men of longer
service to the cause, dismaying to the liberals, and, as a Catholic
and a wet, not calculated to raise much enthusiasm among the
Protestant drys of the South and West. The formerly Republican industrialist would, however, raise a campaign fund
of almost $5,000,000. It could also be said that he put his money
where Smith's mouth was—he was the largest personal contrib-
utor to that fund. Assisting him were four other millionaires
whose presence in the high command was supposed to help persuade the business community that Smith was sound on economic questions: Gerard as national treasurer; Herbert H. Lehman; Jesse Jones, the gombeen man of Houston, Texas; and
Senator Peter G. Gerry. Also high in the campaign councils, of

course, was Bill Kenny, host of the Tiger Room and possessor of a fortune estimated at $30,000,000.

But it was the unpersonable Raskob's appointment which dismayed some of Smith's oldest supporters the most. Born to an Alsatian father and an Irish mother in Lockport, New York, he seemed to have inherited more characteristics from the Teutonic than the Celtic side of his house. He was a shy, inhibited little man, almost furtive in manner. As a son of poverty, much like Smith himself, he had knocked around from job to job in his youth until he became private secretary to Pierre S. Du Pont, of *the* Du Ponts. His shrewdness so impressed Du Pont that he was promoted rapidly, and in 1914 he persuaded his employer to invest heavily in William C. Durant's tottering automobile empire, which became part of General Motors.

Fourteen years later Raskob was chairman of the finance committee of General Motors, vice-president of E. I. Du Pont de Nemours, a director of several large New York banks, and a Knight of St. Gregory (a papal order). He was also the father of twelve children. Politics had not interested him until he became interested in Smith's career which, as a good Catholic, he saw counterpoised to the rise of the Ku Klux Klan and other manifestations of anti-Catholicism in America.

Among those who ended up hating him was a fellow Catholic, Eddie Dowling, the Broadway producer who in 1928 presented a musical titled *The Sidewalks of New York,* in which the famous comedy team of Smith and Dale and a young dancer named Ruby Keeler were featured. It may have been the first of what has now become a familiar, but still strange, happening—the coalescing of show business and politics. Dowling wrote the show, he recalled several years ago, to "further the candidacy of Al Smith for President." The scenario, in fact, was a freely adapted version of Smith's career.

Dowling did not regret the gesture, since the show became a hit, but he came to detest Smith's chief campaign manager.

Raskob, he ruminated, was "a strange little man, a mixed-up man . . . almost a Machiavellian mind, really and truly. . . . He wanted to be Secretary of the Treasury," and finally, in Dowling's estimation, "a cowardly little guy." Much of Dowling's rancor, as he frankly indicated, resulted from the financial disaster visited upon many of Smith's friends because of Raskob's means of financing the campaign during its last desperate stages.

Roosevelt, already identifying himself with the more liberal wing of the party, was also an anti-Raskob man, who considered the appointment "a grave mistake." Twice during the month of July he expressed his fears that Raskob as chairman of the national committee would "permanently drive away a host of people in the south and west and rural east who are not particularly favorable to Smith, but who up to today have been seeping back into the party." Two weeks later Roosevelt, who reluctantly agreed to head a division (Commerce, Industries and Professional Activities) at national headquarters, was writing a friend that "Frankly, the campaign is working out in a way which I, personally, should not have allowed and Smith had burned his bridges behind him." Roosevelt obviously did not agree with the Smith theory that he would get the liberal and Southern votes anyway and that it was the better part of strategy to attempt to split away Republican support in the Northeast and Middle West by presenting himself, in the reflected glitter of the combined wealth of his "fat cats," as the friend of the business community.

Certainly Raskob's efforts as a money raiser were highly successful. For the second time in history the Democrats in 1928 outspent the Republicans on a Presidential campaign. The Democratic National Committee disbursed $5,342,000 against $3,529,000 for the Republicans—and that, it turned out, still wasn't enough for Raskob. Some of the Democratic money flowed in from sources that would dismay the liberals (from Thomas Fortune Ryan, who had made much of his vast fortune out of a foul-smelling New York city traction company's watered stock, for instance). Even so, all contributions were not welcomed, as James W. Gerard has recorded. He was cagey enough to reject $10,000 offered by a pair of New Jersey bootleggers because "we had to be careful of a 'plant' by the other side."

Nor were all the Democratic bigwigs repelled by Raskob and his closed-in personality. Claude Bowers accompanied him to Hot Springs, Arkansas, for the ritual "notification" to Senator Robinson that he was the party's candidate for the Vice Presidency. On the journey, Bowers said, "I found my prejudice against Raskob melting in the warmth of his personality. . . . He was a little man with serious brown eyes. One could almost see his mind work, and it was a good mind. Occasionally he smiled, but most of the time he was serious. During the journey back I was surprised to see him take from his bag a copy of *Ariel*, the André Maurois biography of Shelley. An executive of General Motors reading about the poet would have seemed incongruous even if he had not then been engaged in a political campaign."

At important stops along the way, practical politicians boarded the train expecting a glad-handing, backslapping welcome and certainly a highball and a cigar to sustain them until they got off at the next stop, but instead they were confronted by a "quiet, undemonstrative man of business," as Bowers observed. They, too, found him incongruous, with or without the Shelley biography on his lap. Raskob "gave them his ideas about organization, patterned after that of General Motors," which "drove the joviality from their faces."

Even before Smith formally accepted the nomination, he lost the support of the other most conspicuous Catholic in public life, Senator Walsh of Montana. Walsh wrote Bowers that he could not "wholeheartedly" campaign for Smith because Smith as governor of New York had opposed the Great Lakes-St. Lawrence waterway. He ascribed Smith's attitude on the waterway to the "provincialism" of New Yorkers. Montana and the other Western states wanted the waterway, and Al

Smith couldn't count on Senator Walsh, therefore, to hit the campaign trail on his behalf.

The party became a little restive, too, as Smith delayed until August 22—almost a month after his nomination—his formal speech of acceptance. He fretted over its composition because, he said, it was difficult for him to make a "set speech" after years of talking off the cuff. The demands of radio, carrying the speech to millions across the country, must be met; that meant a script from which he could not deviate. It must be delivered at precisely 7:30 P.M. to reach the audiences in the West and East, North and South, over a coast-to-coast hookup. Smith was the first political candidate to find himself at the mercy of an impersonal medium—one, ironically, for which his temperament, rough voice, and unschooled diction made him ill suited.

He delivered the speech in the Assembly chamber with a battery of plate-sized microphones rearing before him, under the direction of the radio producers and broadcast engineers. A disembodied Smith, rasping over the static, was carried to the nation. His speech was sincere, but not greatly stirring.

"While this is a government of law and not of men, laws do not execute themselves. We must have people of character and outstanding ability to serve the nation. To me one of the greatest elements of satisfaction in my nomination is the fact that I owe it to no one man or set of men. I can with complete honesty make the statement that my nomination was brought about by no promise given or implied by me or anyone in my behalf. I will not be influenced in appointments by the question of a person's wet or dry attitudes, by whether he is rich or poor, whether he comes from the north, south, east or west, or by what church he attends in the worship of God. . . . I am entirely satisfied of our success in November because I am sure that our victory means progress for the nation. . . ."

Several weeks later he began campaigning throughout the nation. Being Irish, he may have been depressed by an ill omen that appeared shortly after he left Albany on the campaign trail. Mrs. Smith had brought back from the Houston convention a small burro named Sam Houston, more or less the Democratic Party symbol, which had been presented by Texas admirers. Sam Houston was given the run of the grounds of the Executive Mansion. Soon after Smith left Albany, the burro caught a cold, and despite applications of an 1810 Napoleon brandy given by his daughter Emily, the burro died. But there were soon visible more dire omens than that.

14

The Two Campaigns

FOR his part, Herbert Hoover would have none of the subterranean campaign against Smith's candidacy. He was a cultivated gentleman with no taste for bigotry or whispered slanders. His own fight for the Presidency was conducted on a fairly lofty plane. Political historians have noted it was the first campaign to be handled almost entirely by a publicity apparatus. All he had to do, in the opinion of his advisers, was to ride the easy swell of complacency, make no mistakes, blurt out no ill-considered statements, and all would be well. Hoover merely reminded the nation that prosperity had been achieved under the Republicans and promised more to come—a chicken in every pot, a car in every garage.

Underground there was a different kind of campaign waged against Smith, much of it by members of his own party who were disaffected by his Catholicism and his stand on the Prohibition issue. Sometimes it surfaced on the public platform, as when the famous evangelist Billy Sunday roared in his fundamentalist passion that as the "Ambassador of God" it was his duty to "defy the forces of hell—Al Smith and the rest of them." Smith's male supporters, the evangelist shouted, were "damnable whiskey politicians, bootleggers, crooks, pimps and businessmen who deal with him," while his female admirers were "streetwalkers."

A whole literature could be composed from the propaganda distributed to frighten Americans into believing that if Smith were elected, the United States would become a satellite of the Roman Catholic Church. Writing about it many years later, Claude Bowers believed that the 1928 campaign should serve as a warning to the country. The underground campaign against Smith was not only un-American, but anti-American. "It was a revolt against the Bill of Rights, and yet millions mobilized under its banner. The Hitler movement in Germany had its origin in a similar appeal to racial and religious hate. If it did not eventuate in fascism in America it tended dangerously in that direction."

Certainly its virulence was unequaled in American politics, not even during the height of the Know-Nothing agitation of the mid-nineteenth century. Sometimes the anti-Catholicism was stated with a defensive politeness, as in official church organs; more often it was the most venomous slander run off on small-town printing presses or mimeograph machines. The country was flooded with pamphlets, broadsides, booklets, three-sheets, and handbills—most of them anonymous. It almost seemed that every flatbed press in the country was clattering away around the clock.

There was the respectable voice of a Methodist periodical published in Atlanta which informed its countrywide circulation: "Governor Smith has a constitutional right to run for President, even though he is a Catholic. This we confess. And we have a constitutional right to vote against him because he is a Catholic. This we assert."

All over the country the Christian soldiers were marching —against fellow Christians. H. L. Mencken made some observations of the crusade in the Baltimore *Sun* of August 24, in which he wrote, "The holy war against Al in the late Confederate States seems to be breaking into two halves. On the one hand, some of the Methodist and Baptist papers begin to be extremely polite to him, and warn their customers that it is unchristian (and, what is worse, unwise) to have at opponents too hotly. On the other hand, there are journals which pile indignation upon indignation, and devote practically all of their space to philippics against Al, Raskob, Tammany, the Beer Trust and the Pope."

The *Baptist Courier* of Greenville, South Carolina, declared that Raskob, a papal knight, was "a private chaplain [*sic*] of the papal household" and "without doubt he has been on his knees before the Pope." It also published an article by a member of the faculty of the Southern Baptist Theological Seminary which warned that the "Pope undoubtedly longs for the wealth and power of the United States to be in his hands" and continued, "He will never give up that hope. He will leave no stone unturned to gain that end. . . . Rome means to get control of the United States sooner or later. Protestants may well understand that purpose."

The *Baptist and Commoner*, an Arkansas journal, published a three-page diatribe under the heading IS THE CATHOLIC CHURCH A CHRISTIAN CHURCH? and answered its own question with a resounding No. The church was "a brutal, hell-born power," and its priests were money-hungry scoundrels. "They are always to be found at the bedside of the dying to extort money for the pretense of making prayers, and on hand to extort from the widow every penny possible for the same pretense. To meet them in the street or in the church, they seem to be devout; but when you come to know them you find that they are hypocrites and filled with iniquity."

The *Baptist Trumpet* of Killeen, Texas, warned that if Smith was elected President, "the Romish system will institute persecutions again, and put the cruel, blood-stained heel upon all who refuse her authority."

The *Baptist Message* of Shreveport, Louisiana, dredged up the occasion when Governor Smith and Mayor Walker greeted Cardinal Bonzano on his way to the Catholic Ecumenical Council in Chicago several years before. Smith escorted the prelate to City Hall, and "there, placing him upon a *throne* erected for him . . . he, Governor Alfred Emanuel Smith, Governor

of the Sovereign State of New York, DID PROSTRATE
HIMSELF BEFORE AND BOWED THE KNEE to this for-
eign representative of a foreign potentate and DID KISS THE
RING on the hand of this foreigner, in token of his ABJECT
SUBMISSION TO THE AUTHORITY OF THE POPE OF
ROME."

The editor of the *Baptist and Commoner,* however, outdid
all his rivals in screeching for Smith's defeat. His editorial
read:

> To vote for Al Smith would be granting the Pope the right
> to dictate to this government what it should do.
> A vote for Al Smith would be the sacrificing of our public
> schools. Rome says to hell with our public schools.
> To vote for Al Smith would be to say that all Protestants
> are now living in adultery because they were not married by
> a priest.
> To vote for Al Smith is to say our offspring are bastards.
> Are you ready to accept this?

Though the above sampling is mostly from Methodist and
Baptist publications, other denominations participated in the
orgiastic demonstrations of intolerance. The whole range of
Protestant opinion from strict Lutheranism to permissive
Unitarianism was heard from. Lutherans, as the oldest of
the Protestant schismatics, were especially warned against elect-
ing a Catholic President. A Unitarian spokesman declared
that members of his sect were persecuted in some Roman Catholic countries, and therefore, an American Catholic should not
be placed in the White House. The Episcopalians, perhaps,
were the most discreet in opposing Smith.

None of the Protestant sects was able to exceed the fun-
damentalists in execrating the church and its followers. One of
their organs was the *Fellowship Forum.* Late in September
the New York *Times* quoted what the *Forum* claimed was an
oath taken by the Knights of Columbus, which other periodicals reprinted and which was given perhaps the widest circula-

tion of all the slanders against the Church: "I will spare neither sex, age nor condition, and I swear that I will hang, waste,
boil, flay, strangle and burn alive these infamous heretics [the
Protestants]; rip up the stomachs and wombs of their women
and crush infants' heads against the wall, in order to annihilate
forever their execrable race. That when the same cannot be
done openly, I will secretly use the poison cup, the strangula-
tion cord, the steel of the poniard, or the leaden bullet. . . ."

Smith was heartsick at the abounding evidence of the hatred
and prejudice which his nomination had aroused. Instead of
setting out on the campaign trail as the Happy Warrior, he was
forced into an angry defensive mood that did not present him
at his ebullient best. The intolerance which welled up against
him, his daughter Emily has related, was "the deepest shadow
in his life—a sorrow all the deeper for having been caused by
his fellow countrymen, who, had they really known him for
what he was, could never in honesty have opposed him on the
grounds they chose."

He was hardly less affronted by the crude jokes retailed
throughout the country about the vulgarity of Al and Katie
Smith, about the figures they would cut as President and First
Lady, and how it would be like putting the comic-strip charac-
ters Maggie and Jiggs in the White House, which would soon
reek of corned beef, cabbage, and home brew. Before the campaign train pulled out, a photographer asked Mrs. Smith to
remove some of her jewelry. Smith evidently took that as a slur
on his wife's taste and angrily told the photographer: "Leave
Katie alone!"

His first campaign tour started on September 16, with his
special train crowded with newspaper correspondents, stenog-
raphers, mimeograph operators, speech writers, and advisers.
In his personal party were his wife, his daughter Catherine,
his son Alfred, Jr., Bill Kenny, Mrs. Charles Dana Gibson, Gen-
erals Charles W. Berry and William N. Haskell of the New
York National Guard, Norman H. Davis, Judge Joseph Pro-

skauer, Bruce Kremer of the national committee, Judge Bernard L. Shientag, and a bodyguard named William Roy.

From then until the end of the campaign he drew larger and often more enthusiastic audiences than his opponent. His style—direct, colorful, and energetic—appealed to all those who could see and hear him in person. Almost invariably he spoke from notes scrawled on two or three envelopes, an hour's speech contained in a few hundred words. At times, however, he would forget the omnipresent microphones and loudspeakers, start pacing the platform and waving his arms, and fall victim to the new technology when whole sentences would be lost while he strayed from the mikes. He was unable to cure himself of such lapses as "woik" for "work," "he don't," and "ain't." He was willing to present himself as the image of Presidential dignity, if possible, but he wouldn't turn himself into a phony or a four-flusher.

And Alfred E. Smith, raw, uncut, and unpolished, pleased at least H. L. Mencken in his Presidential persona. Mencken considered him the most refreshing campaigner since Grover Cleveland. By comparison, Hoover was "a pious old woman, a fat Coolidge," a Coca-Cola beside a foaming seidel of Pilsner. Smith was the antithesis of the American politician despite his aptitude for the profession because "The usual writhing and crawling is simply not in him. Cocky, vulgar, even maybe low, he is never cheap. It would be impossible to imagine him intriguing for the Presidency as Hoover has intrigued for it with the Anti-Saloon League, the Ohio gang . . . all the other degraded pimps and harlots of politics across the table. Al came into the campaign with clean hands . . . he seems to be determined to go out of it with clean hands. . . . Somewhere on the sidewalks of New York, without benefit of the moral training on tap in Kansas and Mississippi, he picked up the doctrine that it is better, after all, to be honest than to lie. It is not a popular doctrine in America. It is dangerous baggage in politics. it gets a man suspected and hated. But it has a merit nevertheless: it makes a man comfortable inside. . . ."

Preceding his first speech in Omaha the night of September 19, Smith and his advisers met with Democratic leaders gathered from all over the Middle West in a suite at the Fontanelle Hotel. They told him their section was bitterly unhappy over the perennial farm-relief issue and intimated that Smith was the man to revive their faith in the American political system. It was William Jennings Bryan territory, of course, but Bryan was dead, having fallen on the fundamentalist field of battle at the Scopes "monkey trial" while doing what he conceived to be the Lord's work. Ten thousand packed the auditorium that night and acclaimed Smith's views on government aid to the farmers.

Much cheered by his reception in that stronghold of the corn country, Smith was encouraged as his campaign train rattled south and west toward Oklahoma City, whistle-stopping through southern Nebraska, Kansas, and northern Oklahoma. The Smith special approached Oklahoma City the night before he was to speak there. It was vividly apparent that he was venturing into hostile territory. On each side of the tracks, against the low sandhills, fiery crosses were burning. The Ku Kluxers were providing their kind of welcome for the man they regarded as both the Devil's Disciple and the Pope's Son. Judge Proskauer in his memoir *A Segment of Our Time* recorded that samples of the hate literature were examined on the train as it approached the Oklahoma capital. "We encountered circulars, handsheets and placards," he added, "that screamed the most dastardly canards," part of a "campaign of bigotry almost unbelievable in its intensity."

Smith had made notes for his Oklahoma City speech on several railroad company envelopes, but he tore them up. If Oklahomans wanted to talk about religion, he'd throw the subject right back in their teeth. When the train arrived early in the morning, 100,000 persons, it was estimated, were gathered to greet him or possibly to see whether he wore horns and a tail. In conferences with Southwestern Democratic leaders later that morning, he revealed his intentions of meeting the religi-

ous issue head on. They failed to dissuade him with their argument that it would only deepen the sentiment against him. All
that day he meditated on his most calefactory speech since he
had taken William Randolph Hearst apart for charging him
with responsibility for the New York milk strike. It might be
artless or quixotic to tackle the subject in the bluntest terms
but he believed the time had come for plain-speaking. He
couldn't pretend any longer that the religious issue was a mo-
mentary aberration from which the country would recover in
the coolness of autumn; it either had to be faced down now, in
the heart of enemy country, or never.*

"I felt deep in my heart," he later wrote, "that I would be
a coward and probably unfit to be President if I were to permit it to go further unchallenged."

The auditorium was thronged that night, the crowd mostly
sullen and hostile, but with an active and vocal segment
of Smith partisans, who kept shouting, "Pour it on 'em, Al!" No
such encouragement was needed; Smith was in a fighting mood,
and the entire Democratic National Committee could not have
managed to keep him from speaking his mind.

"I shall speak openly," he told the restive throng, "on the
things about which people have been whispering to you."

He then recited in detail the things people were saying and
publishing about himself and his religion and their relation to
his candidacy.

Then, his voice rising in volume and emotion, he declared
that "I know what lies behind all this . . . the question of
my religion. Ordinarily that word should never be used in a
political campaign. The necessity for it is forced on me . . .
and I feel that at least once in this campaign I, as the candidate
of the Democratic party, owe it to the people of this country to

---

* He could also have been more tactful, as John F. Kennedy was in his
speech to the Greater Houston Ministerial Association, when he acknowledged
that "There is nothing improper in discussing" the religious issue. Kennedy, of
course, profited from Smith's mistakes of thirty-two years earlier and from the
liberalized policies of his church. It must also be acknowledged that the
Kennedy cool was more likely to be effective than the Smith heat.

discuss freely and openly with them this attempt to inject bigotry, hatred, intolerance, and un-American sectarian division
into a campaign which should be an intelligent debate of the
important issues which confront the American people.

". . . I well know that I am not the first public man who
has been made the object of such baseless slander. It was
poured forth on Grover Cleveland and upon Theodore Roosevelt, as well as upon myself. But, as to me, the wicked motive
of religious intolerance has driven bigots to attempt to inject
these slanders into a political campaign. I here and now drag
them into the open and I denounce them as a treasonable attack upon the very foundations of American liberty!"

The crowd now had fallen silent, soaking in his words almost against its collective will.

"I have been told," Smith continued, looking down on row
upon row of sullen, stony-faced farmers, many of them the
"Okies" who in the next half dozen years would be driven from
their parched plains and themselves distill another kind of the
"Grapes of Wrath," as John Steinbeck would entitle their ordeal. Their hostility welled up from the auditorium as though
he were facing the open door of a blast furnace. What did he
and they have in common aside from American citizenship? He
might as well have been addressing a congregation of Martians.
But he continued, "I have been told that politically it might be
expedient for me to remain silent upon this subject, but so far
as I am concerned no political expediency will keep me from
speaking out in an endeavor to destroy these evil attacks.

"The absolute separation of state and church is part of the
fundamental basis of our Constitution. I believe in that separation and all that it implies. That belief must be a part of the
fundamental faith of every true American.

"Let the people of this country decide this election upon the
great and real issues of the campaign and nothing else. . . . If
the contest is fought along these lines, as I shall insist it must be,
I am confident of the outcome in November."

Had he reached them? Probably not, he thought as he sat

down and listened to part of the audience applauding—mostly those whose yearnings for a postmastership or some other federal job could be fulfilled only by a Democratic victory in November.

The Smith campaign train then headed north toward slightly more friendly territory in the mountain states. Yet when the train paused in Billings, Montana, for half an hour on its way to Helena, newspapers brought aboard told of a KKK cross that had burned for an hour the night before on the crest of Rim Rock overlooking the city. On the rest of that first swing he did not revert to the religious issue but, after the local bands had blared through "The Sidewalks of New York" and various Sousa marches, he discussed waterpower in Denver, raked over the Teapot Dome scandal in Helena, and, returning eastward, found a large crowd in Milwaukee quite predictably enthusiastic over his views on Prohibition (one great Milwaukee brewery was now making chocolate candy, and several of the others were dispiritedly producing something called near beer, weak enough to be legal).

He interrupted his national campaigning to proceed to Rochester, New York, where the state Democratic leaders were conferring on whom they should present as candidate for Governor to succeed Smith. There is some conflict over which of several possibilities Smith really favored. The first two names proposed, according to Jim Farley, were Justice Townsend Scudder of the State Supreme Court, a Protestant and a Mason, and Herbert H. Lehman, Jewish and a member of the Tiger Room circle. The selection of Justice Scudder, of course, would be a refutation of the slanders against Smith on religious grounds. Farley says that "during the discussion of available candidates he [Smith] gave me the distinct impression that his preference was for Scudder or Lehman," rather than Franklin D. Roosevelt, whose name was also brought into the conversations. Farley himself was pushing for Roosevelt's nomination, though FDR was then taking treatments at Warm

Springs, Georgia, was still on crutches, and reportedly did not want to run for office. It was also a matter for consideration that Roosevelt had never run for office in New York State except for his one term as a state senator.

The way Smith's daughter Emily remembered it, however, Smith was unenthusiastic about Scudder because of the "unusual austerity that characterized the man."

His only doubts about Roosevelt, according to Mrs. Warner, centered on his willingness to run. Not long before, in fact, Roosevelt had told Smith, "I need another year or two at Warm Springs."

Many of the conferees, however, insisted that the nomination should go to Roosevelt if he was willing to accept it. Several days before, Mrs. Eleanor Roosevelt had pleaded with them not to take him away from Warm Springs. Smith was delegated to enter their plea. "Because of Mr. Roosevelt's physical condition," his daughter said, "Father was hesitant to bring any pressure to bear on him, especially as the two were in no sense intimate. Mr. Roosevelt had never been one of Father's close political associates or advisers, but now, in the absence of anyone more acceptable to the party leaders, Father decided to support him for the nomination."

Mrs. Roosevelt finally agreed that Smith should call her husband in Warm Springs and inform him that the state leaders wanted him to run for governor. FDR yielded to the claims on his party loyalty. It was a fateful choice for Smith to have made. Soon enough he would know how the legendary Dr. Frankenstein felt after the results of his monster-building became known to him.

After several days of attending to the state's business in Albany, Smith set out on a swing through the bitterly hostile South. There was probably little he could do to combat the feeling against him in the more benighted reaches of that section, but at least he could show the flag. The attacks on him as the campaign progressed, the New York *Times* noted in an editorial, were not abating. "The primary objection to Smith is his Catholicism. His wet views come second; his Tammany affiliations third. But it is hard to tell where one leaves off and the other begins. The simple truth is that there would be only a negligible amount of bolting among Democrats if Smith were not a Catholic, regardless of his Tammany affiliations and his opposition to Prohibition."

On his Southern tour, Smith avoided the subject of religion, considering that he had already expressed himself as fully as possible in Oklahoma City. He drew curious, attentive crowds in Richmond, Virginia and Nashville, Tennessee. The Southerners refrained from burning crosses in his honor, and Smith began to hope that he might be able to maintain the Democratic hold on the South—without it he didn't stand a chance.

When he reached Louisville, however, there was greater evidence of hostility, particularly from the police force. The newspapers rather scornfully reported that on his whistle-stops Smith would tell the crowds, "I hope to meet yez-all personally." Not only were the Louisville police rude, but one policeman accused him of being drunk. That evening, when he appeared at the auditorium to deliver an attack on the Republicans' tariff policy, he found the place unbearably hot. His bodyguard, William Roy, went down in the basement of the auditorium and found a platoon of Louisville police standing guard while the engineers stoked the furnaces.

He saved one of his better speeches for an appearance at Sedalia, Missouri, in fairly friendly territory. Sedalia is located halfway between Kansas City and Jefferson City, the Missouri capital, and Smith drew a larger crowd there than he might have in either St. Louis or Kansas City. The stands at the fairground were crowded when he lashed out at the Coolidge administration's claims to have been economical and to have reduced the federal budget by $2 billion. "Never was a campaign fiction so completely and mercilessly riddled," the New York *World* correspondent wrote. Smith was always at his best in reducing fiscal matters to their understandable essentials, and he was exhilarated by the crowd's response. Missouri was a border state, and Missourians, after all, were at least semi-Southerners.

He was in high spirits when he returned to the Sedalia hotel, and they were undiminished by the discovery that his party had been victimized by the local riffraff. Mrs. Charles Dana Gibson, wife of the artist and sister of Lady Astor, had given part of her money to Norman H. Davis to keep in his wallet because she was afraid of losing it. Mr. Davis' pocket had been picked on the fairgrounds. When he learned of the crime, Smith searched the closets and looked under the bed. Somebody asked him what he was doing. "Sh!" he said, continuing his pussyfoot search of the suite. "We've got to keep this a secret or the campaign will be ruined and the country hicks will get the idea that they can take over all of us New York city slickers."

H. L. Mencken, who had followed his campaign tour of the disaffected South with all but unqualified admiration, a rare thing for that chronic dissident from Baltimore, saw signs that the South was changing, even though most Southerners, particularly the politicians and other members of the Establishment, were unaware of it. The younger Southerners, he observed, were beginning to rebel against the "hegemony of the self-elected saints." They were no longer willing to submit to the "dreadful devices of the medieval theologian. The South," he added, "cannot go on being an intellectual poor-farm. . . . It is growing too rich to submit to them. . . . The very denominational seminaries that were set up to combat learning and propagate ignorance . . . spread the poisons of enlightenment. Not many of their graduates believe that Jonah swallowed the whale. . . . It is Al's good fortune that he has been chosen to lead this movement of deliverance, not only in the South, but everywhere in the land. Win or lose, he is a lucky man, for he will be remembered."

Even the sage of Baltimore, however, refused to predict that Smith could win the election.

From his Southern swing, Smith returned to Albany again to earn his pay as governor. Then he made his final tour of the campaign, barnstorming through Boston, Philadelphia, Baltimore, and Newark. He flailed the Republican record with continuing effectiveness, and the big cities of the Northeast responded to him with the greatest enthusiasm of the campaign. The last few days before November 6 he spent on home ground, speaking to massive rallies in Brooklyn and the Madison Square Garden.

His final word to the electorate was delivered over a national radio hookup from a studio in Carnegie Hall. That event in itself showed how technology was engulfing politics; the day of the pear-shaped tone and the photogenic profile was not far off.

"At no time," he told his radio audience, "did I ever trade a promise for a vote. I have made no promises to any man or group of men. . . . I can enter upon the duties of the greatest office in the world without commitment to anybody except the American people. . . . I shall give this country the best that is in me to bring about a constructive, progressive, and forward-looking administration."

In another twenty-four hours he would learn whether that pledge was good enough for the American people.

15

"Thy Will Be Done. . . ."

*I understand that you were kind
enough to pray for my election,
and I thank you for it. I hear
you're disappointed because
nothing came of it. Well, girls,
remember this—it's in the Bible:
"Thy will be done on earth. . . ."*
—ALFRED E. SMITH *speaking
to the girls at a convent
in Georgia late in 1928*

NOVEMBER 6 was not only election day, but Katie Smith's brithday. No matter how the election turned out, Smith was determined that the other occasion would be properly celebrated, and while the nation was going to the polls that day, Smith occupied himself by ordering a huge birthday cake and making other preparations which had nothing to do with the Presidency. He had the kind of self-respect that allowed him to draw the line between the private and public man. Katie's birthday would be celebrated in the proper spirit whether he was President-Elect or merely the lame-duck governor of New York.

With something more than symbolism, whether the rest of the country liked it or not, he would hear the news of victory or defeat among the men to whom he owed his career. The members of the Tammany Society gathered at the Seventy-First Regiment Armory to hear the returns, and Smith, early in the evening, took his place among them. His wife and children and friends of the family waited in the suite at the Biltmore.

The ordeal of waiting to learn whether the country would accept him as Al Smith, American, or reject him as Al Smith, Catholic—which was the way he saw it then—was mercifully brief. The returns came in quickly by telegraph, and within a few hours it was evident that he would be badly defeated.

As he sat there listening with his friends, his comrades from so many earlier political battles, the unlit cigar in his mouth drooped lower and lower. He was a cigar smoker, not a cigar chewer, ordinarily, but tonight he was so preoccupied by the vision of total defeat that he never lit up. He said little, but he was certain then that the reason he was being so badly beaten was his religion. Even a year and a half later he still held to the belief that he was rejected solely for that reason; he wrote in a magazine article about Richard L. Shiel replying in the English Parliament to the charge that the Irish are aliens in race and religion (as far as England was concerned) and quoted Shiel: "Partakers in every peril, in the glory are we not to be permitted to participate? And should we be told as a requittal that we are estranged from the whole country for whose salvation our lifeblood was poured out?" It would be another nine years before he could bring himself to tell an interviewer that he might have done better in the election if he had possessed more knowledge of and sensitivity to those social conditions and cultural traditions in the hinterland which made him feared and therefore hated.

By 9:30 P.M. the dimensions of his defeat were quite apparent, and he decided to leave the armory and the commiserations of his old comrades to rejoin his family. Time would tell the whole story when all the returns were in: He received 87 electoral votes to Hoover's 444. The popular vote wasn't quite that lopsided: Smith 15,016,443 (40.7 percent) to Hoover's

21,392,190 (58 percent). More crushing perhaps was the fact that Smith had lost New York State while Roosevelt won the governorship by a plurality of 25,564—the cruelest of surprises.

As he rode back to the Biltmore through the election night crowds, he must have pondered the fact that he was now, or soon would be, unemployed. An immense debt had been piled up by his unsuccessful campaign, and his personal finances were in similar disarray. Less than twelve months from that night, with the collapse of the stock market, millions of his fellow citizens would begin to know the same uncertainties of being jobless. He could not have known or even guessed that losing that election was probably the luckiest thing that ever happened to him; for he believed in that much-touted eternal prosperity as much as any Republican. Thus to his victorious opponent fell the piteous task of peering around the corner for a glimpse of that vanished prosperity.

Immediately on arriving at the Biltmore suite—there was no considerable crowd to push his way through, nothing being so thorough, so lonely, as political defeat—he took his wife and children into his bedroom for their first moment of privacy in months. He told them there was only the smallest chance that he would be elected.

"It's God's will," Mrs. Smith said with tears in her eyes. She mentioned the threats which had been made on his life during the campaign and added, "But aside from all that, we'll see more of you now."

Smith put his arm around his wife's shoulder and smiled; when he had married Katie Dunn twenty-five years before, he had considered election to the Board of Aldermen an impossible glory. "You mustn't forget," he told his sons and daughters, "that this is your mother's birthday. Come along now. We'll join our friends and cut the cake."

As Mencken bitterly summed up the election results, "Hoover could have beaten Thomas Jefferson quite as decisively as he beat Al. . . . He let Al bombard them with ideas, confident that ideas would only affright and anger them. . . ."

The 1928 statistics have been subjected to more analysis, perhaps, than those of any other American election. Both academic and journalistic experts have turned them every which way in an attempt to determine just how Al Smith, now virtually a folk hero, could have been defeated by the uninspiring Hoover, who is now remembered chiefly as the Presidential victim (or in extreme cases, the cause) of the depression of 1929-39. It is forgotten how little part the semimystical element of charisma played before charismatic emanations could be magnified, or even manufactured, through the new techniques bestowed by the electronics industry and the profession or craft of political engineering.

It was generally accepted that Smith was beaten on the religious issue, but later commentators have found other elements crucial to the outcome. In her *Rum, Religion, and Votes: 1928 Re-examined* (1962), Ruth Silva concluded that Smith's party affiliation harmed his candidacy more than his membership in the Catholic Church. Miss Silva, however, bases her conclusions on a comparison of the 1928 vote with that of 1924, when Democratic voting strength had ebbed to its lowest point.

Actually, on being subjected to objective analysis, the statistics showed the Democratic Party that it hadn't done too badly under Smith as standard-bearer, considering that it had been the minority party ever since 1860. Smith polled 6,000,000 more votes than any Democratic Presidential candidate in history. He received almost twice as many popular votes as John W. Davis in 1924. In 1924 the Republicans had carried the largest cities by a wide margin, while in 1928 that edge had turned over to the other side.

The importance of the urban vote was not visible to most political experts in 1928, when Main Street was still dominant, but Republicans should have taken alarm at the total vote from the nation's twelve largest cities—New York, Chicago,

Philadelphia, Pittsburgh, Detroit, Cleveland, Baltimore, St. Louis, Boston, Milwaukee, San Francisco, and Los Angeles. In 1920 the net Republican plurality in those cities was 1,638,000; in 1924 it was 1,252,000, but in 1928 it had swung over to a slender Democratic plurality of 38,000.

In *The Future of American Politics,* Samuel Lubell demonstrated that Smith's importance to his party has been unjustly overshadowed by Roosevelt's four terms. The 1928 statistics show that "the Republican hold on the cities was broken not by Roosevelt but by Alfred E. Smith," Lubell wrote. "Before the Roosevelt Revolution there was an Al Smith Revolution. . . . It was Smith who first slashed through the traditional alignments that had held so firmly since the Civil War, clearing the way for the more comprehensive realignment which came later."

Both the Solid South and the Republican North were sundered, Hoover taking more than 200 Southern counties which had never voted Republican before, Smith detaching 122 Northern counties from the Republicans, 77 of which were predominantly Catholic.

Smith had become the "Great Commoner" of the urban masses as Bryan had been for the downtrodden farmers and villagers of a generation earlier. He epitomized and drew the support of the newer immigrants, along with the Irish among the older. The "old" immigrants mostly came from northwestern Europe—England, Germany, the Scandinavian countries—and settled on farms west of the Alleghenies. The "new" immigrants, with 1885 as a rough dividing line, came from Italy, Poland, Russia, Greece, the Balkans—most of them Catholic or Jewish—and since the free land of the frontier had been absorbed by their predecessors, they settled in the cities. Smith naturally became their spokesman; his first social and political cause was the sweatshop laboring force they largely made up. Thus a cleavage between classes, as much as between races, began developing forty years ago; the Democratic Party then began capturing the poorer groups concentrated in the cities, and since their numbers increased in greater proportion than the outlanders, they have since become the decisive political factor.

It was Smith who translated Democracy into the urban party. Before him it had been almost as much a rural party as the Republicans. The transference could be studied in a half dozen Pennsylvania counties. Three which the Democrats had won in 1920 and 1924 were largely composed of the rural and native-born. In 1928 they voted Republican. Three other counties, Elk, Luzerne, and Lackawanna, were mostly engaged in mining and industry and had been Republican since 1896. But in 1928 they voted for Smith. (The latter switch may have been due mainly to the fact that Raskob had insisted on spending much of the Democratic treasury in a vain attempt to swing Pennsylvania into the Smith column. Hoover, however, took the state by 1,000,000 votes.) Relatively new Italian-American and French-Canadian-American voting blocs in the New England industrial towns moved away from the Republican Party and have not returned in any decisive numbers.

An urban revolt had begun in 1928, and Smith was its catalyst. "Smith may be today's 'Forgotten Warrior,'" Lubell concludes, "but the line he drew across the map of American politics has never been erased."

His loss of the Solid South signaled a beginning of the decline of the Democrats' influence in that section, which would also be marked by such dissident movements as the Dixiecrats in 1948 and George Wallace's third-party candidacy in 1968. There was more to Southern restiveness than merely religious prejudice against Smith, as Mencken and others pointed out. The textile industry was moving South and creating a business community which was attracted to the Republican high-tariff policy. The *Nation* commented on this development shortly after the election: "In Georgia, in North Carolina, in Alabama, the industrial development has been enormous. The manufacturers and the managers of mills and factories and many of their employes have become Republicans because they felt it was to their financial interests to do so."

Smith, on the other hand, won two of the most urbanized
New England states, Massachusetss and Rhode Island, where
the slump in textile production caused by the defection south-
ward in search of cheaper labor worked in his favor.

As Walter Lippmann shrewdly noted, the most important
result of the election of 1928 was not the unsurprising revelation that there was a considerable amount of religious prejudice
poisoning the land but that Smith's candidacy had begun the
reconstruction of the Democratic Party, had liberated it from
the Bryanesque West and the old base in the South.

The defeated candidate was in a mood of the deepest disen-
chantment during the days following the election. It was something of a wrench, certainly, to transport himself, both mentally
and physically, from the excitements and hopes of the Presidential campaign—which he really expected to win, according
to James W. Gerard, the treasurer of the Democratic National
Committee, since there was then no proliferation of polltak-
ing to prepare him for defeat—back to the comparative drab-
ness of the Executive Mansion in Albany, the lease of which
was shortly to expire. He lost no time in clearing his desk of
the accumulated business, then took a long vacation in the
South.

At first the loneliness of defeat was not so bitterly evident.
A huge crowd had welcomed him back to Albany. Then, with
the state's business cleared away, he went South in a private car
—Bill Kenny's—and was constantly laved by the consolations
and ego strokings of Kenny, Raskob, and other members of the
party.

On the way to Biloxi, Mississippi, where Smith haters were
thicker than boll weevils, his train was greeted by cheering
crowds, until he wondered how he could have lost the election.

En route, in Georgia, the train halted for a sentimental side
journey. Smith visited a convent school where the girls had
prayed for his election. After his defeat they had written him
of their bitter disappointment. "I understand you were kind

enough to pray for my election," he told the girls, "and I thank
you for it. I hear you're disappointed because nothing came of
it. Well, girls, remember this—it's in the Bible: 'Thy will
be done on earth. . . .' "

On his return to New York, he attended one of the few banquets in the past decade at which he was not the guest of honor
and chief adornment. The leaders of the state Democratic Party
gave the dinner for Governor-Elect Roosevelt and the new lieutenant governor, Herbert H. Lehman, at the Lotus Club. Smith
was invited to sit on the dais, but all the attention was focused
on the beaming FDR, the new star of New York Democracy.
Morose and silent, Smith felt like an old character man shoved
into the wings by a new and more magnetic personality whose
name had just gone up in lights on the marquee outside.

During a break in the festivities, Smith walked out of the banquet room and down the corridor to the men's room, accompanied by his old friend, Eddie Dowling, the Broadway actor-
producer.

While they were occupied at the urinals, as Dowling has recalled, Smith was bemoaning the bleakness of his prospects. He
would soon be out of office, off the state's payroll for the first
time in years. He didn't have any money saved up, and he didn't
know what he was going to do to earn a living.

Raskob, virtually Smith's shadow, had slipped into the men's
room on their heels and listened to Smith's recital of his personal troubles.

"Don't worry, Al," Raskob told him, according to Dowling's
recollection. "I'm going to build a new skyscraper—biggest
in the world—and you're going to be president of the company."

In that curious setting Smith learned that his future was assured, that his admirers had provided him with a job that
would last to the end of his life and guarantee that he would
move up to Fifth Avenue rather than back to Oliver Street.

Raskob, as Dowling remembered the incident, told Smith
that he was putting up the Empire State Building on the site of

the old Waldorf-Astoria principally as a means of providing Smith with a well-paying job. But Dowling, who now disliked Raskob, remembered that the industrialist some time before had told him he'd seen the Eiffel Tower, and "it burned him to think the French had built something higher than anything we had in this great country of ours. . . . Then he claimed he was building the Empire State to give Al a job. . . . That wasn't so at all."

Power, even when it doesn't corrupt, can become an addiction even with the best of men. As the time approached for him to hand over the governorship to Roosevelt, Smith was finding this was true in his own case. He had been governor long enough to regard it as a job with tenure. With that illusion gone, a new one took its place. As governor emeritus, as titular head of the national party, as the most eminent Democrat in the state of New York, he trusted that he would retain a certain influence over the management of the state government. He did not take into account Roosevelt's own considerable ego or the fact that inevitably a feeling of rivalry would spring up between them.

All this was complicated by the judgment of Smith, as a self-made city man, of his successor as a country squire, an amateur, a nice fellow to have on your side and make stirring speeches in your behalf—but essentially a lightweight. Smith underestimated Roosevelt as a man and as a politician—and that was the essence of what became a shattered friendship, a wary enmity. Everything considered, it was something of a miracle that they had been friends; it would have been a greater one if, under the pressure of conflicting ambitions, they had not come to a bitter misunderstanding. There were also the conditions under which Roosevelt came to Albany. Smith had not carried him into office, Roosevelt had made it on his own by running ahead of the national ticket. Doubtless he had also learned from Jim Farley that he was not Smith's first choice for the nomination.

The Rooseveltian strategy in winning the election must also have worked against a continuation of the old easy relationship. He had started out his campaign by denouncing bigotry, as applied to Protestant intolerance of a Catholic candidate. Then his distant cousin, Nicholas Roosevelt, warned him that he needed a Republican swing vote. The religious issue in New York State had taken a slightly different twist. Roosevelt's opponent was Albert Ottinger, who was Jewish. When the vote was tallied and analyzed, it was apparent that more than 100,000 upstate Republicans had voted for Hoover, then switched over to the Democratic column to cast their ballots for Roosevelt —or against Ottinger.

The Smiths celebrated Christmas in the Executive Mansion, then started moving their possessions to a suite at the Hotel DeWitt Clinton as was customary for the outgoing governor. The Roosevelt family's trunks arrived from Hyde Park and were placed in the hallways. They were lined up outside the door to the second-floor living room in which Smith and his family gathered on their last night in the Executive Mansion. To dispel the gloom of their dispossession, Smith ordered a bottle of champagne opened. He dipped his fingers into his glass, went to the door and sprinkled champagne on one of the Roosevelt trunks, saying, "Now, Frank, if you want a drink, you'll know where to find it."

A sadder task than moving out of the mansion, for Smith, was disposing of all the birds and animals in his backyard zoo. He spent much of his last days in office arranging for new homes for them in various zoos and parks around the state.

Even after formally handing over the governorship, Smith dismayed Roosevelt by staying on in Albany. Week after week went by, and the Smiths stayed on at the Hotel DeWitt Clinton. The ex-governor simply wanted to help Roosevelt in making the changeover easier, join in any policymaking decisions, influence him on one or two appointments. He also wanted to help "Frank" work out the problems of an executive budget, on which he considered himself an unrivaled expert.

That wasn't the way it looked to Governor Roosevelt or Mrs. Governor Roosevelt. To them it appeared that Smith was trying to intrude, trying to continue running the state government. "I was not greatly surprised," wrote Mrs. Roosevelt in her autobiography (*This I Remember*), "when after his defeat it became evident that he thought he was going to retain a behind-the-scenes leadership in the state. It would not work; and he soon discovered that it would not work. . . ."

Smith, of course, wanted to protect the jobs of some of the people he had brought into the state government, often at considerable sacrifice to their personal lives. He hoped that Roosevelt would retain Mrs. Belle Moskowitz as a sort of *chef de cabinet* because of her great expertise in social problems, but Roosevelt had Louis Howe firmly in mind for that position.

He also pressed Roosevelt to keep Robert Moses on as secretary of state, an office in which he had performed with great efficiency. Moses, however, was definitely not a Roosevelt man. He had opposed FDR's nomination for governor, saying, "He'll make a good candidate but a poor Governor"—and Roosevelt's intelligence service, under Howe, was excellent. Also Roosevelt and Moses had clashed three years before, when FDR, as chairman of the Taconic State Park Commission, had appointed Howe as secretary at a salary of $5,000 a year.

After he had conferred with Roosevelt on the Moses matter, Smith told his daughter Emily, "I told Frank that I had no desire to pick his appointees for him. Any Governor should do that for himself. But I said that Bob Moses had a great record and a lot of ability, and on that account I thought it would be a good idea to keep him on as Secretary of State."

Roosevelt's curt reply was, "He rubs me the wrong way."

A third unsuccessful plea was entered on behalf of Commissioner of Conservation Alexander MacDonald, who was a Republican, but whose administrative abilities Smith considered invaluable to the state. He believed that Roosevelt agreed to keep MacDonald on, not yet acquainted with Roosevelt's habit of blurring his yeses, nos, and maybes when confronted with a discomfiting suggestion. Shortly thereafter he learned that Mac-

Donald had been let go, along with Mrs. Moskowitz and Robert Moses. MacDonald was replaced by Roosevelt's Hyde Park neighbor Henry Morgenthau, Jr., of whom Smith had a low opinion. "Henry might have ideas and principles and professions," Smith told a newspaper writer, "but, in the face of any more dominant influence, he would either conceal or deny them."

He was undoubtedly irked by the fact that Moses' job went to Ed Flynn, the supple Bronx County leader, who had replaced him (Smith) in the late Mr. Murphy's paternal favor.

The New York *World* had predicted that there would be a clean sweep of Smith officeholders: "The appointment of organization Democrats to supplant some of the Smith Independents already forecasts a change in the political picture." Roosevelt quickly carried out that program to build his own organization; already Jim Farley and Louis Howe, his chief advisers, were urging him to shape his actions toward a run for the Presidency in 1932.

Smith, not yet aware of those ambitions, was also rebuffed when he asked that Roosevelt show him an advance copy of his first message to the 1929 legislature. Roosevelt agreed to the request. But somehow the copy was not sent over to Smith's hotel. In the message Roosevelt addressed himself principally to rural problems and barely made polite mention of his predecessor.

Smith finally got the message and, no doubt trailing sulfurous private oaths, took Mrs. Smith to Florida while he worked over the proofs of his soon-to-be-published autobiography, *Up to Now*. The memoirs of a defeated political candidate ordinarily are not a fast-moving item in the bookstores, but his financial condition was eased when the *Saturday Evening Post* bought the book for serialization.

On his return North, he was delighted by evidence that some highly respected people, ranging from a large part of the Harvard faculty to Winston Churchill, who was enduring his own

exile from politics at the time, still held him in high regard. Alfred North Whitehead, the British philosopher, was to give
the chief address of the evening when forty Harvard professors
who had supported his candidacy invited Smith to attend a dinner at which he was the guest of honor. Whitehead praised
Smith's career in an urbane and scholarly address. Smith was
anxious over having to follow so erudite a man to the center of
the high table, but he launched into a vigorous half-hour speech
on the problems of governing a state and sat down to
what Judge Proskauer called "tumultuous applause."

A short time later Smith was invited to dinner by Bernard
Baruch. The financier was then playing host to Winston
Churchill on one of his frequent American visits. Baruch asked
Churchill whether there was anyone he would particularly like to meet, and the latter immediately replied, "Al
Smith." The two men got along splendidly—both specimens
of the total political animal. Later in the evening Smith had
an engagement to speak at Tammany Hall, and Churchill insisted on accompanying him. During intervals in Smith's
speech, many an Irish face clouded with bewilderment at hearing an English voice call out approvingly, "Heah, heah!"

During those first months of being out of office and out of
power, Smith exhibited many withdrawal symptoms. They
wore thin the old rude charm, the old Charlie-me-boy exuberance. When *Up to Now* was published, George Oppenheimer,
then publicizing books for the Viking Press, launched a hopeful
campaign on its behalf and found the ex-governor in a bale-
ful mood. For the benefit of newspaper photographers and the
newsreels, and ultimately the book, Oppenheimer staged a
scene at which he would present Smith with the first copy while
the cameras clicked or rolled. Smith appeared, as Oppenheimer
recalled, in "a humor that completely belied his label, 'The
Happy Warrior.' His mood grew blacker when he was told
the newsreel was to be in sound . . . he had not prepared anything to say. I, on the other hand, was fully prepared, having

rehearsed for several days in front of a mirror. . . . The Governor's ill humor increased my stage fright to such an extent that, when we were lined up for the cameras, I advanced to the desk, gracefully tripped over a camera cable, righted myself, and said, 'It gives, Governor Smith, me great pleasure to present you with the first copy of your autobiography, *Up to Now.*'

"Not only had I breached syntax, but I had made my speech sound as if the book I was handing him was the first copy distributed up to now. The Governor glowered fiercely; one of the girls in his office . . . snickered delightedly; and the cameraman called 'cut.' Luckily I made the next take without untoward incident and the Governor delivered a graceful speech of acceptance."

Nevertheless, Oppenheimer hung a signed photograph of the occasion on his wall, showing him and Smith with their formidable noses in profile. Robert Benchley, on examining the photograph, commented, "It must be a double exposure. There are no *two* noses like that anywhere."

Up to Now divulged few political secrets, and perhaps for that reason, and the fact it had been serialized, its sales were disappointing. Smith accepted it as just another in a series of bad breaks, explaining, "My constituents don't know where to look for a bookstore."

He was now fifty-five years old, and it seemed to him that there was something eating away at the center of things, leaving a hollowness that saddened him. Shortly after his autobiography was published, he went over to watch the workmen tearing down the old Waldorf-Astoria on Thirty-Fourth Street, on the site of which the Empire State Building would pierce the skyline of midtown Manhattan. Later he told a friend:

"In the banquet room where I've spoken so many times and attended so many dinners, it was pathetic. Those great gold and brass moldings and decorations in the corners that I supposed were really costly—nothing but gilded plaster. And the chandeliers! They looked magnificent hanging, but on the floor

—just junk. I went thinking I might pick up something for my apartment, but there was nothing there worth having. It was pathetic."

In a very few months he and the rest of the country were to learn that their world was hollower and falser than the plaster cornucopias on the walls of the old Waldorf-Astoria.

PART III
Tragic Warrior

What are the roots that clutch . . .
Out of this stony rubbish? . . .
A heap of broken images, where
the sun beats. . . .
I will show you fear in a
handful of dust.
—T. S. ELIOT

16

The Walls Came Tumbling Down

SMITH'S depressed mood lingered for months. A climacteric of whatever source, physical or psychological, seems to have held him in its grip. Some of his former comrades might have been forgiven for hopefully ruling him out as a power broker when he announced, "As far as running for office again is concerned—that's finished." They preferred to ignore another statement Smith made indicating he had not lost *all* interest in political affairs, that he would continue to fight for the principles he considered right.

One of those a trifle too eager to believe that Smith was dropping out of the political game entirely was Mayor James J. Walker. Smith had all but carried Walker to City Hall in his arms, but Beau James was long on personal charm, a trifle short on political gratitude. Naturally Smith was pained when he heard that Walker had expressed the opinion that other than religious prejudice was responsible for his losing the Presidential election. "He exchanged the old blue serge suit for a white tie and tails," Walker blithely remarked, "the brown derby for a top hat. He took off the square-toe brogans with which he had climbed from the sidewalks of New York to dizzy heights and put on a pair of pumps. It takes a damn good acrobat to do that while at the top of the ladder." *

Then, too, Walker was challenging Smith's influence in New York City itself by maneuvering to force Judge Olvany to resign as Grand Sachem and replace himself with a Walker man. Smith studied these encroachments on his position as No. 1 Democrat and found them all of a piece with Governor Roosevelt's attitude toward him. He could only conclude that he was being frozen out of both the New York and Albany poles of state politics. The bitterest aspect, from his viewpoint, was that he considered both men his protégés. Walker more than Roosevelt, of course.

At a social function Walker and Smith overheard Judge Olvany say that he was quitting because of his health.

Smith snapped, "Did you lose your nerve?"

Walker, pretending ignorance, told Olvany, "I would have appreciated it, George, if you had given me twenty minutes' notice."

A short time later Olvany did resign, and Walker dictated the choice of his replacement as head of Tammany Hall, John F. Curry, who was not a Smith man.

Late in March, 1929, Smith called up Walker and asked to see him at City Hall. The New York *Times* had just published an editorial which led off by inquiring, "Who, if anybody, at the present moment is the acting mayor of New York?" Walker had been out of town when the editorial was written; Joseph V. McKee, the president of the Board of Aldermen, and his deputy, Charles A. McManus, were vacationing in the South. There was, in fact, a wave of disillusionment washing over the Walker administration. A fun mayor with a nice taste in tailoring and show girls could be tolerated just so long. The big town was upset by hints of corruption in the background of

---

* Another remark of Walker's that Smith did not appreciate came at the opening of the Empire State Building on May 1, 1931, when Walker cracked that it looked like the kind of place "some public official might like to come and hide."

the murder of Arnold Rothstein, the top gambler, and taxpayers' groups were growing restive at Walker's fiscal policies.

On top of all that—perhaps more serious than any of the other charges to Smith, the straitlaced family man—the gossip columns were reporting that Walker was being seen everywhere and all the time with Betty Compton, the musical comedy star, whom he later divorced his wife to marry. To Smith, the flip little man sitting behind the mayor's desk at odd hours was giving the party a black eye that all the makeup on Broadway couldn't hide.

As Walker later related to Dudley Field Malone, his interview with Smith was something close to a showdown.

"Jim," Smith started off, "do you still regard me as the head of the party in New York State?"

"I'll regard you any way you wish," Walker replied, a little evasively. "What do you want me to do?"

"I want you to promise me you won't run for reelection."

"Do you want the job yourself?"

Smith shook his head.

"What's the score then?" Walker asked.

"You'll be defeated if you run," Smith said flatly.

"That kind of prospect," Walker retorted, "didn't stop you."

Smith then listed all the things people were saying and writing about Walker's absenteeism, his inattention to the duties of his office, but not mentioning the rumors about Betty Compton.

"This is only a straw in the wind," Smith added. "The wind is getting stronger and stronger. And you'll be blown sky-high."

"Why don't you tell me the real reason?" Walker demanded.

Smith stared at him without replying.

"Then I'll tell you," said Walker angrily, "without all this beating around the bush. It's because I have a girl. Isn't that what's bothering you?"

"It's bothering a lot of people."

"As a matter of fact, I wasn't going to run. I'm sick of living in a glass house I never asked for." (This, surely, was a lapse of memory. Smith remembered, if Walker did not, that interview at the Half Moon Hotel on Coney Island.) "But now I'm going to run!"

"You'd better pray for a miracle," Smith remarked, then left the mayor's office.

But it didn't take a miracle to elect Walker as mayor of New York, not even with Fiorello LaGuardia, the Fusion candidate, as his hard-hitting opponent. Walker winked, grinned, and wisecracked his way past charges that his administration was riddled with corruption and was easily reelected. It was not the best thing that ever happened to him. Smith's advice, if not his sense of prophecy, was sound.

Mr. and Mrs. Alfred E. Smith, Sr., were now in residence at 51 Fifth Avenue—dream street of the native New Yorker. Smith was on salary at $65,000 a year as president of the Empire State Building, which would dwarf every other structure in the tallest city in the world. There were 14,000 millionaires in the United States, and Smith couldn't see any reason why he shouldn't eventually join their ranks. There was nothing in his philosophy that frowned on a man making a million if he didn't have to ruin a lot of other people doing it.

He was titular head of a company whose promoters included such gilt-edged names as Pierre S. Du Pont, John J. Raskob, Louis G. Kaufman, and Ellis P. Earle. When Empire State, Inc., completed its 102-story building, he would manage a structure with a population the size of a small city.

At the same time he was eased into the banking business. This really sealed his new position as a man of affairs; there was no one regarded with more awe in the money-minded twenties than a banker. New banks were sprouting like mushrooms in a wet woods. In New York City banking had just entered a sort of ethnic phase. A group of Jewish garment manufacturers had formed the Bank of the United States. Francesco M. Ferrari and an Italian group had established the City Trust Company. The Irish decided they had to have their own bank, too. James J. Riordan, Smith's old friend and benefactor, organized the County Trust Company with the support of wealthy contractors, many of them familiars of the Tiger Room. Smith was invited to sit on the board of directors of the County Trust.

He moved into a suite of offices at Madison Avenue and Thirty-Sixth Street, from the windows of which he could watch the progress being made in tearing down the Waldorf and building the Empire State. Belle Moskowitz had opened her own public relations outfit in Manhattan, and Smith saw to it that she handled the publicity for the Empire State. Smith also signed on a young woman named Mary Carr, who had worked at Democratic national headquarters during the campaign, as his secretary.

He eased himself into a comfortable, lucrative routine centered on the office and the penthouse apartment down Fifth Avenue near Washington Square. In addition to his Empire State job and his bank directorship, he was serving as an editor of the *New Outlook* and writing, or collaborating, on a weekly column for the McNaught syndicate, which appeared in the New York *World* among other newspapers. Both the National Broadcasting Company and the Columbia Broadcasting System offered him air time whenever he wanted to speak on any subject he chose for a national radio audience. Almost every day he met such old friends and supporters as John J. Raskob, Bill Kenny, Jim Riordan, Terence McManus, George McNamee, and Dan Mooney over the luncheon table. His once-lean figure soon began to acquire the respectable convexity of a budding capitalist.

It was a serene life, even if the canker of his defeat continued to gnaw. Much of what he did, as a suddenly anointed executive, was simply to okay other people's plans. There was nothing creative, venturesome, or exciting about it. The trivia of existence, as with most Americans, absorbed him for most of his waking hours.

On the surface everything seemed tranquil, almost humdrum, as the autumn of 1929 deepened. A few insiders un-doubtedly knew that the economy was being held together by a rope of sand, but Smith was as much an innocent about Wall Street as any bootblack sinking his life savings into RCA. The country's attention was focused on such matters as the celebra-tion of the fiftieth anniversary of the invention of the electric light bulb at Menlo Park, New Jersey, where Thomas A. Edi-son's friend Henry Ford had reconstructed the village as it looked in 1879. There was a fuss in the newspapers over Car-negie Foundation charges that more than 200 colleges were subsidizing their football players. Ernest Hemingway's *A Fare-well to Arms* and Oliver La Farge's *Laughing Boy* were being discussed by the kind of people who buy best sellers. A New York cemetery was offering a luxurious mausoleum with at-tached rooms—"a symphony in marble"—which it claimed was "in the reach of everyone's pocketbook." A Japanese biolo-gist claimed that he had discovered a technique for changing racial characteristics, even the color of skin, which would ho-mogenize the physical appearance of all mankind. Trivia. . . .

In September the stock market had risen to new highs; then it began fluctuating violently, but with a downward trend. Everyone reassured each other that it was only a temporary in-stability, even though by the third week in October the Dow-Jones Averages were down 50 points from their September peak. Speculation had become a way of life, with practically no margin required for plungers in the market and the Securities and Exchange Commission not even a gleam in anyone's eyes. Hoover had continued the easy-money policy of his predeces-sors despite warnings from the Federal Reserve Board that the discount rate was too low. By midsummer of 1929 certain indicators pointed to an advancing low-pressure area, coming on as inexorably as a storm rounding Cape Hatteras. Business inventories had trebled in one year to $1.8 billion, and con-tracts for residential building declined by more than $1 billion in one year to $216,000,000. Industrial production was going down; unemployment was going up. In August the Federal Reserve Board finally persuaded the President that the discount rate should be raised to 6 percent.

That measure still didn't cool off the stock market. AT&T topped the 300 mark, and General Electric was up to 396. On October 24, there was a sharp break in the market, and by noon the situation was so serious that a group of leading bankers created a pool of $250,000,000 to shore up the prices. For the next several days Wall Street tried to restore confidence while the price index bobbled uncertainly.

On Tuesday, October 29, a panic erupted on the floor of the Stock Exchange, more than 16,000,000 shares were traded—sold, that is, at any price they would bring—and $14 billion in paper value simply evaporated before the gong rang. It was all over. The great boom had ended, and it would take another generation before people started believing those who maintained that prosperity could be made everlasting.

Then came winter and the start of a decade-long depression. Al Smith was not among those ruined by the Wall Street collapse, simply because he didn't have enough money to play the market. His job was safe, because the foundations of the Empire State Building had already been laid and its backers, for the most part, had not been caught short in the market crash. So construction went on, and the Empire State rose story by story even as the country's hopes sank lower and lower.

Even then, perhaps, he didn't realize that losing the election of 1928 was the luckiest thing that ever happened to the Democratic Party—and himself. Could President Alfred E. Smith and Secretary of the Treasury John J. Raskob have prevented the Wall Street collapse and the consequent depression? Not likely. And if Smith and the Democrats had been caught in the fallout, the political history of the next decades would have taken a very different turn.

Even with his excellent salary, Smith did not entirely escape the consequences of the crash, though he felt them less than most of his fellow citizens. Just ten days after "black Tuesday," on November 8, 1929, Jim Riordan committed suicide. Riordan was one of his oldest and closest friends, and Smith wept when he heard the all but incredible news. To a good Catholic, that meant his friend was damned through all eternity for taking his own life. Smith and other friends of the dead man could only conclude that Riordan had been driven insane by financial worries.

And that conclusion brought up the matter of the County Trust Company, which Riordan had headed. He had killed himself on a Friday. The news of his suicide was withheld until after the bank was closed for the weekend. If a run on the bank were to be averted, the depositors had to be reassured before its doors opened Monday morning. By then it was announced that John J. Raskob had taken over the presidency and Smith had become chairman of the board. Those members of the Tiger Room crowd who weren't wiped out the previous week —and there were a number of cagey ones in addition to Raskob, who had got out from under that summer even while loudly proclaiming that the market was sound—came to the rescue of the County Trust and put up enough money to keep the bank from closing. Somehow the County Trust weathered the storm, though the Italians' City Trust failed and the Jews' Bank of the United States foundered in a flurry of grand-jury indictments.

The Riordan suicide disclosed a situation disastrous to many of Smith's closest friends, a situation which broke up many friendships in the old Tiger Room crowd. During the last weeks of the '28 campaign, the Democratic National Committee had run out of funds, largely because Raskob insisted on sinking $1,000,000 in the vain hope of swinging Pennsylvania into the Republican column. All the true believers in the Smith inner circle, like Smith himself, were convinced that he would win out, but it would be a close finish. Raskob pleaded that they couldn't let Al lose just because they were shy a million or two in campaign funds. The loyal Jim Riordan came up with a solution: The County Trust Company would lend the Democratic National Committee the money it needed.

After Smith was elected President, there would be plenty to make up the deficit and pay off the loan. The law prohibited corporations from making campaign contributions, so all of Smith's closest friends, as Raskob explained it, would have to sign the note for $1,500,000. And the faithful signed—Eddie Dowling, Tim Mara, Jack Gilchrist, George Getz, Mike Meehan, Herbert Bayard Swope, Joe Haggerty—though some of them would have been hard pressed, they knew, if the note were called.

Raskob solemnly promised, as Dowling and others recalled, that the signers would never be called on to pay off the million and a half.

Riordan's suicide and the precarious condition of County Trust made it necessary to collect—immediately. In response came a howl of outrage and genuine pain from the endorsers of the note. Most of them by now had their backs against the wall, and besides Raskob, as a multimillionaire, could have picked up the tab without suffering much damage. But Raskob was a businessman, and he hadn't put his promise in writing.

"When John Raskob asked these fellows to sign this note and promised that the note would never be called," Eddie Dowling said in recalling the bitter memory years later, "I think he did that with his tongue in his cheek. First of all, he could not personally give a million and a half dollars to a candidate running for a high office. . . . He had to have co-signers to make it legal. If Smith had won and gone into the White House, I don't think Raskob would have called the note. . . . But Smith lost. He's a dead candidate. So, as he picked up the chips and thought of all the men who had signed that note—these were lifelong friends of Al Smith's—I suppose his reasoning was why shouldn't they share. Why shouldn't they? And so he called the note."

Dowling was present, he said, when Raskob appeared in the office of Tim Mara, the sports promoter, to demand that Mara come through with his share.

"You can go to hell," Mara told Raskob, "to get that $50,000 out of me."

The crash, its aftereffects, revelations, and recriminations, broke up the old Tiger Room gang. Some members, going with the coming man, drifted over into the Roosevelt camp. Others were too busy trying to save their businesses. The Society for the Perpetual Adoration of Alfred Emanuel Smith simply stopped functioning, though many of its members would always look back on the 1928 campaign as their finest hour.

Smith was saddened as old friends fell out, and rumors spread of double-dealing in the months before the Wall Street collapse.

Mike Meehan, who had become a multimillionaire before he reached forty, had made his fortune speculating in radio stocks. A short, bouncy, red-haired Irishman, he had encouraged all his friends to plunge on the same issues, particularly Jim Riordan. But Meehan had sold out just before the crash. Apparently he did not tip off Riordan to do the same. The result, as Riordan's friends saw it, was that Riordan was cleaned out, his bank almost closed, and Riordan himself committed suicide.

Raskob's activities before and during the market collapse also failed to endear him to ex-comrades of the Smith campaign. The enduring friendship between Raskob and Smith, under those circumstances, caused many of the latter's longtime supporters to wonder how he could stomach the man. Raskob had been associated more or less clandestinely with the William Crapo Durant stock-speculating consortium, Durant being the man from whom he and Du Pont had taken over General Motors. In the spring of 1929, Durant, with a $4 billion pool invested in Wall Street by himself and his associates, had gone to the White House and warned that the stock market was waterlogged, that most speculators were operating on credit, and that if the Federal Reserve Board did not reverse its tight-money policies, the balloon would come down with a crash. When Hoover and the Federal Reserve failed to act on his warning, Durant quietly went about liquidating his holdings in the market. This had to be done surreptitiously, or it might bring about a panic. While he was selling the euphoric spirit of the bull market had to be maintained. "To promote a job of large-scale public relations," Wall Street historian Dana L. Thomas has written, "the Durant group turned to John Jacob Raskob. . . . As the Durant group began quietly to get from under, Raskob went around the country making speeches urging Americans to get deeper and deeper into the market, tossing optimistic prognostications about the future of stocks as casually as a bridesmaid tossing out nosegays." Raskob himself, of course, was one of those who escaped the debacle.

Many of Smith's friends wondered how he could hope to resume his political career with the much-hated Raskob as his chief promoter and closest friend. But at the time, during 1930, Smith still affirmed he was through with politics. The Empire State had reached its full height of 102 stories, and Smith was working a full day at trying to round up tenants for its thousands of offices. It would be years, in fact, before the skyscraper started to pay off. He was preoccupied with business affairs even as the political tide started turning against the Republicans. The fall elections of 1930 placed a Democratic majority in the House of Representatives and installed many Democratic governors in the statehouses. When it was suggested that he should begin thinking about the 1932 national election, Smith would laugh and say, "What do you think I am? Another William Jennings Bryan?"

With Hoover in disgrace and the Republican claims to having invented prosperity now a bad joke, the Democratic nomination in 1932 obviously would be worth a great deal more than in 1928. But Smith refused to commit himself on the subject of making another run for the Presidency, indicating only that he wasn't interested at the moment. Battle lines, however, were being drawn behind the scenes. Governor Franklin D. Roosevelt was working through Jim Farley and Louis Howe to sew up the nomination for himself. And it was discernible to the naked eye that a split was developing in the party itself, that it was dividing into liberal (Roosevelt) and conservative (Smith-Raskob) camps.

There was also a visible difference of opinion on how to tackle the Prohibition issue. Smith wanted it brought out in the open and disposed of; it had already muddied the more vital issues of two Presidential campaigns, as he saw it. When the Democratic National Committee met in March, 1931, Raskob and his chief collaborator, Jouett Shouse—a new power in the conservative wing of the party—urged that the repeal of the Eighteenth Amendment forthrightly be made part of Democratic policy. They found out, however, that Roosevelt and Farley had ganged up on them, entered into an alliance with Southern members of the national committee—the price for which, as Roosevelt learned in 1938, was handing over control of national legislation to the Southern bloc in the Senate—and had the committee votes to defeat the Raskob proposal.

A tactical victory for Roosevelt, it enabled him to avoid taking a stand on Prohibition and provided him with the Southern support which Smith was never able to secure. The Southerners, as one of their number, Cordell Hull of Tennessee, put it, had decided to back FDR as "the most effective way of killing off Smith." If Prohibition was Smith's bugaboo, Smith was the Southern Democrats'.

A period of guerrilla war, of underground maneuvering and prowling among delegates to the national convention, now began between the Smith and Roosevelt forces. Smith and his old friend "Frank" were out of touch. The governor did not ask the ex-governor to come up to Albany and advise him on state governmental problems. Smith found no reason to go up to Albany, though he had spent much of his adult life in the state capital. If it was also a war of nerves, it was more wracking to the Rooseveltians, because they were all but officially committed to the contest for the Presidential nomination while Smith stayed on the sidelines and kept his own counsel.

17

Hearst's Revenge

As the 1932 campaign began shaping up, there was the usual large field of Democratic contenders eager to unseat the candidate presumptive of the Republicans—Hoover again—including Roosevelt, Governor Ritchie of Maryland, Newton D. Baker of Cleveland, who had been Wilson's Secretary of War, John N. Garner of Texas, and Alfalfa Bill Murray, the picturesque governor of Oklahoma. And possibly Smith. The latter still had not come out openly against Roosevelt, though he was given the opportunity by various emissaries from the Roosevelt camp. One of the first to sound him out on Roosevelt's behalf was Clark Howell, the publisher of the Atlanta *Constitution*, who reported back on the conversation to Roosevelt, who was under treatment at Warm Springs.

"Socially," Smith was quoted by Howell, "we are friends. He has always been kind to me and my family, and has gone out of his way to be agreeable to us." He might also have pointed out that he had supported Roosevelt's renomination for governor in 1930, but he angrily added, "Do you know, by God, that he has never consulted me about a damn thing since he has been governor? He has taken bad advice and from sources not friendly to me."

Howell advised Roosevelt to talk to Smith himself, and by "handling him diplomatically," the publisher was certain that "he will come around all right." It was good advice, but Roosevelt always preferred to work by indirection, to avoid such uncomfortable confrontations as would be involved in asking Smith to step aside.

While Roosevelt's advisers were urging him to head off a break, Smith's were bringing in reports of a stop-Smith campaign being conducted by the Roosevelt forces in the South and West. The Roosevelt men whispered to the fence-sitters that Smith and Raskob were the prime movers in a Wall Street conspiracy to kill off Roosevelt's chances.

A reply was made to those whispered innuendos at the Jefferson Day banquet in mid-April, 1932, also to such speeches as Roosevelt was making as that at Oglethorpe University in Georgia when he declared that "we cannot allow our economic life to be controlled by that small group of men whose chief outlook upon the social welfare is tinctured by the fact that they can make huge profits from the lending of money and the marketing of securities."

Raskob controlled preparations for the celebration, and the party leaders on the dais included Smith, Garner, Baker, Robinson, Harry Byrd of Virginia, and the nominees of 1920 and 1924, James M. Cox and John W. Davis—but not Governor Roosevelt.

Smith got up and delivered a hard-hitting speech which could not be viewed by the Roosevelt forces as much of a comfort to their man. By inference, he attacked Roosevelt as a demagogue willing to stir up a dangerous current of class prejudice and hatred to further his own ambitions.

"The country is sick and tired of listening to political campaign orators who tell us what is the matter with us," Smith, red-faced, his voice harsh with anger, his fist pounding the lectern, told the banqueters. "Few, if any, of them know what the cure is. We are told that we must restore the purchasing power of the farmer. Fine! Of course we must. But *how* are we going to do it? We are told that public works is a stopgap. Whoever said it was anything else? It is at least better than nothing and infinitely better than a continuance of the disguised dole. . . ."

He then sounded more like Hoover's defender than a comrade-in-arms of his fellow Democrat, Governor Roosevelt, and there was a stirring of surprise in his audience.

"Oratory," he continued, "puts nobody to work. . . .

"At a time like this, when millions of men and women and children are starving throughout the land, there is always the temptation to stir up class prejudice, to stir up the bitterness of the rich against the poor, and of the poor against the rich. . . . I protest against the endeavor to delude the poor people of their country to their ruin by trying to make them believe that they can get employment before the people who would ordinarily employ them are also restored to conditions of normal prosperity.

"I announce tonight an exception to the statement," he roared, that he would "not be for or against any candidate," that he would stay neutral during the preconvention campaigning. "I will take off my coat and fight to the end against any candidate who persists in any demagogic appeal to the masses of the working people of this country to destroy themselves by setting class against class and rich against poor!"

Read in cold type, it would appear that Smith's Jefferson Day speech was not only a defiant brief for the Bourbons, for what FDR later called the "economic royalists," but a plain statement of opposition to Roosevelt. It could hardly be interpreted in any other way, and when Smith had finished the speech, the men on the dais, most of them, applauded heartily, but the assembled rankers gave him a scant five seconds of applause, according to the New York *Times* reporter who covered the event.

Certainly the Jefferson Day speech should have discouraged Roosevelt's men from entertaining any hopes that Smith would support FDR's candidacy even if he didn't enter the lists himself. Two of Roosevelt's top brass, Jim Farley and Ed Flynn, both formerly fervent Smith men, made the trek to the upper reaches of the Empire State Building to take soundings on Smith's attitude.

As Flynn recalled his conversation with Smith, the latter "gave it to me in a very forceful way. He told me that he was completely through with politics and that no one could induce him to enter the political arena again. He opened a drawer in his desk, pulled and spread before him a number of papers, and said, 'Ed, these are all debts that I must clear up. Financially I am in an extremely bad position.'

"Then he told me that various members of his family had been in the stock market without his knowledge, had suffered great losses, and were heavily in debt. This situation had been brought about by John Reardon [sic], who was president of the County Trust Company at that time and had been a good friend of Smith's. When the crash occurred, Reardon [sic] had committed suicide, and it was only with Reardon's [sic] death that Smith learned of his family's involvement. Smith felt that in honor he must assume the obligations his relatives had incurred, and he assured me that it would probably take him the rest of his life to clear up these family burdens."

Lieutenant Governor Lehman was told the same thing, according to Flynn, who added, "I certainly believe that Smith spoke the truth both to Lehman and me. No doubt many considerations entered into his subsequent change of plans. It began to be clearer and clearer that the candidate of the Democratic ticket would stand an excellent chance of being elected. Smith's immediate friends began to bring great pressure on him. If he yielded, it was due to a human weakness."

With Jim Farley, Smith was more evasive. He received Roosevelt's right-hand man with "extreme cordiality," Farley recalled, but wouldn't come out and say whether he was in or out of the race. But later Smith told Congresswoman Mary T. Norton of New Jersey, "Farley betrayed me. Wait and see him betray Roosevelt." (Farley finally split with Roosevelt in 1940 over the third-term issue.)

Meanwhile, during the months preceding the nominating convention, Smith was under intense pressure from Raskob, Shouse, and other conservative Democrats, who believed that Smith was the only barrier between the country and a dangerous liberalism. Their feelings of alarm were increased by Roosevelt's celebrated "forgotten man" speech, a symbol he borrowed from the works of William Graham Sumner, a Yale professor and extremely conservative pioneer sociologist. In Sumner's writings, the forgotten man was just the opposite of the meaning Roosevelt attached; he was one who "just when he wants to enjoy the fruits of his care, is told that it is his duty to go and take care of some of his negligent neighbors . . . it is all wrong to preach to the Forgotten Man that it is his duty to go and remedy other people's neglect. . . . It is a harsh and unjust burden which is laid upon him. . . ." Thus Roosevelt, or rather his speech writers, had completely twisted around Sumner's meaning. But that wasn't what aroused Smith and his friends; it was the demagogic slant of Roosevelt's jeremiad, his advocacy of the sort of makeshift remedies which Smith as governor had snorted at and rejected as "fur coats for elephants."

Smith was also embittered—and no doubt these feelings were worked on, Iago-like, by Raskob—by the sort of deals the Roosevelt camp was making in order to grab the nomination. The Roosevelt men had struck a bargain with Jimmy Hines, the West Side boss, and were trying to make inroads into Tammany Hall, which Smith regarded as his fiefdom. They had also come to terms with James M. Curley, the Boston party leader whose appeals to Irish separatism were abominated by Smith, largely because the Massachusetts leader Senator David I. Walsh was a Smith man. While decrying FDR's fraternal embrace of Hines and Curley, however, Smith himself was not fending off Boss Hague or the Jersey City machine. He was especially outraged by the way Roosevelt attracted to his standard certain Southern party leaders (among them Dan Roper of South

Carolina, who was to be rewarded with a Cabinet post), many of whom had "sat out" the 1928 campaign.

Undoubtedly Roosevelt, having started building the ground-work of his campaign almost the moment he was inaugurated as governor of New York, had a sizable head start. FDR was the front-runner, and Smith was the last best hope of an informal stop-Roosevelt movement. Among those intent on stopping Roosevelt was William Randolph Hearst, whose journalistic organs were joining in a thunderous paean of praise for Garner of Texas, but Hearst, of course, couldn't bear the thought of the nomination's going to Smith again. The rival Scripps-Howard chain, however, came out strongly for Smith in a front-page editorial: "As Roosevelt generalizes, Smith is specific. As Roosevelt loves delay, Smith loves action. Irresolution is ingrained in one, boldness in the other. . . . In Franklin Roosevelt, we have another Hoover."

Two weeks after Roosevelt formally made known his candidacy, Smith called a press conference at his Empire State offices and passed around his own announcement:

"So many inquiries have come to me from friends throughout the country who worked for and believed in me, as to my attitude in the present political situation, that I feel that I owe it to my friends and to the millions of men and women who supported me so loyally in 1928 to make my position clear.

"If the Democratic National Convention, after careful consideration, should decide it wants me to lead I will make the fight; but I will not make a pre-convention campaign to secure the support of delegates.

"By action of the Democratic Convention of 1928 I am leader of my party in the nation. With a full sense of the responsibility thereby imposed I shall not in advance of the convention either support or oppose the candidacy of any aspirant for the nomination."

With that announcement, the "feud" between Smith and Roosevelt the newspapers were talking about was solidified. Roosevelt and his supporters believed that Smith had had his chance and couldn't prevail against the prejudices too many voters held and that the party needed a candidate who could gain wide support, particularly among Republicans and independents. Smith and his friends just as firmly contended that Smith was not only the titular but actual leader of the Democratic Party—and besides, almost anyone could beat Hoover. They felt that Smith deserved another chance, had worked for it and earned it through the years Roosevelt was playing the country squire.

Smith knew it would be an uphill battle, that he would have to offset the whispered charges from the Roosevelt and other camps that he had become the captive of Wall Street interests, that he was playing Trilby to Raskob's Svengali.

Thomas Cochran, an old friend who had become a partner in J. P. Morgan & Company, went up to the Empire State offices to offer whatever help he could, saying, "It is probable that I am the only member of the firm of J. P. Morgan who voted for you in 1928. But they are all for you now, and what I'd like to know is what we can do to help."

"Tom," replied Smith, holding up his hand in pretended alarm, "just don't tell anyone."

His daughter Emily said later that Smith "did not expect to win the nomination for himself" but was determined to be a strong, if not decisive, influence on the choice.

But the attitude he showed others, as the convention assembled in Chicago on June 27, indicated he may have nursed hopes that the nomination would fall his way. Roosevelt was far out in front, but he did not have enough delegates pledged or instructed to him to win the nomination on the first ballot. It would take 770 to nominate under the two-thirds rule, and according to the New York *Times,* the votes each candidate could count on included:

Roosevelt	485
Smith	94
Garner	90

There were lesser pledges of support for Reed, Murray, Ritchie and several other contenders. Obviously it would be a wide-open fight, with the eventual distribution of Garner's supporters a crucial factor. And Garner meant Hearst, who had cemented an alliance between California and Texas that guaranteed Garner his solid bloc of 90 votes.

Unchallenged though he was in later conventions, Roosevelt in 1932 was something of an unknown quantity. Walter Lippmann expressed much of the current skepticism about FDR when he wrote that the primaries had shown he was not "the idol of the masses, opposed only by international bankers, the power trust, and Mr. Raskob," that the urban working classes had suspected "something hollow in him, something synthetic, something pretended and calculated." H. L. Mencken was also skeptical of Roosevelt's posture as the shield and buckler of the forgotten man and was certain only that whatever the outcome of the convention "the row will end with sore heads on both sides . . . the fight will be carried on in a berserker and suicidal fashion.

"No one," Mencken explained, "really likes Roosevelt, not even his own ostensible friends, and no one quite trusts him. He is a pleasant enough fellow, but he has no more visible conscience than his eminent kinsman, Theodore Dentatus. His chief support at this moment does not lie among people of his own place and kind, but among the half-witted yokels of the cow and cotton States, and these hinds prefer him, not because they have any real confidence in him, but simply because they believe he can split New York, and so beat Al Smith and the Pope."

Mr. Mencken despaired of the Republic in whose future he had never demonstrated any conspicuous faith, because the Republicans renominated Hoover and the Democrats were "committed irretrievably to fraud and imbecility."

The in-fighting between Smith and Roosevelt began well before the convention was called to order. The Smith camp had hoped that Jouett Shouse would be installed as permanent chairman of the convention, but the Roosevelt forces jammed through their own favorite, Senator Thomas J. Walsh of Montana. At the sessions of the Platform Committee, of which he was a member, Smith demanded that a plank favoring outright repeal of the Eighteenth Amendment be adopted. His plea for candor on the issue was successful. His forces were also successful in defeating a move by the Roosevelt troops to have the two-thirds rule amended and a simple majority required to nominate.

Smith was unmovable when Roosevelt's men made last-minute attempts to arrange a compromise. One ambassador of goodwill sent up to the hotel suite which served as his headquarters was Ed Flynn, who later termed it an "extremely painful interview." Smith apparently considered him a traitor, as one of Boss Murphy's old boys, for having lined up with the often anti-Tammany Roosevelt.

"Ed," Smith angrily told him, "you are not representing the people of Bronx County in your support of Roosevelt. You know the people of Bronx County want you to support me."

Flynn replied that was probably true, but that he'd decided to back Roosevelt at a time when Smith was saying he wouldn't return to politics. They parted on unfriendly terms.

Claude Bowers, who was attending the convention both as a delegate and a newspaper correspondent and who would be appointed Roosevelt's Ambassador to Spain, also called on the Smith headquarters and found its centerpiece in a more amiable mood, "cordial, jovial and without the slightest indication of nervous strain"—it was only Roosevelt men, evidently, who made him nervous. One of his followers, Bowers later related, suggested that Smith appear before the entire New York delegation and demand its unqualified support. "Oh, no," Smith replied. "I wouldn't do that. I never would do that. Every man is entitled to his opinion."

At a caucus of the New York delegation that night, Smith was greeted by an ovation, while Lieutenant Governor Lehman, as a Rooseveltian, was booed. Mayor Walker, already under investigation by Governor Roosevelt, was given the loudest cheers of all.

Roosevelt's name was placed in nomination, and the organ blared out "Happy Days Are Here Again," which then became the Roosevelt anthem. Smith arrived at the convention hall just as Roosevelt's nomination was being seconded. He was walking briskly along a runway leading to the floor when he heard Roosevelt's name mentioned from the platform; his face darkened; then he turned on his heel and said to a newspaper-man accompanying him, "I can go back to the hotel and listen to that over the radio."

Thus Smith, just when his presence might have helped stem the Roosevelt tide, elected instead to sit out most of the convention in his hotel suite. He listened over the radio as his name was placed in nomination by Governor Joseph B. Ely of Massachusetts. Ely eloquently pleaded that the "prejudices of our Protestant ancestors" had been eliminated by the honorable records compiled by many Catholic officeholders. "The small voice of the inarticulate souls of millions of Americans," he declared, "begged for the leadership of one of their own."

The demonstration that followed Ely's speech was the longest and most enthusiastic of the convention, augmented by the galleries which had been packed with Smith supporters by Raskob and Shouse. Yet there was a chill of defeat around Smith headquarters. He would not or could not come out fighting with everything he had. For days it had been rumored that Smith would take the platform and destroy Roosevelt with one of his famous demolition efforts, but the former Happy Warrior stayed in his hotel suite. "The Al of today," Mencken thought, "is no longer a politician of the first chop. His association with the rich had apparently wobbled him and changed him." William Allen White, an anti-Smith man, believed that Smith was "afraid, for some queer reason, to put his wrath behind the punch."

Smith's sudden withdrawal from the hostilities, just at the

critical moment, has never been explained. He detested the idea of Roosevelt's winning the nomination, yet he did not come out swinging. It is still the one great mystery of his career.

On the first ballot both he and Roosevelt showed more strength than the preconvention forecasts indicated:

Roosevelt	666
Smith	201
Garner	90

The favorite sons were so far out of the running that it was obvious they would carry little weight in the final struggle. Garner and his 90 votes from Texas and California were the key, but it was William Randolph Hearst, pulling wires from his California retreat, who could turn the key. The Garner block, along with the fence-sitters who would rapidly join the scramble for the bandwagon, could give Roosevelt the nomination.

For thirteen years Hearst, with his elephantine memory for those who had, in his opinion, done him wrong, had been brooding over the comeuppance which Alfred E. Smith had administered to him. More than anyone else, Smith had killed off his political career, and besides that, Smith had black-guarded him so effectively from the platform of Carnegie Hall that his influence in New York never approached that of the pre-1920 years. The Chief had suffered grievously at Smith's hands, and as a rich, willful, egocentric man he was ill equipped to handle such sufferings with grace or philosophy, certainly not with forgiveness. He distrusted Roosevelt and his glib formulas for succoring the forgotten man, regarded him as unreliable; but he *hated* Smith, and he forgot that an honest enemy is often preferable to an uncertain ally.

Hearst, savoring his revenge in the leisurely fashion of the true gourmet, decided to keep the convention in suspense and would take phone calls from no one but his personal contacts.

That left Smith plenty of time to wonder whether he hadn't lost his only real chance for the Presidency by attacking Hearst so relentlessly on the issue of New York City milk prices.

Hearst held out for two more ballots, knowing that though he himself had never made the White House, he was now, finally, able to dictate the Democratic nominee. On the second and third ballots the positions of the three contenders were relatively unchanged. On the second, it was Roosevelt 677, Smith 194, Garner 90. On the third, Roosevelt 682, Smith 190, Garner 101—a barely perceptible movement. The convention adjourned at dawn. Deals would have to be made that day, before the delegates reconvened that evening. Some of Roosevelt's support, particularly in the Deep South delegations, was beginning to slip.

Farley, as leader of the Roosevelt forces, was close to desperation. "We did little more than hold our own on that [third] ballot," he wrote in his memoirs. "Our situation was desperate. There were indications that we could not hold our delegates through the fourth ballot. . . . The crisis was at hand."

With tears in his eyes, he appeared before the California delegation and pleaded, "Boys, Roosevelt is lost unless California comes over to us on the next ballot."

All that day Farley and the other Roosevelt men dickered with Hearst through various third parties. Smith made one effort in that direction, though he could not bring himself to attempt any negotiations with Hearst himself. He asked Judge Proskauer to call Garner in Washington and sound him out on swinging over the Texas delegation; Garner refused to take the call. Probably, by that time, he knew it was all sewed up for him and for Roosevelt.

With his considerable histrionic instinct, Hearst waited until the last possible moment before calling his personal representative in Chicago, Colonel Joseph Willicombe, and commanding a redeployment. Willicombe in turn called Hearst's Washington representative, George Rothwell Brown, and

passed along the message to Garner: "Mr. Hearst is fearful that
when Roosevelt's strength crumbles it will bring about either
the election of Smith or Baker. Either would be disastrous. Tell
Garner that the Chief believes nothing can now save the country but for him to throw his delegates to Governor Roosevelt."
First, however, Hearst insisted that Roosevelt must pay the
price for his support. Garner would receive the Vice Presidential nomination. FDR would promise not to meddle in European affairs and not to adopt an internationalist stance in
any way reminiscent of Woodrow Wilson, whom Hearst detested and whom Roosevelt adored. It did not take Roosevelt
long to forswear his old fealty, at least for the moment. The
deal was made.

Smith was seated in the gallery that evening when the convention reassembled, still weary from the previous all-night
session.

It did not take him long to learn the fate of his last throw of
the dice.

California, coming up early in the balloting, showed what
had happened over the long-distance wires that busy afternoon.

William G. McAdoo, leader of the California delegation
and a man with his own unhappy memories of Alfred E. Smith,
spoke the fateful words into a microphone:

"California casts forty-four votes for Franklin D. Roosevelt."

The galleries, largely sympathetic to Smith, booed lustily
in counterpoint to the roar of outrage from Smith's bloc—New
York, Massachusetts, and Connecticut. (Claude Bowers believed it "was a mistake, in view of the Smith-McAdoo feud,
since it gave to the action the appearance of a prearranged revenge." But it was Hearst's, not McAdoo's, thirst for vengeance that was satisfied. "In Spain two years later he [McAdoo]
was my guest . . . he told me that he had realized the danger
of having him make the announcement and that he had urged
the choice of someone else, but without effect.")

That vote, coupled with Texas', started the landslide.

An effort was made to halt it when John F. Curry, as leader

of the New York delegation, demanded time to poll his followers. He wanted all the boys on record as having supported
Smith to the bitter end. Jimmy Walker was missing and had to
be hauled out of bed by Dudley Field Malone, who rushed him
to the convention hall in a taxi. It was Walker's moment of
truth. A man with a supreme sense of discretion, about to be
tried before Governor Roosevelt on charges that he was unfit
to be mayor, would have cast his vote for Roosevelt. With his
insouciant courage, with that chipper defiance which New
Yorkers like to think is typical of their breed, Walker blithely
announced, "I vote for Alfred E. Smith." His comrades
cheered, and up in the gallery Smith grinned and said, "Good
old Jim. Blood is thicker than water." Smith's boys would go
down fighting to the bitter end—the last great consolation of
their hero's political career.

State after state switched their votes to Roosevelt, all but
Smith's diehards. The final vote was Roosevelt 945, Smith 190,
12 for several other candidates.

The Smith supporters rebuffed all pleas that the nomination
be made unanimous; the delegations from Massachusetts,
Connecticut, and New York sat stony-faced in their seats as the
organ pealed out "Happy Days" and Roosevelt men danced
in the aisles. Later in the evening Smith's embittered followers
tore down Roosevelt posters in the various Loop hotels and
ripped them to shreds.

James W. Gerard, treasurer of the national committee, was
indignant over the refusal of the Smith bloc to join in the
hosannas. Down on the convention floor he looked up Mrs.
Charles Dana Gibson and hurriedly told her, "You're a great
friend of Smith's. You go up there," he pointed up to the gallery
where Smith was sitting with his arms folded, his face mask-
like and chalky with the disappointment he was trying to conceal, "and tell him he has to come down here to the floor and
move to make the nomination unanimous."

Mrs. Gibson agreed to act as Gerard's messenger but returned a few minutes later to report Smith's adamant reply:

"I won't do it . . . I won't do it . . . I won't do it . . . I won't do it."

The other traditional leaders of the party—Cox, Davis, Baker, Jim Reed—were equally dismayed and enraged by the upstart's victory. None could be coaxed to the microphones to say a good word for the nominee, until finally Reed agreed to speak. When he did, it was to remind the party it must "get back to the old principles and old methods"; he spoke lovingly of Washington, Jefferson, and the economic philosophy of John Stuart Mill. But it was too late. The new dispensation, the four terms of Franklin D. Roosevelt, had arrived.

It was announced that Roosevelt was flying to Chicago to address the convention. By the time his plane landed an aura of triumph was already beginning to form around him. Millions would hear his confident message to the convention over the national radio hookups.

By that time Smith and his party were speeding East. He caught the first train available after Roosevelt was nominated. At some point in those two journeys, Roosevelt in a plane overhead, flushed with victory, Smith on his train, sunk in defeat, must have crossed paths—and that was about as far apart as they would stand in the coming years. In politics, sportsmanship is the luxury of the winner.

18

The Leader in Exile

IN the ensuing weeks it appeared to Roosevelt and his campaigners that Smith was indulging himself in a monumental Achillean sulk. It was important to them that Smith, in the sacred name of party unity, agree to announce his public support of Roosevelt, even if he would not actively campaign in that cause. He represented a large segment of the party, after all, particularly in the East; with his urban following he was strong where Roosevelt was weakest.

Even while the Smith train was rolling eastward from the convention, an effort to seal the breach was made. On Mrs. Roosevelt's instructions, Judge Bernard Shientag boarded the train when it reached the New York Central division point at Harmon, New York, and made overtures on Governor Roosevelt's behalf. Smith listened, but remained noncommittal. All the way homeward he let off steam to Judge Proskauer and other intimates, not merely over his defeat, but the way Roosevelt had arranged it through the Hearst-Garner-McAdoo alliance.

A further outlet for his feelings was a dinner given him by his convention staff on July 20, the menu for which saluted him as "the man with a record who had a program, the moral victor of the battle of Chicago" and was headed by a quotation attributed to Shakespeare, "Politics is a thieves' game. Those who stay in it long enough are invariably robbed." The menu included:

"Celery Farley," "Branchless Olive Roosevelt," "Nuts McAdoo," "Roast Boned Michigan Boulevard Squab (one in every pot)," "Salade de Saison Politique," "Coupe Empire State with Mortgage," "Tea Bishop Cannon."

Judge Proskauer, the Moskowitzes, and other veteran supporters were present, and reported that Smith had never been in better form, taking over the entertainment program, singing, dancing, and telling funny stories.

He could joke about it, but he was still sore about his defeat at the national convention. No doubt his attitude was accurately reflected by his wife. The Smiths appeared at a party fund-raising dinner, and James W. Gerard heard Mrs. Smith say, quite loudly: "Who is Frank Roosevelt to be running for President of the United States?"

Eddie Dowling, too, noted that Smith was still nursing a grudge over the events in Chicago. Dowling had become a Roosevelt enthusiast, which was bad enough. What caused a complete break in his friendship with Smith was the fact that just after Roosevelt was nominated, while Smith glowered down at the platform from his seat in the gallery, Dowling had grabbed the microphone and sang a parody of "Three Blind Mice," in which he poked fun at Raskob, Smith, and Shouse.

Deliberately, Smith let Roosevelt and his supporters stew until the Democratic State Convention assembled to pick a nominee for governor. The question was whether he would side with Roosevelt and favor Lieutenant Governor Herbert H. Lehman as Roosevelt's successor—which would be interpreted as a favorable sign by FDR—or whether he would join John F. Curry, the Tammany leader, in his opposition to Lehman. Smith thus was caught up in conflicting loyalties. Lehman was an old friend, he had tried to stay fairly neutral between Smith and Roosevelt, and in 1928 he had contributed $500,000 to the Presidential campaign fund. All this outside the fact that Lehman was an able man and would make a good governor. Smith also owed a debt of political loyalty to Tammany and Curry, the latter having held the New York delegation firmly in line for Smith in Chicago.

Behind closed doors, just before the convention opened, Smith slugged it out with Curry, having decided to back Lehman all the way.

If the Democrats did not nominate Lehman, Smith told Curry, he would run for mayor of New York City the following year and snatch control of Tammany Hall away from Curry.

"On what ticket?" Curry demanded.

"On a Chinese laundry ticket," Smith retorted, "I can beat you and your crowd."

Curry was forced to yield.

As Claude Bowers described the scene in the convention hall that evening, Smith was given an ovation when he marched up to the platform. Roosevelt was also seated there. This would be their first meeting in years. The noisy hall quieted down as the delegates held their breath over what would happen next. "With a debonair smile and manner, Smith shook hands with everyone in the front row as he approached the center. Roosevelt, in the meanwhile, had risen. Finally reaching his successful rival, Smith thrust out his hand cordially, and he was reported to have greeted him familiarly with 'Hello, old potato,' though this was afterward denied. The scene was dramatic, and the convention roared approval. For the benefit of the photographers Smith, whatever his inner thoughts and feelings, held onto Roosevelt's hand, beaming. . . ." Democracy was saved!

No other course was possible, not for a man who had been a Democrat since before he was old enough to vote. He would take the stump for Roosevelt and the Democracy, whether his heart was in it or not.

First, however, his attention was riveted on the spectacle of Jimmy Walker on trial before Governor Roosevelt. Those hearings must have been viewed with mixed feelings by Smith. Until Walker had attained the mayor's office, Smith had been a sort of surrogate father, and frequently a Dutch uncle, to the younger man. He had warned him against becoming a playboy, but Walker had ignored his advice. Now that Walker was in real trouble, Smith may have sympathized with him personally, but he himself had always been strictly honest, and the testimony against Walker could not be shrugged off. There were charges that Walker had profited from transportation franchise deals, that he had shared a safety-deposit box with a missing and mysterious "financial adviser," and an earlier preliminary investigation conducted by Samuel Seabury had concluded that Walker was guilty of malfeasance, misfeasance, and nonfeasance in office.

After twelve uncomfortable sessions under the magisterial eye of Governor Roosevelt, Walker lost much of his witty charm; his only defense was that the answers to Roosevelt's questions would have to be answered by the missing Russell T. Sherwood. Roosevelt took the case under advisement and pondered for weeks what to do about Beau James. With great relief, no doubt, he was taken off the hook by Tammany Hall.

The Tammany leaders were convinced that Roosevelt would "throw the book" at Walker. The evidence against the mayor was pretty strong, and if Roosevelt let him off, the Republicans would scream that a deal had been made for Tammany's election support.

Smith, Curry, Max D. Steuer, Boss McCooey, and other Tammany chieftains conducted a star chamber session of their own, with Mayor Walker present. The question: Should Walker resign and spare the party a possible disgrace, or should he wait until Roosevelt announced his decision?

At a meeting in the Hotel Plaza, Walker later told his biographer Gene Fowler, Smith finally cast himself in the role of Father Abraham.

"Jim," Smith told him, "you're through. You must resign for the good of the party."

The only one of his Tammany comrades who stood by him, Walker said, was McCooey of Brooklyn, who said that "he'd rather meet defeat with me than win without me."

Late that evening Walker announced his resignation. A few days later he sailed for Europe to join Betty Compton in Paris, and that was the end of a career which Smith had sponsored, nurtured, and finally terminated.

Smith struck out on the campaign trail independently, without consultation with Roosevelt, his advisers, or the national committee. His appearances in the big Eastern cities drew large crowds, and he hammered effectively at the failures of the Hoover administration. Hoover had not managed to make either his public works or his relief programs work because his administration and the Republicans were not pulling together. "In the picture of the twenty-mule team pulling the borax wagon," he pointed out, "if all the mules do not pull the wagon does not move. And in the Republican administration, nineteen of the mules are lying on the ground asleep and the twentieth is giving a halfhearted pull." Even more wholeheartedly he campaigned for Lehman's try at the governorship.

As the election approached, the betting odds, offered by professional gamblers, which had been five to one in favor of Hoover, began tipping toward Roosevelt. It was testimony not only to Roosevelt's popular appeal and the widespread disillusion with the incumbent, but of the Democratic Party's quadrennial ability to pass a miracle. The Democrats fight among themselves up to the last roll call of the nominating convention, until it appears that they have opened so many old wounds they can't possibly survive; then all turn to the joyous task of falling upon the Republicans. It appeared to H. L. Mencken, too, that Hoover's dullness as a speaker, his inability to popularize an issue were as self-defeating as Democratic unity was self-propelling. "He is the sort of man who, if he had to recite the Twenty-third Psalm, would make it sound like a search warrant issued under the Volstead Act." Then, too, Mencken believed that Hoover had been oversold to the people in 1928. His sponsors had "advertised him as a master mind, and he himself let it be known that he was loaded for any kind of economic bear that might come down from the woods." Instead, he had turned out to be a "shifty and shabby politician, his back to the wall."

The Hoover landslide of 1928 was reversed in 1932, Roosevelt winning a popular vote of 22,800,000 to Hoover's 15,700,000, and the Republicans losing all but six states.

Smith went up to Albany for Lehman's inauguration as governor on January 1, 1933, and intended to stay in the capital for several days to visit with old friends. He was called back to New York by a telegram telling of Belle Moskowitz's death, which caused him to weep openly. Mrs. Moskowitz had been seriously injured in a fall down the front steps of her home on the Upper West Side but appeared to be recovering. Then suddenly complications set in, and she died.

No one, not even Smith himself, had worked harder for his success than Mrs. Moskowitz; no one, not even his wife or mother, had believed in him more or labored harder to make a rather easygoing man live up to his potential.

"She had the greatest brain of anybody I ever knew," he told newspapermen who met his train at Grand Central.

As the new administration took power in Washington and Roosevelt gathered his brain trust and the nation began to lift its head at the promise of a New Deal, Smith, according to his family and friends, began to hope that he might be summoned back to public office. Eagerly, then wistfully, he waited for word that his experience, his political and administrative aptitudes were required in Washington to help cope with the greatest domestic crisis in American history. It was the season of breadlines, the bank holiday, the worst unemployment the nation had ever known. These were matters with which Smith had coped, perhaps in lesser forms, and certainly no one except Roosevelt had a larger share of the public's confidence. He was still waiting and hoping as late as May, 1933, by which time the biggest jobs at Roosevelt's disposal were already filled.

He believed that America's situation was as desperate as if the country were at war with a foreign enemy and that it must beware of drastic remedies which might prove worse than the economic disease from which it was suffering.

"And what does a democracy do in war?" he rhetorically asked in a newspaper interview. "It becomes a tyrant, a despot, a real monarch. In the World War we took our Constitution, wrapped it up and laid it on the shelf and left it there until it was over."

Perhaps it was to help guard against such "despotism" that he wanted to play a role in confronting the national emergency. Yet he waited in vain for any word from Washington. The capital was in a frenzy of experimental planning, of vast dreaming and table turning, of agency forming and bureaucratic empire building; high places were found for college professors, social reformers, not a few crackpots, Southerners who had dragged their feet during the national election campaign, even a number of Republicans—but there was no room at the inn for Alfred E. Smith.

"The administration should call upon the ablest, the soundest, and the most experienced men we have. But that is not being done," he remarked in the spring of 1933. "I know that at times there seems to be a dearth of ability in one party or the other, but that's not the situation now. The Democratic party has many men of exceptional ability, but judging from Roosevelt's appointments so far he isn't going to use any of them."

This was the greatest country in the world, he said, as he viewed with mounting distrust the series of panaceas applied by the Roosevelt administration in its search for a cure-all. "Our energy, our ingenuity, and our natural resources would seem to make almost anything possible. But Franklin Roosevelt and these 'brain trusters' of his are giving the people the idea that the government *owes* them something, and that is wrong. No government can support its people. *They* must support the government.

"Not even this country of ours can foot the bill if everybody who wants a dole is given one. But that is what Roosevelt and his New Deal brain trusters seemed to be heading for; and unless they are stopped, you and I may never live to see the time when this country will get back to the fundamental principles it was founded on."

That statement might well have served the conservatives of 1969 as it did in 1933, those who, like Smith, thought the New Deal was a cover word for Socialism. He was quicker than most to see that the pump priming of the Roosevelt administration's various agencies—some of which bloomed and died as quickly as those of the Johnson administration's antipoverty program between 1965 and 1968—would be an endless process. It was halted, as the truism goes, only when the war in Europe began in 1939 and industry and agriculture were revived by orders from the belligerent nations abroad.

By the summer of 1933 he realized that Roosevelt would never send for him, that his public life was ended. There was a flurry of speculation that summer that Tammany's sachems might persuade him to run for mayor as their only hope of defeating the Fusion candidate, Fiorello H. LaGuardia, who commented, "It looks as though I have frightened them. They know I can beat anybody but Smith." Smith, in any case, refused to run. He had too much pride to descend the ladder merely to ease the qualms of the boys on Fourteenth Street. So he was left to his brooding over the loss of power and position. Possibly he recalled a quotation from his old idol, Bourke Cochran, which he had memorized as a youth: "Is the politician happy? Far from it. When the scepter of power finally drops from his nerveless fingers, he is condemned to an isolation the more unbearable because of the adulation to which he has become accustomed."

Roosevelt hetmen always maintained that the Smith-Roosevelt feud was one-sided, that Smith's was the sorehead, the attitude of a bad loser. This view was expressed by Jim Farley before he himself broke with Roosevelt in more bitterness than ever existed between Smith and Roosevelt. Farley believed it was "a case of two extremely able and popular public men, each of whom cherished an understandable ambition to be President of the United States. . . . For some reason, known only to himself, Smith always had a tendency to underrate the ability of his successor. . . . Roosevelt's genuine confidence in the Happy Warrior was not returned, and they were never as close as the public imagined. In the salty language he used in private conversation, Al had been known to refer to F.D.R. as a visionary and to speak lightly in other ways regarding the latter's knowledge of public questions."

Why, then, with all that "genuine confidence" in Smith, didn't Roosevelt find a responsible post in his administration for him or at least make the offer of one? It may have been that with all the social and economic experimenting fostered by the New Deal, Roosevelt felt that Smith's conservatism simply wouldn't fit in, that he felt Smith wouldn't make a good team player after having his own way for so many years. Probably, too, he would not have been comfortable with Smith sitting in his Cabinet, their old roles reversed. Many of his chief aides— Hopkins, Ickes, Tugwell, General Hugh S. Johnson and the rest—were virtually unknown before FDR brought them to Washington. He couldn't afford to have Smith playing the prima donna in a cast already supplied with temperament.

Joe Proskauer believed it was the political and psychological differences between the two men that kept Smith out of the Roosevelt Cabinet. Smith, as Proskauer analyzed him, was "essentially a simple and uncomplicated being. He was direct in speech and action. He lacked completely those subtleties which made Roosevelt complex. He came to believe that those complexities and contradictions which Roosevelt's most loyal supporters found in him evidenced that instability which indeed did show itself at times in subsequent events. He was distrustful of Roosevelt's use of his great personal charm as a technique for solving the most vexatious problems. . . . Smith believed that this complete confidence of Roosevelt in his ability to win by this technique would lead to some tragic error." Proskauer cited the Yalta agreements as an instance of that kind of mistake. Smith was also distrustful, Proskauer said, of Roosevelt's "human frailties," of an ambition "excessive to a point of public peril," of his "impatience with legal restraint."

There could be no reconciliation between the two men, Proskauer believed, because their philosophies were so divergent it was difficult to comprehend how they could be members of the same party. Smith was "profoundly disturbed by the Roosevelt arrogation of power in the national government. He opposed wholeheartedly the centralization in the national government of the functions of relief. He believed that these were functions of the states and that the invasions of the rights and duties of the states in this respect would lead to a dangerous disturbance of individual liberty and of the American federal system. He was ardently for the underdog; but he believed that the underdog would be the worst sufferer from the impairment of the American tradition. He had no confidence in the theory that assault on those who have was the way to help those who do not have. . . ." It was Smith's opinion, finally, that Roosevelt was handicapped by a "lack of sober judgment, of painstaking investigation and a propensity to play hunches to a dangerous degree. . . ."

Robert Moses also believed that Smith and Roosevelt basically had little in common. He dismissed as "balderdash" the theory expressed by Frances Perkins before a meeting of the American Historical Society: "It dawned on her, she said, that by the use of psychology and psychiatry, hidden motives behind the acts of political figures are suddenly illuminated. Smith, she said, was rejected by the people in 1928, and therefore resented Roosevelt and became obsessed with the idea that Roosevelt didn't like him and invented reasons for returning the compliment."

The real underlying reason for the split, according to Moses, was that Smith and Roosevelt "were essentially very different people. Smith was an urban democrat with basic sympathy for the masses, but in economics he was a congenital conservative.

Roosevelt was a country-squire liberal. They really had little in common but membership in the same party. Smith thought about economies in many ways like a Southern conservative Democrat. So did Jam Farley. Roosevelt showed after 1932 that he wanted no part of Smith, and Smith no doubt was resentful, but the cleavage is not to be explained on theories of the head-shrinkers of the American Historical Society."

In almost every basic attitude they differed, Moses has noted. Regarding religion, Roosevelt was an "easygoing and traditional Episcopalian, while "Smith's religion was an enormous and decisive influence on his life and thought," which made him "a political evolutionist" and "a believer in discipline" and in the "slow, sure, laborious process of human improvement."

Smith, Moses added, "did not understand Roosevelt's mental processes and was therefore suspicious of them. It was a little like Gladstone observing Disraeli on the tightrope. He couldn't quite believe Ben Dizzy would reach the other side. Roosevelt was intuitive, Smith was logical. Smith had hunches but did not improvise. Smith was an organizer, Roosevelt an evangelist." To attempt an explanation of their estrangement on the basis of "personal enmity" was nonsense in Moses' opinion. "As I look back, it seems that if their respective friends, advisers and kitchen cabinets had been a little less fanatical, at least some of these differences might have been reconciled. . . ."

But it was a sad thing for Smith that he never received the summons from the White House because, as Oscar Handlin has remarked, his exclusion "crippled Smith as a politician. He had never been a theoretician, but had always formed his opinions through contact with concrete problems. Now condemned to be a bystander and a detached critic, he would ever after rest his judgments on the experience of an earlier, bygone era. His ideas would become rigid, unresponsive to new situations. . . ."

Personal problems, too, probably contributed to his abrupt turn from all forms of liberalism. He was involved in law suits over the County Trust Company affairs, the collection of Tim

Mara's $50,000 note, and a fight over the control of the Meehan Coal Company. Making a go of the Empire State was another constant concern. Hundreds of its offices were empty; it had been finished just about the time many businesses were collapsing, and its gorgeous pinnacle now seemed to New Yorkers a symbol of all the twenties' ruined hopes.

Many of his friends, Raskob and Kenny excepted, had gone broke during the early years of the Depression, and Smith could never keep his hands in his pockets when a friend was in trouble. For a generous man it wasn't easy being affluent during the Depression. Either he grew calluses on his conscience, or he was likely to be tapped out most of the time. Smith's lordly salary was subject to a constant leakage. Anyone who could get past his secretary, Mary Carr, was certain of making a touch.

He did find considerable consolation in his role as a grandfather, with a large supporting cast supplied by his sons, daughters, sons-in-law, and daughters-in-law. His children and their families all lived in the New York area, Emily (Warner) in Southampton, Catherine (Quillinan) in Rye, the others closer by. By the time of his seventieth birthday, the Smith clan, fully assembled, filled a large room. All his grandchildren were instructed to address their letters to Santa Claus in care of the Empire State Building, because that was where their Santa Claus was headquartered. When his son Walter's daughter, the six-year-old Catherine, was operated on for removal of her appendix, he sat by her bedside all night, and when he went back to his apartment, he wouldn't allow anyone to use a telephone until he heard from her doctor that she was coming along fine.

Much of his leisure was spent with the uptown friends he had made in the twenties—the old neighborhood around Oliver Street caught only an occasional glimpse of him flashing by in his chauffeured limousine—with cards or golf their alternating recreation. He had become a fanatic about golf. At cards the favorite was what was called the Alfred and Katie Smith Special Poker Game. The stakes were low, but the rules were wild. They played with a pack of sixty cards, some marked as elevens and twelves, eights and deuces wild, the whole thing an abomination to purists.

During that first year of the New Deal, he knew one moment of triumph when he was selected as one of the delegates to the state convention called to repeal the state's Prohibition law. In appointing him, Governor Lehman had pointed out that "if it were not for him, we would still face prohibition for years to come." On the day the convention opened, he marched up Capitol Hill in Albany with 10,000 persons cheering him along the way and another 4,000 gathered on the Capitol lawn. The night beer came back—legally and at potable strength—there was no happier tankard man in the country.

19

Carrying the Liberty League Banner

LATE in 1933 Smith began openly attacking the Roosevelt administration. For months he had watched the New Deal at work and now he had come to the conclusion that it was exhibiting a dangerous radicalism, that its remedies were ill considered, that it was interfering too much with the normal processes of business. He had become a captain in the forces of the backlash, soon to be organized and financed by Wall Street and big industry. His enemies, of course, accused him of having sold out to his wealthy friends, but his record as governor was a credible defense against that charge. He had always deeply distrusted radical changes of any kind.

In successive issues of *New Outlook,* of which he was a member of the editorial board, he harshly criticized the administration for taking the United States off the gold standard and creating what he termed "baloney dollars," and he wrote editorials under such self-explanatory titles as "Does the Star-Spangled Banner Still Wave?" "Where Are We Going?" and "Is the Constitution Still There?"

Condemning the New Deal's inflationary policies, he declared that the Democratic Party was not necessarily fated to be "always the party of green-backers, paper-money printers, free silverites, currency managers, rubber-dollar manufacturers and crackpots." The attitude he expressed toward elastic dol-

277

lars manipulated by Washington experimenters was all of a piece with his long detestation of William Jennings Bryan and his free-silver crusade.

The New Deal's spawning of new agencies—the old fur-coats-for-elephants syndrome—also attracted his sense of the ridiculous. "It looks," he wrote in the December (1933) *Outlook,* "as if one of the absent-minded professors had played anagrams with the alphabet soup. The soup got cold while he was unconsciously inventing a new game for the nation, a game which beats the crossword puzzle—the game of identifying new departments by their initials." The whole process of providing relief for the millions of unemployed was being bastardized, he believed. "Halfway between a lemon and an orange is a grapefruit; halfway between a 'public work' and a 'relief work' is a 'civil work.' Up to now the Federal establishments have been increased to include an AAA, an FCA, a PWA, an FERA, an NRA, a CCC, a TVA, an HOLC, an RFC—and now we have a CWA. . . . The reason for the new CWA [Civil Works Administration] is, however, crystal-clear. It was created to hide the failure of another existing agency. It was set up because the PWA, or Public Works Administration, had broken down. Instead of acknowledging the failure of the Public Works Administration and reorganizing it along sensible lines to insure action, this crazy, top-heavy structure, choked with redtape and bureaucracy is being left as it is and out of it is being created the new Civil Works Administration."

The NRA, the Blue Eagle program so vigorously administered by the colorful General Hugh Johnson, was in his opinion unconstitutional. "It is all very puzzling, and the bewildered observer, hoping ultimately for an honest test of the issues in the courts, is further confounded by the suggestion that the President could ask Congress to create a few more Supreme Court judgeships and fill them with men sympathetic with the aims of the National Recovery Act. That would indeed be a new deal." As it happened, the Supreme Court agreed with Smith that the NRA was unconstitutional; it regulated practically every aspect of a man's conduct of his business. But Smith was also alarmed by the first hint—later to become an actuality —that Roosevelt wanted to pack the Supreme Court so it would be more amenable to his legislation and executive orders.

The battle lines between Smith and Roosevelt were drawn. The latter had become the leader and spokesman of the opposition within their own party.

In the bitterness of that conflict, Smith did not hesitate to act as the obstructionist in matters affecting the careers of old friends who had switched sides. Ed Flynn of the Bronx, for instance. President Roosevelt wanted to appoint Senator Royal S. Copeland—who, incidentally, owed his seat to Hearst's intervention a decade before—as Ambassador to Germany and have Flynn appointed U.S. Senator from New York in Copeland's place. The appointment, however, would have to be made by Governor Lehman, and Lehman owed the governorship, in large part, to Smith's all-out support at the 1932 state convention.

Governor Lehman wouldn't name Flynn to the Senate until the latter had gone to Smith for his blessing. "It was apparent as I talked with Smith," Flynn later recalled, "that the sores and hurts made at the [national] convention had not yet been healed. He told me that he could not give me an answer because he would have to consult his friends. . . ." Flynn pleaded that he needed an immediate decision because the Senate was about to adjourn and the Copeland ambassadorial appointment would have to be confirmed by that body, but Smith insisted that Flynn would have to call him the next day. The next day Smith "still equivocated and said he could not make up his mind just what he wanted to do. I pointed out that delay was just as disastrous to the plan as a blunt refusal to go along with the suggestion." Thus Flynn lost out on the biggest plum of his career, and Smith paid off a grudge, possibly easing his conscience by reflecting that it would be a bad thing for so slavish a Roosevelt follower to be named to the Senate.

Dirty pool was the name of the game, and the Roosevelt forces played it with equal enthusiasm.

Roosevelt struck back at Smith through one of the latter's closest friends, Robert Moses, whom FDR did not like in any case. Early in 1934 Mayor LaGuardia appointed Moses as a member of the Triborough Bridge Authority, which was responsible for a vast construction program to bridge the East River between Manhattan and its opposite shore. Immediately after the appointment was announced, Mayor LaGuardia was summoned to Washington by Secretary of the Interior Harold Ickes, who was also administrator of the PWA program and the vast funds at its disposal. Ickes noted in his diary that LaGuardia was called on the carpet "at the instance of the President."

New York's PWA projects were in dire jeopardy, Ickes told LaGuardia, because of the Moses appointment. "Moses," as Ickes confided to his diary, "is a bitter personal enemy of the President's. The President and such friends as Jim Farley and Louis Howe think that Moses would leave nothing undone to hurt the President and we don't want to do any business with Moses. He is a very close friend of Al Smith."

LaGuardia stalled on firing Moses, but the New Dealers pressed the matter with all the enthusiasm of a Sicilian vendetta. Finally, Ickes had to announce that New York's PWA funds were cut off. Deliberately playing politics with funds to relieve the city's hundreds of thousands of unemployed was something even Roosevelt's then enormous prestige could not withstand; the administration was under furious attack in newspapers not only in New York, but throughout the nation, and the PWA funds were restored. Two years later, at the opening of the Triborough Bridge, Moses introduced Ickes and all the other speakers but one, President Roosevelt. FDR was as capable of nursing a grudge as Smith.

By then Smith was completely alienated from Roosevelt, a large part of his party, and the majority of his fellow citizens, who generally upheld the administration's bold measures to break the grip of the Depression.

To charges that he had "sold out to Wall Street," he presented an attitude of bitter defiance. He would not apologize for having become a cog in the capitalist machinery. "I didn't have a rich aunt or rich uncle to take care of me. . . . No one who has gone through what I went through in 1928 is going to be worried by sneers and epithets. . . . Unless you're ready to subscribe to the New Deal 100 percent and sign your name on the dotted line, you're a prince of privilege, you're a reactionary, or you're an economic royalist."

Late in the summer of 1934 the Liberty League was organized to offer a shelter to those who believed that Roosevelt was embarked on a revolution subtly designed to carry out the same functions as the Bolshevik model in Russia. Its chief aim was to make propaganda. Its chief spokesman was Al Smith, but public dissections of the New Deal were also conducted by Jouett Shouse, its president, James P. Warburg, Nicholas Roosevelt, John W. Davis, Governor Ritchie of Maryland, and former Governor Ely of Massachusetts. Raskob and other anti-Rooseveltians subscribed to a war chest large enough to hire a corps of publicists, economic and political strategists.

If the New Deal was the revolution, the Liberty League was the counterrevolution—the last charge of the imperial guards. Aside from arousing the electorate against the New Deal and all its works, its purpose was to deny the Democratic nomination to Roosevelt in 1936.

Liberty League speakers ranged the country for more than a year, and its publicity men filled the columns of newspapers disenchanted with Roosevelt. For a time it seemed to be making inroads into Roosevelt's massive public support. Farley, as chief strategist for FDR's renomination, conceded that the league for a time had "quite an influence," that its pamphlets and other publications had a wide circulation, and that it "constituted a formidable threat."

The league's activities were shaped toward a climax in January, 1936, the beginning of another election year. On January 24, John W. Davis, the Democratic standard-bearer of 1924, assailed the "despotism" of the New Deal before the New York State Bar Association at the Waldorf-Astoria. The second part of the one-two punch at the administration was to be Smith's address before the Liberty League dinner the following night at the Mayflower Hotel in Washington. It was also to be broadcast over a national radio hookup.

That evening of January 25 Smith advanced to the microphone—his old enemy, which he had stigmatized as "just a piece of cold metal suspended on a string . . . it could not produce an original idea or an original thought in a century." Before him were 2,000 of the wealthiest people in the country, all in evening dress, a sea of aristocratic noses, bare feminine shoulders, purplish sclerotic cheeks, and plump bellies—"a memorable gathering of the pompous plutocrats who signed the checks which kept the Liberty League operating," as Farley scornfully noted. It is impossible not to wonder whether it occurred to Smith to ask himself: What the hell am I doing here? Until eight years before, he had had nothing in common with the people sitting there behind their puddles of melting baked Alaska. What was Al Smith of South Street doing in that crowd, offering solace to those who needed it least, reading the lines that ripped into what they feared most?

Quite possibly, though, such thoughts never occurred to him, not after the years of bitterness and frustration which had driven him into this plush and bejeweled enclave. Perhaps he simply considered himself one of them, one of the Bourbons arrayed against the faceless millions outside. And undoubtedly he considered himself enlisted in a righteous cause, fighting an administration whose actions led him to believe it was striking down constitutional government and plotting the eventual subversion of the Republic.

At any rate he delivered one of the more forceful speeches of his career, his definitive indictment of Roosevelt and the New

Deal. He started out by saying that he had no personal ax to grind, that he had abandoned all hopes of resuming his political career, that he was motivated simply by concern for the future of his grandchildren, his party, and his country. It hurt him to attack a Democratic administration, but he considered that he was placing "patriotism above partisanship."

He was brought to this denunciation of the New Deal because he feared that the nation was endangered by Roosevelt's pitting class against class, by substituting "government by bureaucracy" for "government by law." He arraigned Roosevelt for having renounced the 1932 Democratic platform plank by plank and "draining the resources of our people into a common pool and redistributing them" according to the whims of New Deal ideologues.

"How do you suppose all this happened?" he demanded. "Here is the way it happened: The young brain trusters caught the Socialists in swimming and they ran away with their clothes. . . . It's all right with me if they want to disguise themselves as Norman Thomas, or Karl Marx, or Lenin, or any of the rest of that bunch, but what I won't stand for is allowing them to march under the banner of Jefferson, Jackson, or Cleveland!"

He then issued a call to all those Democrats in Congress not hopelessly bedazzled by Roosevelt to reread the Constitution, "stop compromising with the fundamental principles laid down by Jackson, Jefferson and Cleveland," and live up to their oaths of office.

His windup, hurled with all the passion at his command, by inference charged the Roosevelt administration with having established a second Kremlin in the White House:

"There can be only one Capital—Washington or Moscow.

"There can be only one atmosphere of government—the clear, pure, fresh air of free America, or the foul breath of Communistic Russia.

"There can be only one flag—the Stars and Stripes, or the red flag of the godless union of the Soviet.

"There can be only one national anthem—'The Star Spangled Banner' or 'The Internationale.'

"There can be only one victor. If the Constitution wins, we win. But if the Constitution. . . .

"The Constitution cannot lose! The fact is, it has already won, but the news has not reached certain ears."

The speech set the tone and stated the theme for anti-New Deal propaganda for years to come; Secretary of the Interior Ickes called it the "gospel of reaction." The Republican New York *Herald Tribune* described it as a "masterly summary of the case against the New Deal" and predicted that "this same deep feeling will find an echo in countless hearts." Events proved, however, that the country was not greatly stirred.

Even Smith's old admirer, H. L. Mencken, a man much concerned with style, believed that Smith had lost his touch, that his Liberty League speech was "another and massive proof of his loss of professional technique." The legendary Smith would "never have got himself up in long tails and a white tie and gone to a dinner of Palm Beach crocodiles and boa constrictors to make it. He would have worn his old brown derby, and loosed it before an audience of his ancient lieges—horrible, hairy, human. There would have been 1,000 New York firemen in the gallery armed with gongs and firewhistles, and down on the floor they would have been supported by 10,000 garbage haulers, white wings and cops in mufti, howling like hyenas at every pause in the flow of syllogisms. . . . But the Al of today wears a boiled shirt, prefers champagne to schooners, and plays golf instead of pinochle."

During the next several months, the Liberty League claimed to have secured the allegiance of a sizable proportion of delegates to the national convention from most of the Northeastern and Middle Atlantic states. Thereupon they provided the monster figure the New Deal propagandists were looking for. Instead of attacking the hapless Republicans, soon to nominate the decent, earnest, but lackluster Alf Landon of Kansas, they concentrated their fire on the "plutocratic" Liberty Leaguers and raised the fear that the "reactionaries" were plotting to seize power and turn the clock back a hundred years. Actually the Liberty League, knowing it had little chance to block Roosevelt's renomination, hoped at least to claim a share of influence over shaping the platform.

Smith attended the nominating convention in Philadelphia, heading a group of dissidents that included Bainbridge Colby, Wilson's Secretary of State; ex-Senator Reed of Missouri, ex-Governor Ely of Massachusetts, and other voices from the past. They called on the convention to repudiate the New Deal —an entirely quixotic gesture of protest. Two days after the convention opened, on June 25, a group of Smith diehards demonstrated in the gallery and had to be quelled by the police. Smith walked out of the convention before it renominated Roosevelt and Garner by acclamation.

He was now entirely alienated from his party. In October he announced that he was supporting Alf Landon for the Presidency. Shortly before the election, which provided an overwhelming victory for Roosevelt, he remarked before an audience in Albany that he did not believe Roosevelt himself was a Communist or Socialist but that something sinister was taking over in the country. "There is some certain kind of foreign 'ism' crawling over this country. What it is I don't know. What its first name will be when it is christened I haven't the slightest idea. But I know that it is there."

Perhaps the supreme irony of his political turnabout was that it made him an involuntary ally of his ancient enemy, William Randolph Hearst. The Hearst empire was in trouble, and the Chief was inclined to blame Roosevelt and federal taxation policies; all the more galling because he had boosted Roosevelt into the White House. On the editorial pages of the Hearst papers had blossomed a surprising proposal that Smith head a "genuine Jeffersonian Democratic ticket." He didn't care, Hearst wrote, that he and Smith had been enemies for years. "Nor do I care whether he pronounces the word 'radio' in a manner to suit the professors of the brain trust. He pronounces the word 'America' properly and patriotically, and that is all that matters in these widely disloyal days." The politics of revenge makes the strangest bedfellows.

20

Night Superintendent of the Zoo

ONE of the more appealing stories about Al Smith in his later years was told to the author by an attendant at the Central Park Zoo shortly after Smith's death. The Smiths had moved up from the lower or Washington Square end of Fifth Avenue and lived in a large apartment at No. 820 looking across Central Park and its zoo. The proximity of the zoo apparently was what chiefly attracted the animal-loving Smith, and he spent much of his spare time there. He regarded himself as an unpaid volunteer member of the staff. At night, the attendant said, whenever one of the tigers had a toothache or an animal roared in pain, Smith would throw a coat over his pajamas, put on bedroom slippers, hurry across Fifth Avenue and into the park. Then he would consult with the attendants on the proper remedies and sit up most of the night with the suffering beast.

Robert Moses was then park commissioner, and arranged a ceremony at which Smith was appointed "honorary night superintendent" of the Central Park Zoo. Smith was given the keys to the various animal houses and paid a purely honorary salary of $1 a year.

He often took dinner guests across the avenue to visit the zoo. One of the tigers had succumbed to Smith's charm and had been taught to perform one particular trick on signal.

When Smith and his guests arrived in front of his cage, Smith would suddenly growl in his harshest and most menacing voice: "LaGuardia!" The current mayor was making things difficult for all loyal sons of St. Tammany. On hearing the word, the tiger would snarl loudly, unsheathe his claws, and leap at the bars of his cage.

Aside from his affinity for tigers, Tammany or otherwise, Smith grew closer to the church as he aged. He devoted much time to Catholic charities and even a study of church doctrine, which had never before much interested him. It was almost as though he were trying to puzzle out why the majority of Americans had rejected him for being a Catholic; he had succumbed to the old man's tendency to look backward and ask himself where he went wrong. More than most men he was simply guided by his conscience, but even a good man can question himself.

He waited until he was sixty-four years old before he and Katie and a large party of friends—including Mr. and Mrs. Daniel J. Mooney, Justice and Mrs. Edward J. McGoldrick, and Bishop Fulton J. Sheen, then teaching at the Catholic University in Washington—embarked on a trip to Europe. Anywhere across the water would always be terra incognita as far as Smith was concerned, and the newspaper columnist Ben DeCasseres rightly called him "the modern Innocent Abroad," adding, "He brings them no discourses on Homer or Dante or Emerson. What he brings them is an administrative and organizing brain that is the equal of any in Europe or America." Pope Pius XI received him at the papal summer palace near Castel Gandolfo, where the villagers believed that Smith was the President of the United States. Later Smith said he was "never prouder than I was today, when I could call him 'Father' and he called me 'Son.'" Subsequently he was invested as a Privy Chamberlain of the Cape and Sword, a member of the Pope's official household.

Smith and his party then toured France, England, and Ireland. He was received by Mussolini and Churchill. The day after they arrived in Ireland he visited his grandmother's native village and met people who claimed they were his relatives. After a quick tour of the lakes of Killarney, they headed for Cobh and a ship home. Smith couldn't get back fast enough. He returned to New York thanking God, as he said, "for permitting me to be born in His country." He had seen Europe and once was enough.

Viewing America from abroad, however, had not convinced him that Roosevelt and his administration were acting in the country's best interests. He wondered just how much difference there was between a Roosevelt and a Mussolini. During his visit to Rome, Mussolini twice asked Smith "if there was anything in the Constitution of the United States to prevent a President from having a third term," then pointedly and with "a pronounced smile" asked, "How is the New Deal?"

Nor could he approve of the Roosevelt administration's attitude toward the German-Jews seeking a refuge from Nazi repressions or toward the Civil War in Spain. Possibly for political reasons, touching as they did on the millions of American unemployed, Roosevelt refused to urge the amendment of immigrations laws to admit Jewish refugees from Hitlerism. Smith considered that wrong, because most Americans were descended from refugees of one kind or another. He also charged that the immigration laws were based on "fantastic Aryan theories rather than American principles," but FDR didn't budge.

In the Spanish Civil War, the administration appeared to be biased toward the republican cause, even though it was partly led and influenced by Communists. They destroyed churches and killed priests. American liberals, however, labeled Franco's revolution a Fascist movement, and the administration was discreetly anti-Franco. At the 1938 State Constitutional Convention, of which Smith was a delegate, he was a member of the anti-New Deal Democrat splinter group, which brought him into opposition with his old friend Senator Robert F. Wagner, who led the loyalist delegation. Smith futilely advocated lower

real estate taxes and condemned the government for "throw-
ing money around the way we used to throw sawdust on the
old barroom floor."

He mellowed a bit with the years, felt less personal bitterness toward Roosevelt. The two men were still estranged, but
word reached Smith that whenever mutual friends visited the
White House, Roosevelt invariably asked "How is the old boy?"
—meaning Al Smith.

But Smith remained a dissident, convinced that Roosevelt
was excessively ambitious and much too inclined to view himself as indispensable. It had become a yearly custom, marked
on city-desk calendars of all the New York newspapers, for the
press to interview Smith on his birthday. On December 30, 1939,
when the reporters gathered in his Empire State office, he was
asked for his opinion of the New Deal and the widely discussed
possibility that Roosevelt would seek a third term.

On the third-term issue, he commented, "I have always
thought that two terms are enough for any man. . . . That
has been an unwritten part of the Constitution since the days
of Washington."

Answering other questions, he declared that "the fundamental policy of the New Deal has been to challenge the American
form of government. . . . It just won't do to ignore the Constitution, or to circumvent it after 150 years. . . . If the platform comes out in fulsome praise of the New Deal, it will be
time to get the walking shoes out again."

He stayed away from the 1940 convention because he was certain it would turn into another Roosevelt coronation. Listening to it on the radio, however, he was greatly disturbed when
Senator Carter Glass offered Jim Farley's name in nomination, citing the fact that Jefferson had warned against a third
term for any President, and the galleries were swept by prolonged booing and hissing. The New Deal troops were so well
drilled and single-minded that they reacted with outrage at
the thought of any man supplanting Roosevelt. Farley then
joined the anti-Roosevelt ranks.

Smith "took another walk," as he put it, during the 1940 election campaign and supported Wendell Willkie, the Republican candidate. He joined Willkie's campaign train during its swing through the Eastern cities. The crowds cheered him, but when it came time to vote, it was evident that Roosevelt had captured his urban following. He ripped into the New Deal's "reckless" spending and dissected the claim that FDR was indispensable. "Experience can't possibly be an argument for breaking the third-term tradition, because if you offer that argument now you have to admit that at the end of the third term he has four more years of experience, and at the end of a fourth term you might just as well elect him for life!"

Another anti-Roosevelt crusade had ended in failure, FDR's hold on the electorate was seemingly unbreakable. From then on, Smith seemed to be resigned to living out the rest of his life under a Roosevelt administration. Roosevelt's policy of lend-leasing supplies to the Allies against Hilter was immediately approved by Smith in a national radio broadcast, which earned him a grateful cable from Winston Churchill, now Britain's Prime Minister. It also brought a subsequent invitation to drop by the White House the next time he was in Washington. Smith accepted, and he and Roosevelt more or less patched up their personal, if not all their political, differences. They spent an hour talking about old times; less comfortable subjects were avoided. It was obvious that the country would soon be at war, and Smith realized that their disagreements on domestic policy, on aspects of the New Deal which had antagonized him, would fade into insignificance.

Pearl Harbor catapulted the country into a war on two fronts, but Smith was too old for any kind of service in the war administration. His son Alfred was commissioned a captain in the Army, and his son-in-law Major John Warner also went back into uniform.

Smith continued to preside over the affairs of the Empire State Building, now slowly beginning to pay its way. For years only about two-thirds of its office space had been rented. The

King of Siam, on visiting the building, remarked that he felt right at home there because his country also had white elephants. But at least the Empire State was no longer a standard vaudeville joke or an easy target for stand-up comics who referred to it as "The Empty State Building," "The 102-Story Blunder" or "Smith's Folly."

Smith's functions were largely ceremonial, but he showed up every day in his office on the thirty-second floor and sat behind his desk in the high-backed leather chair from the Executive Mansion in Albany. The staff handled all the rental and maintenance problems, while Smith served as attention getter, greeter, and publicity man deluxe. Royalty and movie stars were given a personal guided tour. So, occasionally, were the more ordinary people who made the Empire State Building the city's No. 1 tourist attraction. One elderly and timid visitor, hesitating before entering the elevators that zoomed with breathtaking speed, asked Smith whether she could expect to go up or down. "It all depends," Smith told her with a grin, "on the kind of life you've lived."

The millions of dollar admissions helped tip the financial balance for the Empire State. Just in and by itself the building was a smash hit, drawing more than a million visitors a year, especially after the spectacular film *King Kong* showed the giant gorilla climbing to the pinnacle of the Empire State with a disheveled Fay Wray in his grasp and defying the combined assault of the U.S. armed forces.

Few VIP's passed through New York City without the ritual visit to the Empire State, a drink, a cigar, and possibly a splendid ceremonial lunch with the Honorable Alfred E. Smith. One of those shortly before the war had been Winston Churchill, who, a few days later, was knocked down by a taxicab and hospitalized. Smith hurried to the hospital, knowing Churchill would need emergency treatment of a kind doctors wouldn't prescribe. He insisted on being left alone with the British statesman, to whom he announced: "I suppose you think of me as a politician, but just now I am a diagnostician and have brought you a little medicine."

He then produced a bottle of Scotch from his hip pocket.*

By the time of his seventieth birthday on December 30, 1943, his health and his wife's were failing. The occasion was warmed by letters and telegrams from President Roosevelt, ex-Governors Nathan Miller and Herbert H. Lehman, Governor Thomas E. Dewey, Wendell Willkie, Alf Landon, Walter Lippmann, John D. Rockefeller, Jr. Twenty-six members of the family assembled in the Fifth Avenue apartment that evening for the celebration.

It was the last time he had anything to celebrate. Early that spring Mrs. Smith was taken to St. Vincent's Hospital and on May 4, 1944, she died of heart failure. The family knew that he would not long survive her. His daughter Emily and her children moved into the Fifth Avenue apartment to fill up some of the empty space, but her father was merely going through the motions of existence. That summer he complained of intestinal disorders, and early in September he was taken to St. Vincent's Hospital, then several weeks later transferred to the hospital of the Rockefeller Institute. His heart was failing. His last earthly concern was to ask his secretary, Mary Carr, to bring the checkbook so he could pay his outstanding bills.

An old friend, Father John Healy, was summoned. Smith opened his eyes, looked at the priest and asked: "Am I dying, Father?"

"Yes."

"Start the Act of Contrition."

Early in the morning of October 4 he died of lung congestion and an acute heart condition. Two days later he lay in state at St. Patrick's Cathedral, and close to 200,000 persons

---

* Aside from whiskey, Smith and Churchill had in common a tremendous admiration for the orations of the late William Bourke Cochran. Churchill earlier in his career had mentioned or quoted Cochran so often in his speeches that his wife threatened to walk off the platform if she heard the name again.

filed past his bier, though many of them, in that critical year of the war, had their own sorrows.

The tribute was deserved. No American political figure had conducted himself more honorably. That his highest aspirations were not fulfilled was not, perhaps, of crucial importance. He could not have prevented the Depression of the thirties or headed off World War II or solved the social problems, involving both class and race, which the Depression and the war only temporarily concealed. It was of greater importance that the last sixteen years of his life were largely wasted when his special understanding could have done much to confront those problems before they assumed vast proportions. The fact that his candidacy in 1928 demonstrated the way to successive victories through a coalescing of urban factions was less important than the example he presented to all ethnic groups and the paramount lesson he endlessly expounded that people of all kinds can live together and make democracy work. Roosevelt and his theorists believed that once the economy was restored, all social problems would be solved, or solve themselves, in consequence; but Smith denied (in 1940) that "security is the essence of freedom" and intuitively realized that there was more to a man's life than the size of his paycheck. It is the problem that underlies the unrest of today.

The Happy Warrior ended as a tragic one, but the tragedy was as much America's as his own.

Afterword

Acontinuing glow surrounds the memory of Alfred E. Smith. Each year, at the Waldorf, there is the Alfred E. Smith Memorial Dinner. In October, 1968, several weeks before the national election, the dais was decorated with the presence of such notables as Nixon, Humphrey, Rockefeller, Lindsay, Dewey, Farley. The occasion was particularly impressive to the British newspaper correspondent Patrick O'Donovan, who called it "perhaps the most important political occasion in America." O'Donovan also wrote:

"Alfred was a Catholic politician. He was the first to make the grade. He was incessantly Governor of New York State. He had a vaguely Irish air, brown bowler hat and walking stick. He was a genial and professional politician. He was defeated for the Presidency, to the wounding of America, by Herbert Hoover.

"It was said that he was an ignoramus. He is said to have telephoned for a gun to be sent round and on being questioned said—'G as in Jesus, U as in Europe and N as in pneumonia.' He was, in fact, the fine flower of American democracy, sophisticated, efficient, honest and the sort of person you would be proud to have at your table. So each year, under the crimson aegis of the Catholic Church, which comes as near as you can to the Crown in America, the power men of this country dine in memory of this essentially lovable but quite dead politician."

That seems to sum it all up rather nicely—the memory, the legend. And it is the legend that survives.

Notes on Sources

The complete listing of many sources listed below under their author's surnames may be found in the Selected Bibliography, which follows.

1. Under the Brooklyn Bridge

Some of the material and much of the atmosphere in this chapter was gathered at random some years ago, much of it in the ubiquitous bar and grill establishments of the neighborhood, when the author was a reporter on the New York *Journal-American*, on South Street, a few hundred yards from Smith's birthplace. This was not scholarly research, but it helped in recapturing some of the essence of Smith's early life. It should be added that Smith did not leave behind any collected papers, letters or reminiscences except for his autobiography. What he did, in any case, clearly and unambiguously spoke for the man.

The Oscar Handlin comment on Smith's patriotism is contained in his *Al Smith and His America*, 79.

Details of Smith's ancestry and birth may be found in his autobiography, *Up to Now*, 3-8, and the affectionate memoir of his daughter, Mrs. Emily Smith Warner (with Hawthorne Daniel), *The Happy Warrior*, 23-28.

Smith's recollection of his boyhood was reprinted in *Recreation Magazine*, December, 1939.

Same source for his recollection of membership in the St. James' Union.

The description of his mother was offered by Henry Moscowitz and Norman Hapgood, *Up from the City Streets*, 15.

2. A Diploma from the Fish Market

Smith's recollection of picnics and Sunday excursions, *Recreation Magazine*, *op. cit.*

Girl's memory of Smith as a sporty youth, Henry Pringle's *Alfred E. Smith*, 107-8.

Details of his various jobs, *Up to Now, passim.*

3. Running with the Tiger

Survey of Tammany's depredations, William H. Allen's anti-Smith and anti-Tammany campaign document, *Al Smith's Tammany Hall*, 27-28.

His career in the commissioner of juror's office, Pringle, *op. cit.*, 116-17.

Claude Bowers' anecdote on Smith's courtship, *My Life*, 205.

Election night interview with Smith, New York *Morning Telegraph*, November 6, 1903.

4. A Freshman in Albany

Smith's recollections of his first night in Albany, *Up to Now*, 69-70.

Gene Fowler's description of the State Capitol, *Beau James*, his biography of James J. Walker, 32.

Senator James W. Wadsworth on Smith, quoted by Pringle, op. cit., 145.

Smith's prank on the girl visitors from the East Side, *ibid.*, 149.

Smith on Boss Murphy, *Up to Now*, 121.

His guardianship of Jimmy Walker, Fowler, *op. cit.*, 55-56.

5. Turning Point

Smith on his fellow legislators' carelessness in appropriating state's money, quoted in Moscowitz and Hapgood, *op. cit.*, 60.

Moscowitz's description of Smith as vice-chairman of the Factory Commission, *ibid.*, 70.

Frances Perkins' quote on Factory Commission's activities, *The Roosevelt I Knew*, 22.

The New York *Times'* profile of Smith, March 29, 1913; Albany *Knickerbocker Press'* comment, January 21, 1913.

Description of Governor Sulzer's personality, Pringle, *op. cit.*, 169.

Warren Moscow on Smith's setting the tone of the state government, *Politics in the Empire State*, 11.

Smith on the widowed-mothers' pension, *Up to Now*, 129-30.

6. Accumulation of Prestige

Frances Perkins' description of her visit to Boss Murphy, *The Roosevelt I Knew*, 24-25.

Smith's speech on the Widows' Pension Act is included in his *Progressive Democracy, Addresses and State Papers of Alfred E. Smith*, 159-62.

Smith on Walter Barnes, Jr., *Up to Now*, 140.

Smith's reply to Barnes included in *Progressive Democracy*, 162-69.

Hapgood and Moscowitz on his mastery of state government, *Up from the City Streets*, 129.

Charles Evans Hughes' observation on the same subject, *ibid.*, 130.

7. A Tin Star Worth $105,000

New York *Tribune* account of the Smith block party, September 22, 1915.

New York *World* on his candidacy, September 25, 1915; New York *Tribune's* endorsement, September 29, 1915.

Smith's embarrassment over Judge Swann's introduction, Pringle, *op. cit.*, 180-81.

David Burner's analysis of Smith's political methods, *The Politics of Provincialism,* 24.

Robert Moses' first meeting with Smith, Cleveland Rodgers' *Robert Moses: Builder of Democracy,* 23.

Mayor Hylan's appointment of Magistrate Douras, W. A. Swanberg's *Citizen Hearst,* 327.

Smith's opinion of Mayor Hylan, Moscowitz and Hapgood, *op. cit.,* 145.

Smith's charges against the Public Service Commission, New York *World,* November 2, 1918.

His mother's first vote, *Up to Now,* 164.

8. Smith Takes on Hearst

Smith's troubles with his dog Caesar, *Up to Now,* 85-86; Pringle, *op. cit.,* 233.

The anecdote of Smith being approached by a former schoolmate for a city job is related in Raymond Moley's *27 Masters of Politics,* 19.

Reconstruction Commission report, quoted in Rodgers, *op. cit.,* 25.

Felix Frankfurter on Smith's success as governor, quoted by Moley, *op. cit.,* 18.

Edward J. Flynn recounted his escapades with Smith's nephew in his *You're the Boss,* 14.

Hearst's anger over the Luce appointment, New York *Times,* May 9, 1919.

Hearst's charges against Smith regarding the milk trust, New York *American,* October 1, 1919.

Smith quoted on Hearst, New York *Times,* October 19, 1919. Hearst's reply, *Times,* October 28, 1919.

Smith's Carnegie Hall denunciation of Hearst is included in *Progressive Democracy,* 371-84.

Consequences to Hearst of Smith's attack, Swanberg, *op. cit.,* 327.

The Smith-Walker dispute over the Walker Bill, Fowler, *op. cit.,* 52-55.

9. Downtown Boy Moves Uptown

Smith on the danger of Presidential yearnings, quoted by Pringle, *op. cit.,* 42.

Bourke Cochran on Smith nomination, *Up to Now,* 209.

Description of state convention political types, Pringle, *op. cit.,* 49.

New York *World* report on Hearst's Senatorial ambitions, January 22, 1922.

Smith's awareness of the virtue of silence, Pringle, *op. cit.,* 46.

Farley's account of his efforts at the state convention as Smith's manager, *Behind the Ballots,* 33-37.

Edward Flynn's observations on Boss Murphy's attitude, *You're the Boss*, 36.

Hearst brigade's flight from Syracuse, New York *World*, September 29, 1922.

10. The First Hurrah

Oscar Handlin on Smith's political significance, *Al Smith and His America*, 82-83.

Smith's January, 1924, message to the legislature, Albany *Times-Union*, January 3, 1924.

Threats against Smith over Mullan-Gage Act, *Up to Now*, 268.

Edward Flynn on Smith's Presidential ambitions, *You're the Boss*, 80.

Arthur Schlesinger on Smith's liberal followers, *The Crisis of the Old Order*, 24-25.

Frances Perkins on Mrs. Moskowitz's help to Smith, *The Roosevelt I Knew*, 51-52.

Description of the 1924 national convention scene, Pringle, *op. cit.*, 308.

Smith's account of truce meeting with McAdoo, *Up to Now*, 288-89.

11. Up at the Tiger Room

The Tiger Room and its membership were described by Eddie Dowling for the Oral History Project, Columbia University Library. The author is indebted to the project for the use of this and other interviews.

Smith's sponsorship of Walker and the Coney Island meeting are described in Fowler, *op cit.*, 69-71.

Smith's open letter to Hearst, New York *American*, September 3, 1925.

Emily Smith's wedding details, Pringle, *op. cit.*, 123-24.

First Smith-Raskob meeting related by Eddie Dowling, Oral History Project interview.

Smith's Metropolitan Opera speech was covered by the New York *Times*, October 31, 1925.

Times' comment on Ogden L. Mills' clinker, November 4, 1925.

Louis Howe report on Mrs. Smith's European tour may be found in the Louis Howe Papers, dated April 15, 1925, in the Louis Howe Papers, Franklin D. Roosevelt Library, Hyde Park.

Howe to FDR on Smith's drinking, *ibid.*

Oswald Garrison Villard's comment on the same subject, *The Nation*, November 30, 1927.

H. L. Mencken on Smith Presidential boom, *A Carnival of Buncombe*, 141-45.

Moses' analysis of Smith's administrative talent, New York *Times Sunday Magazine*, August 1, 1943.

12. The Remaking of an Image

Professor Lindsay Rogers' candid recollections of his work in the Smith campaign were recorded for the Oral History Project at Columbia.

Proskauer-Smith conversation on the Marshall letter was reported to his daughter by Proskauer, *The Happy Warrior*, 183-84.

Moses' recollection of "editing sessions," his *A Tribute to Governor Smith*, 21.

Smith and grandfatherhood, Warner, *op. cit.*, 198-99.

Samuel Lubell's analysis of the city-country split, *The Future of American Politics*, 34-35.

Milton-McAdoo letter quoted in Edmund A. Moore's *A Catholic Runs for President*, 114.

Claude Bowers report on his FDR conversation, *My Life*, 177-78.

William Allen White's attitude toward Smith is analyzed in Moore, *op. cit.*, 128-30.

Bowers' description of Smith at the Biltmore, *My Life*, 187-89.

Smith's meeting with supporters at the Lotus Club, *ibid.*, 189-90.

13. Once Again the "Happy Warrior"

Herbert Hoover's exposition of his philosophy was contained in his *American Individualism, passim*.

Mrs. Warner's description of her father during the convention, *The Happy Warrior*, 201-2, 203.

Dowling on Raskob, Oral History Project interview.

Roosevelt's opposition to Raskob was expressed in letters dated July 11 and 25, 1928, and may be found in the Roosevelt Papers, Hyde Park.

James W. Gerard recalled his fund-raising activities for the Oral History Project at Columbia.

Bowers' observations on Raskob, *My Life*, 199.

The burro incident is recalled by Mrs. Warner, *op. cit.*, 208-9.

14. The Two Campaigns

Claude Bowers on the anti-Smith underground campaign, *My Life*, 203.

Methodist periodical on Smith candidacy, *Wesleyan Christian Advocate*, quoted by Michael Williams, *The Shadow of the Pope*, 192.

Mencken's survey of the anti-Smith campaign in religious periodicals was published in the Baltimore *Sun*, August 24, 1928.

Fellowship Forum broadside quoted by the New York *Times*, September 29, 1928.

Mencken on Smith's "clean hands," *A Carnival of Buncombe*, 185.

The account of FDR's selection as candidate for governor is recounted in Farley, *op. cit.*, 79; Warner, *op. cit.*, 221-22.

New York *Times* analysis of factors inimical to Smith's candidacy, October 3, 1928.

Mencken's observations on the campaign tour, Baltimore *Sun*, September 3, 1928.

Smith's final radio appeal, quoted in New York *Sun*, November 6, 1928.

15. "Thy Will Be Done. . . ."

Hotel scene as Smith and his family listen to the election returns, Warner, *op. cit.*, 228.

Mencken summation of results, Baltimore *Sun*, November 12, 1928.

Samuel Lubell's analysis of election, *The Future of American Politics*, 34-41.

The Nation's comment, November 21, 1928.

Smith's speech at the Georgia convent, quoted by Bowers, *op. cit.*, 206.

Smith told of Empire State project by Raskob, related by Eddie Dowling in his OHP interview.

Smith's toast to FDR, Warner, *op. cit.*, 231.

Smith's comment on Henry Morgenthau, Jr. quoted by Arthur Krock in an Oral History Project interview.

New York *World* prediction that Smith men would be swept out of office, December 30, 1928.

George Oppenheimer's recollections of launching the Smith biography, *The View from the Sixties*, 82-83.

Smith on tearing down the Waldorf, New York *Sun*, November 6, 1928.

16. The Walls Came Tumbling Down

Jimmy Walker's challenge to Smith is described in Fowler, *op. cit.*, 132-33.

A fascinating recent account of how the Wall Street crash came about may be found in Dana L. Thomas' *The Plungers and the Peacocks*, 200-11.

Raskob's calling in the campaign fund note was recalled by Eddie Dowling in OHP interview. The Tim Mara episode, *ibid.*

The Mike Meehan-Jim Riordan involvement is told in Thomas, *op. cit.*, 216-18.

Smith scoffing at 1932 candidacy quoted in Frank Graham's *Al Smith: American*, 217.

17. Hearst's Revenge

Howell's account of his talk with Smith quoted by Handlin, *op. cit.*, 154.

Smith's Jefferson Day speech, New York *Times*, April 14, 1932.

Edward Flynn's recap of his sounding out Smith, *You're the Boss*, 85-86.

Thomas Cochran offer of help in Smith candidacy, Warner, *op. cit.*, 252.

Mencken's expression of skepticism regarding FDR, Baltimore *Sun*, May 2, 1932.

Flynn's "painful interview" with Smith, *You're the Boss*, 94.

Farley's recollection of his plea to the California delegation, *Behind the Ballots*, 24.

Claude Bowers' recollection of talk with McAdoo in Spain, *My Life*, 245.

Gerard "orders" Smith to move for a unanimous nomination, recalled in his OHP interview.

18. The Leader in Exile

Dinner menu composed by Smith's convention staff quoted in Graham, *op. cit.*, 218.

Mrs. Smith's comment on FDR candidacy, Gerard interview, OHP.

Dowling on Smith's grudge over the convention platform incident, Dowling interview, OHP.

Smith tells Mayor Walker to resign for the good of the party, Fowler, *op. cit.,* 200-1.

Mencken on Hoover's campaign, Baltimore *Sun,* October 10, 1932.

Smith on the desperation of the country's situation, interview in New York *Times,* February 8, 1933.

Jim Farley's view of the Smith-Roosevelt split, *Behind the Ballots,* 77-79.

On the same subject, Joseph M. Proskauer, *A Segment of My Time,* 65-71; Moses, *op. cit.,* 39-40.

19. Carrying the Liberty League Banner

Smith's criticisms of the New Deal were contained in articles published by *New Outlook,* of which he was an editor, September, 1933, to January, 1934.

Smith thwarts Flynn's Senatorial appointment, Flynn, *op. cit.,* 147-48.

Farley on the Liberty League's influence, *Behind the Ballots,* 292-95.

Smith speech before Liberty League dinner, New York *American,* January 26, 1936.

New York *Herald Tribune*'s editorial on the speech, January 27, 1936.

Hearst's praise of Smith, New York *American,* August 29, 1935.

20. Night Superintendent of the Zoo

Smith's opposition to Roosevelt policy of not admitting German-Jewish refugees, interview in New York *World-Telegram,* December 31, 1939.

Smith's visit to Winston Churchill in the hospital is recounted in Warner, *op. cit.,* 305.

Details of Smith's death and funeral were gleaned from the New York *Times, Herald Tribune* and *Journal-American,* October 1-6, 1944.

Selected Bibliography

ALLEN, WILLIAM H., *Al Smith's Tammany Hall*. New York, 1925.
BOWERS, CLAUDE, *My Life*. New York, 1962.
BURNER, DAVID, *The Politics of Provincialism*. New York, 1968.
FARLEY, JAMES A., *Behind the Ballots*. New York, 1938.
FLYNN, EDWARD J., *You're the Boss*. New York, 1947.
FOWLER, GENE, *Beau James*. New York, 1949.
GLAZER, NATHAN, AND MOYNIHAN, DANIEL P., *Beyond the Melting Pot*. Boston, 1963.
GRAHAM, FRANK, *Al Smith, American*. New York, 1945.
HANDLIN, OSCAR, *Al Smith and His America*. Boston, 1958.
HOOVER, HERBERT, *American Individualism*. New York, 1922.
LUBELL, SAMUEL, *The Future of American Politics*. New York, 1952.
MENCKEN, H. L., *A Carnival of Buncombe*. Baltimore, 1956.
MOLEY, RAYMOND, *27 Masters of Politics*. New York, 1949.
MOORE, EDMUND A., *A Catholic Runs for President*. New York, 1956.
MOSCOW, WARREN, *Politics in the Empire State*. New York, 1948.
MOSCOWITZ, HENRY, and HAPGOOD, NORMAN, *Up from the City Streets*. New York, 1927.
MOSES, ROBERT, *A Tribute to Governor Smith*. New York, 1962.
O'CONNOR, RICHARD, *Hell's Kitchen*. Philadelphia, 1958.
OPPENHEIMER, GEORGE, *The View from the Sixties*. New York, 1965.
PERKINS, FRANCES, *The Roosevelt I Knew*. New York, 1946.
PRINGLE, HENRY F., *Alfred E. Smith: A Critical Study*. New York, 1927.
PROSKAUER, JOSEPH M., *A Segment of My Times*. New York, 1950.
RIORDAN, W. L., *Plunkitt of Tammany Hall*. New York, 1905.
RODGERS, CLEVELAND, *Robert Moses: Builder of Democracy*. New York, 1961.
SCHLESINGER, ARTHUR M., JR., *The Crisis of the Old Order*. Boston, 1957.
SMITH, ALFRED E., *Progressive Democracy, Addresses and State Papers*. New York, 1928.
———, *Up to Now*. New York, 1928.

SWANBERG, W. A., *Citizen Hearst*. New York, 1961.

THOMAS, DANA L., *The Plungers and the Peacocks*. New York, 1967.

WARNER, EMILY SMITH (with HAWTHORNE DANIEL), *The Happy Warrior*. New York, 1956.

WHITE, WILLIAM ALLEN, *Masks in a Pageant*. New York, 1928.

Index

Index